London

Edited by Marianne Mehling

London

A Phaidon Cultural Guide

with over 290 colour illustrations
and 6 pages of maps

Phaidon

Contributors: Maria Paukert M.A., Dr Helmut Scharf, Dr Hubert Stadler

Photographs: Marion Müllmayer

Phaidon Press Limited, Littlegate House, St Ebbe's Street, Oxford OX1 1SQ

First published in English in 1988
Originally published as *Knaurs Kulturführer in Farbe: London*
© Droemersche Verlagsanstalt Th. Knaur Nachf. Munich 1985
Translation © Phaidon Press Limited 1988

British Library Cataloguing in Publication Data

London : a Phaidon cultural guide.
  1. London (England)—Description—1981-
  I. Knaurs Kulturführer in Farbe London
  und Umgebung. *English*
  914.21'04858   DA684.2

  ISBN 0-7148-2504-2

Translated and edited by Babel Translations, London
Typeset by WM Print Limited, Walsall
Printed in West Germany by Druckerei Appl, Wemding

Cover illustration: Tower Bridge (photo: ZEFA Picture Library (U.K.) Ltd.)

Foreword

Earth has not anything to show more fair:
Dull would he be of soul who could pass by
A sight so touching in its majesty:
This City now doth, like a garment, wear
The beauty of the morning; silent, bare,
Ships, towers, domes, theatres and temples lie
Open unto the fields, and to the sky;
All bright and glittering in the smokeless air.
Never did sun more beautifully steep
In his first splendour, valley, rock or hill;
Ne'er saw I, never felt, a calm so deep!
The river glideth at his own sweet will:
Dear God! the very houses seem asleep;
And all that mighty heart is lying still!

This is William Wordsworth's enthusiastic response one morning early in the last century to crossing Westminster Bridge, gateway to central London for travellers arriving by coach from Dover. Nowadays travellers from all parts of the world visit this famous capital city, reaching it by car or train from one of the channel ports, or by flying direct to Heathrow or Gatwick airports. And in London itself people now get around in taxis, or on buses, or by Underground. Alternatively, if you want to get to know the town from closer quarters still, you can motor your own way through the exhausting chaos of the capital's traffic.

The quiet town known to Wordsworth, under a bright, clear sky, has changed very considerably. The 'towers, domes, theatres and temples' described by the poet remain, however, and can still be admired by the modern visitor, even if they are often hidden among high-rise buildings. The fascination exercised by the buildings, streets, alleyways, squares, monuments and bridges of London has also remained, and even the most critical visitor is likely to be captivated.

The area known as the City of London, a mere square mile, is now the centre of business and commerce and also the site of St Paul's Cathedral, Sir Christopher Wren's masterpiece. Wren was the 'architect of London' who changed the face of the city after the Great Fire of 1666. The City is linked by Fleet Street, traditional home of the press, to the former City of Westminster, where Westminster Abbey, the Houses of Parliament, and the government buildings of Whitehall are situated.

Adjacent is St.James, the 'palace quarter'. If London is the Brompton Road, Regent Street and Oxford Street, where one can buy exquisite goods of all kinds, it is also Soho, the pleasure quarter, which on a misty night sometimes still seems to be haunted by the ghost of the notorious Jack the Ripper, and Hyde Park, where at Speakers' Corner anyone is free to express an opinion and get things off his or her chest.

London boasts impressive churches, palaces, houses, museums, art galleries and monuments of all kinds, countless large and small theatres, offering unforgettable experiences for every taste. It is a huge metropolis of 30 boroughs, in which art and culture stand side by side with rubbish, the decent with the shocking, and poverty with wealth. London has world-famous sights alongside gems known to scarcely anyone, but which repay the trouble taken to discover them.

This book is a guide to the treasures of London. Its text and pictures deal with world-famous attractions in the city centre which are a must for every visitor; but the book also points out churches, houses, palaces, museums, monuments and other objects of interest in the suburbs or out-side the boundaries of London, such as Windsor Castle. And it also deals with treasures not mentioned in every guide, but nevertheless worth a visit.

The sights in the London section appear under a number of categories (see opposite). In the section on Greater London, the towns and boroughs are arranged in alphabetical order of place name for easy reference, as with other guides in the series. The heading to each entry in this section gives the name of the town/borough and a reference to the map on pp.190/1. Within each entry the main sights are printed in bold type: less significant objects of interest appear under the heading **Also worth seeing** and places in the vicinity under **Environs**. At the end of the book is a list of the principal sights of London and an index of places mentioned in the text, as well as an index of notable artists.

London

Inhabitants: 2,000,000
Inhabitants: Greater London: 6,765,000
Plan: pp.32/33

Map of the Underground: pp.34/35
Greater London pp.190/91

It is now almost 2,000 years since the legions of the Roman Empire, far from home in the cold, inhospitable North, founded a military and trading base which itself was to become the capital of a world empire. London was the capital of the British Empire, at the height of its power under Queen Victoria in the nineteenth century, and now capital of the British Commonwealth of Nations, which emerged from this empire and was created in 1931 by the Statute of Westminster.

London is also one of the world's largest cities, seat of the Royal Family, of government, of Parliament, of an Anglican and a Catholic archbishop, several universities, polytechnics, academies, important research institutions and scientific societies. The Stock Exchange and world-famous banks have made London a centre of world finance, and the famous auction houses of Sotheby and Christie established its reputation as a centre of art dealing. Magnificent palaces like Buckingham

Tower Bridge, one of the London landmarks

Palace, Kensington Palace and St.James's Palace, and, outside the boundaries, Hampton Court and Windsor Castle, underline the point that London is still a royal city; the Houses of Parliament and other buildings interesting for both their interior and exterior architecture are worthy seats of government and administration. Numerous monuments stand as reminders of turning points in the history of both city and country, and the people who made this history. They also remind us of tragedies like the Great Fire of 1666. The British Museum and the Victoria and Albert Museum are world-famous, likewise the National and Tate Galleries. St Paul's Cathedral, reminiscent of St Peter's in Rome, and Westminster Abbey have long been among the great churches of Europe.

But London is not just a city of splendid silent monuments and historic sights in stone and marble. London is alive—alive in its streets and squares, always full of noisy traffic, with the characteristic red double-decker buses towering above it. The extensive, beautifully tended parks are a marked contrast—oases of peace and recreation. And London lives in its citizens, who also make it a city of contrasts. There are those with titles, great or splendid names, most of them with a well-filled bank account. Their trademark is the Rolls-Royce, or other expensive cars with well-known names. And of course they wear dark suits, and carry umbrellas, not just because of the proverbially capricious weather; their hat is the characteristic bowler. They are at home in the West End and in the City, where great financial deals are made, or also in the major shopping streets like Regent Street and the Brompton Road, where inherited money or money they have earned themselves returns to circulation. They also meet on great social occasions such as Royal Ascot ot Henley Regatta. In stark contrast to these we find colourful, imaginatively dressed punks or other trendsetters, who have developed a lifestyle of their own,

determined to be different, and to make their mark. Between these two extremes are the ordinary Londoners, whose way of life is scarcely different from that of any other Europeans. Or perhaps it is. It's true that there is hardly another metropolis in which the rush hour and day-to-day chaos proceed in as orderly a fashion as they do here, as is shown by the famous queue, to be found in London just as much as elsewhere in England, and probably the result simply of a sense of tidiness. And there is hardly another European people with such a sense of tradition and delight in remaining true to it—whether it is Pearly Kings and Queens, the Lord Mayor's Procession, the State Opening of Parliament or the Trooping of the Colour. And there is another striking feature: all democracies have conflicts, and everyone has a right to different opinions and views and to denounce and attack injustice. However there is one matter upon which all Londoners agree: the monarchy and its representatives. The Royal Family is not just the First Family, but also the most popular and loved.

There is also a firm reminder that half the world was once ruled from London, and that many of the subjects of this Empire came to see the capital, enjoy its style, to spend or invest money, to be educated about traditions now established in their own lands as well, to start a new life here, to work here or simply to exist here, which seemed more attractive to some of them in London than in their homelands, of which many are now part of the Third World. All these Asians, Indians and Africans have brought their own traditions and way of life with them, and add another chracteristic and interesting shade to the palette of the metropolis. And the most poverty-stricken of them are an additional problem for the city, which anyway shares the problems of all major cities: overpopulation, pollution, refuse, traffic chaos, crime, unemployment and poverty, and

'Big Ben', the famous bell-tower ▷

sometimes also racial tension and even race riots. The contrast between rich and poor is particularly stark if, after visiting somewhere smart like Chelsea, Belgravia or a fashionable shopping street, you wander into some little alleyway in Soho or a part of the East End which is not intended for tourists and visitors, and in which socially deprived or impoverished locals and immigrants who haven't 'made it' are fighting for survival alongside each other or in ghettos. Such metropolitan contrasts are also to be found in Rome, Paris or New York. London is a metropolis which is worth seeing, discovering and exploring. Anyone who has once stood in front of the magnificent buildings, strolled through the splendid streets and squares, seen the countless attractive streets and houses or wandered through the little alleyways, is certain to return.

History and cultural history

Pre-Roman period (before 55 BC)

It has been surmised that by c. 500 BC Iron Age Celts were settled in the London area.

Roman period (55 BC – AD 410)

55BC: *Caesar* mounted his first British campaign.

AD43: The Emperor *Claudius* invaded Britain with several legions and made it a Roman province. The military and trading centre of *Londinium* was founded on the north bank of the Thames, at a point where the tides were no longer so noticeable. It had an early wooden bridge, and a citadel on the site of the later *Tower*. Roads radiated from here and were measured from the 'London Stone'. They stretched as far as the Scottish border.

AD60: The Roman Governor Suetonius was driven out by a revolt led by Queen *Boudicca*, and London was plundered and partially destroyed. After the Romans had defeated the revolt and rebuilt the town, it flourished economically, and became capital of the province.

c. AD70–80: A fort with an area of ten acres was set up on the site of the modern City, and it was from here that the medieval and modern cities developed.

View of London by night

This was also the site of the *Mithraeum* with nave and two aisles, discovered near Walbrook.

From 240: London was the administrative capital of one of the four Roman provinces in Britain.

286–7: Revolt of the Roman admiral *Carausius*, who commanded the British fleet against the Franks and Saxons. He seized Britain from the Emperor *Diocletian*, declared himself Emperor and made London his capital.

314: First mention of London as a bishopric.

367: London attacked by the Picts, Scots and Saxons.

c. 402: Roman troops withdrawn from Britain to protect Rome against the assaults of the Goths.

449 (traditional date): End of Roman rule in Britain, which was conquered by the Germanic Angles, Saxons and Jutes.

Anglo-Saxon period (*c.* 450–1066)
c. 450–1066: Development of the *Saxon style* in architecture.

457: Britons fleeing from the Anglo-Saxons sought refuge in London.

596: *Augustine* commissioned by *Pope Gregory the Great* to bring Christianity to the Anglo Saxons.

604: London mentioned for the first time as a royal centre of the Anglo-Saxon kingdom of *Essex*. London became the centre of a newly-founded bishopric, and *Augustine* consecrated *Mellitus* as the first bishop, with a cathedral.

610: The *East Minster* (on the site of the later *St.Paul's Cathedral*) became the first bishop's church.

c. 650: An Anglo-Saxon king's tomb ship, discovered N. of London in 1939, was presented with valuable Frankish and Byzantine gifts. The treasure is now in the British Museum.

757–821: *Offa* and *Coenwulf* made London into a Mercian royal residence.

827: *Egbert*, King of Wessex, overlord of the Anglo-Saxon Kings.

839: London attacked by the Danes.

851: London plundered by the Danes.

872: London rebuilt, but recaptured by the Danes.

878: King *Alfred* (871–899) defeated the Danes at Edington, reconquered and fortified London, which flourished once

Houses of Parliament by night

more. First moves towards municipal self-government ('Folkmoot').

886: London became part of Wessex in the division of England under *Alfred the Great*.

894–996: London attacked by the Danes.

1013&14–16: London occupied by the Danes.

1016–35: England ruled by the Danish King *Cnut* or *Canute* (c. 994–1035), who captured London in 1016 and later imposed a tax.

1042–66: Reign of *Edward the Confessor*.

1065: Consecration of the first *Westminster Abbey*.

Norman period (1066–1154)

1066–1200: Norman style in architecture.

1066: Norman Duke *William the Conqueror* crowned King of England in Westminster Abbey after the Battle of *Hastings* (14 October). London submitted only after guarantee by treaty of her ancient rights and freedoms.

1078: William the Conqueror built the *Tower* for the protection and control of London. It was completed *c.* 1300, and

served as a residence into the 16C. The *White Tower* is the heart of the complex; *St.John's Chapel* and the *Wakefield Tower* (Crown Jewels) are also Norman in origin. The strongly-fortified castle was later used as a state prison.

1085–86: William the Conqueror commissioned the *Domesday Book*, the account book of the feudal administration of the royal taxes, recording all possessions for taxation purposes.

1097: *Westminster Hall* built as part of the Norman Royal Palace (now part of the Houses of Parliament).

1100–35: London expanded to replace *Winchester* as the English capital under *Henry I*. The independent, self-ruled city now became dependent on the King.

12C: First work on *Lambeth Palace*, seat of the Archbishop (present building dates from 1829–34).

1106: Nave of *St.Saviour* built.

1123: Building of the Norman-Gothic *St.Bartholomew*, the oldest surviving church in the City.

1132: Royal *charter* granted municipal freedoms and offices of self-government (*Lord Mayor* and council).

Piccadilly Circus, the 'gateway to Soho'

The Plantagenets (1154–1399)

1156: London the official capital of England.

c. 1166: Miracle and mystery plays performed as precursors of the modern theatre.

1176–1209: *Old London Bridge* built, the first stone bridge over the Thames. It was the only one of its kind until the 18C and survived until it was pulled down in 1832.. This was the first stone bridge to be built in Europe since Roman times.

c. 1180–1300: *Early English style.*

1185: Consecration of the *Temple church*, one of the oldest in London. The chancel of the round church was not completed until 1246.

1189–99: *Richard I* (Richard the Lionheart) granted the citizens of London rights over the Thames, in exchange for payment.

1192: The first Mayor of London elected by the Guilds was *Fitz Aylwin*, who forbade wooden walls and thatched roofs to protect houses against fire.

13C: Great *Dominican, Franciscan, Carmelite* and *Carthusian monasteries* built outside the City.

1215: Under pressure from the barons, King *John Lackland* acceded to *Magna Carta*, settling questions of municipal privilege, trade, fiefs, taxes and the selection of bishops. The rights of the City of London were also confirmed, and became a model for the constitutions of other English towns. If the Lord Mayor of London wished to be confirmed in office he had to go to neighbouring, independent Westminster, the seat of King and Parliament. The *Lord Mayor's Show* is still an annual event: the newly-elected Lord Mayor processes to Westminster, now itself a part of London.

1245–69: *Westminster Abbey* built on the site of an earlier church dating from 1050–65 and an even older Benedictine monastery (building continued in the 14,16 and mid 18C); it is a major work of the Decorated style, and indeed of medieval architecture in London. It was rebuilt by Henry III in order to give Edward the Confessor a more glorious tomb.

1247: *Bethlehem Hospital*, oldest hospital for the insane in the world.

1272–1307: Reign of *Edward I*. The

View of Waterloo Bridge and the City of London

View of the National Theatre

clergy were barred from legal practice by the foundation of the *Inns of Court* for the training of secular lawyers.

1280: *Hanseatic League* represented in London.

1290: *Jews* expelled from London.

1300–80: *Decorated style.*

14C: *London manuscript of organ music.*

1312: Dissolution of the *Knights Templar*; their estates passed to the Knights of St; John who sublet to the Inns of Court which took over after the Reformation.

1332: Division of the *Common Council* into two houses, one for the lords spiritual and temporal, one for knights, citizens and country parishes.

c. 1340: Birth of poet and statesman *Geoffrey Chaucer* (d.1400) in London. His principal work, the 'Canterbury Tales' dates from *c.* 1387–1400.

1348: The *plague* claimed 75,000 lives in London.

1350–1520: *Perpendicular style.*

1377: With about 40,000 inhabitants, London was one of the largest cities in Europe.

1381: London taken in the course of the Peasants' Revolt led by *Wat Tyler*. The situation of the peasants gradually improved despite bloody suppression.

1382: The English reformer *John Wyclif* (*c.* 1320–84) condemned at the *Council of London* and later declared a heretic. His supporters, the *Lollards*, were bloodily persecuted. (Hus and Luther were influenced by his views, which had a socialist cast).

House of Lancaster (1399–1461)

1411–1439: Building of the *Guildhall*, the City town hall, restored and given a new façade in the 17&18C.

1450: *Jack Cade*, leader of a political revolt against *Henry VI*, declared himself ruler

Royal Albert Hall

of London from 3–5 July; a little later he was killed while fleeing.

1455–85: *Wars of the Roses*, the *White Rose* (of *York*) fighting the *Red Rose* (of *Lancaster*) for the crown of England.

House of York (1461–1485)

1472: Guild of musicians established in London.

1476: *Book printing* introduced in London; first book press in England opened under *William Caxton* (1424–91).

1483: *Richard III* had his nephews *Edward* and *Richard* murdered in the Tower in order to seize the crown.

House of Tudor (1485–1603)

1485: *Henry VII* first Tudor king.

1485–1558: *Tudor style* in architecture.

16C: Trading companies brought about economic upsurge in London.

1503–19: Magnificent *Henry VII Chapel*,

in Perpendicular style, added to Westminster Abbey.

1509–47: Reign of *King Henry VIII*.

1510: Foundation of St.Paul's School in London.

1526: First visit of the Augsburg painter *Hans Holbein the Younger* (1497 or 98–1543) to London, where he painted a group portrait of *Thomas More's* family.

1532: Holbein became painter to the court of Henry VIII and finally settled in London (portraits of English nobility).

1534: Henry VIII passed the *Act of Supremacy,* caused by the breach with Rome, and founded the independent Anglican Church. Numerous churches and monasteries dissolved, and replaced by five hospitals and hostels for the old. Constant growth of the population brought social problems for London.

1535: *Thomas More,* Lord Chancellor from 1529–32, executed in London for high treason as a result of differences with the King. His principal work *'De optimo statu rei publicae deque nova insula Utopia'* appeared in 1516. First dealings in stocks and bonds in London.

1537: Hans Holbein the Younger painted the *Whitehall Dance of Death* and allegorical pictures in the *Steelyard*.

1558–1603: Reign of Queen *Elizabeth I*, after whom the *Elizabethan style* is named. She encouraged science and the arts, especially acting (*Swan, Rose* and *Globe theatres*). The Tower ceased to be the Royal residence.

1563: Decree of *legal social aid* to deal with social problems in London.

1567: *London Stock Exchange* founded for trade in insurance and bonds.

1570: The Stock Exchange acquires its own premises in the *'Royal Exchange'*.

1575: Population of London approximately 180,000.

1579: *Sir Thomas Gresham*, merchant, financier and founder of the London Stock Exchange, founded *Gresham College*.

1588: Further upsurge of trade and economy after the *victory over the Spanish Armada*.

1592: *William Shakespeare*, (1564–1616) first mentioned as an actor in London.

1597: Richard Burbage's troupe founded the London *Globe Theatre*.

1598: Rise of the London *Merchant Adventurers*, a group of top merchants who soon dominated English export trade.

House of Stuart (1603–1714)

1603: *James I* first King from the House of Stuart.

1603–25: *Jacobean style* named after James I.

1605: *Gunpowder Plot* of the Catholic nobility under *Guy Fawkes* betrayed; he and his fellow conspirators against James I and Parliament executed.

1607: *John Thorpe* built *Holland House*.

1619–22: *Inigo Jones* built the *Banqueting Hall* in late Renaissance style (1625 with ceiling paintings from the studio of Rubens).

From 1625: *Caroline style.*

1631–8: *Covent Garden* market place, designed by *Inigo Jones*, built.

1623: The Flemish painter and engraver *Anthony van Dyck* (1599–1641) became court painter to *Charles I* in London, where he was celebrated as a portraitist of court society. One of his principal works is *'King Charles I on Horseback'*, (c. 1636).

1635: *Leicester Square* designed and built.

1637: *Hyde Park* became the first public park, used mainly by the aristocracy. The park was originally a possession of Westminster Abbey, then confiscated by Henry VIII and later used for hunting. The *Great Exhibition* was held here in 1851.

1642–6/8: In the Civil War London supported Parliament against the absolutist tendencies of the Stuart kings. For this purpose a municipal army and parliamentary army were raised.

1649: London was instrumental in the fall of Charles I, who was executed in Whitehall. *Oliver Cromwell* took over the business of government as Lord Protector.

1652: First *coffee house* opened in London.

1656: First opera performed in the *Opera House* in London. *Sephardic Jews*, i.e. Jews from North Africa and the Near East were allowed to settle in London again *(Petticoat Lane).*

1660: *General George Monk*, who fought for Cromwell in the Civil War, supported the restoration of the Stuart monarchy after the Lord Protector's death. He occupied London, which followed promonarchist policies after it had been granted certain rights. The *Restoration* was completed by the recalling of the House of Stuart under *Charles II* by Parliament. London had more than half a million inhabitants, roughly a tenth of the national population.

1662: *John Graunt* (1620–74) laid the basis of modern *population statistics* with his principal work *'Natural and political observations upon the bills of mortality'*.

1665: The *plague* claimed 68,500 lives in

Dock in Southwark ▷

London. *Bloomsbury Square* designed and built. First appearance of the official *'London Gazette'*.

1666: Four-fifths of the central part of the City burned down in the *Great Fire*. 13,200 houses and 89 churches destroyed. The scientist and architect *Sir Christopher Wren* (1632–1723), named head of rebuilding work in the same year, submitted a general building plan on generous modern lines in 1668, but was unable to carry it out. The City was certainly rebuilt in stone, but the medieval street network was followed, and became even more cramped than before. He rebuilt 55 new churches, largely in the English baroque style, to the 14 which survived the fire. Many of them were destroyed in the 19C or damaged in the Second World War.

Post 1666: *Merchant Taylors' Hall* built.

1675–1710: Wren built *St.Paul's Cathedral* in English baroque style on the site of earlier 7,10 and 11C buildings. This mighty church with its drum dome 361 ft. high is the largest in Christendom after St.Peter's in Rome.

1680: Wren builds *St.Bride's* and *St.Mary-le-Bow*.

1682–4: Wren builds *St.James,* Piccadilly.

1688&9: *Glorious Revolution* . *Declaration of Rights* and *Bill of Rights* promulgated against James II. *William of Orange* succeeded the fleeing monarch as *William III*; establishment of constitutional monarchy. London's municipal rights were confirmed, and the restrictive city wall was removed.

1692: Foundation of numerous *public companies* caused the London Stock Exchange to flourish.

1694: Plague, fire and revolution were things of the past. Foundation of the *Bank of England* to finance a war with France. The City became the centre of European and international trade and finance.

1702: Death of William III in London.

1703: Work began on *Buckingham House* (rebuilt by *John Nash* in 1825; new main façade by *Sir Aston Webb* in 1913). The English physicist, mathematician and astronomer *Sir Isaac Newton* (1643–1727), whose principal work *'Philosophiae*

Queen Elizabeth and Prince Philip at the wedding of Prince Andrew and Sarah Ferguson

naturalis principia mathematica' (containing the Newtonian axioms) appeared in 1687, became President of the *Royal Society* of the *London Academy.*

1704: The *Orangery* at *Kensington Palace* designed by Hawksmoor, later modified by Vanburgh.

1705: Opening of *His Majesty's Theatre.*

1709–10: The composer *Georg Friedrich Händel* (1685–1759) moved to London, where he conducted operatic performances with modest success. He was more successful with his oratorios (including *'Messiah',* 1742).

House of Hanover (1714–1901)

1714: *George I* became the first king from the House of Hanover.

1714–1830: *Georgian Style* in art.

1717: First *Grand Lodge* of the *Freemasons* founded in London, representing a modern, liberal, humanitarian trend.

1719: Händel became director of the new London Opera House.

1720: *Old Haymarket Theatre* opened in London.

1721–6: Church of *St.Martin-in-the-Fields* built.

1723: *James Anderson* published the constitution of the Freemasons ('Old Duties').

1725–30: Palladian villa *Chiswick House* built with interior and gardens by *William Kent.*

1730–33: *James Gibbs* built the new *St.Bartholomew's Hospital* (founded 1123) in the Palladian style.

1731: Death in London of the writer and politician *Daniel Defoe* (b.*c.* 1660), known for his socially aware writings imbued with the spirit of enlightened Puritanism (including *'Robinson Crusoe',* 1719).

1731–52: *George Dance* built the Mansion House in neoclassical style.

1732: The Grand Lodge of Freemasons in London admitted Jews. Foundation of the *Academy for the Preservation of Ancient Music.*

1741: The English actor and playwright *David Garrick* (1717–1779), director of the Theatre Royal, Drury Lane, played Shakespeare's Richard III.

1744: Foundation of the firm of *Sotheby,* now the oldest and largest auction house in the world.

1746–55: *Canaletto,* the Italian painter, worked in London.

Sarah Ferguson and Prince Andrew, the 'bridal couple of 1986'

The Horse Guards

1750: Westminster Bridge built, the second bridge over the Thames.

c. 1750: First specifically English furniture style created in London by *Thomas Chippendale* (1718–79).

1757: The painter, graphic artist and art theoretician *William Hogarth* (1697–1764) became court painter. He was considered a master of the portrait and social satire (*'A Rake's Progress'*, 1735, *'Mariage à la Mode'*, 1745). Birth in London of the painter, graphic artist and poet *William Blake* (d.1827), a forerunner of the pre-Raphaelites. He illustrated literary works by himself and others (including Edward Young's *'Night Thoughts'*).

1759: Opening of the *British Museum*, private collections endowed in 1753.

1760: Last remnants of the *town fortifications* removed to make possible a connection with Westminster.

1763–6: The Austrian composer *Wolf-gang Amadeus Mozart* (1756–91) spent time in London during his three-year tour. He composed his first symphony, and also six violin sonatas dedicated to the Queen of England.

1768: Foundation of the *Royal Academy of Arts*. The portrait painter *Sir Joshua Reynolds* (1723–92), principal representative of the English rococo school, became President of the Royal Academy of Arts.

1771–8: *Robert Adam* built *Apsley House*.

1774: The painter *Thomas Gainsborough* (1727–88) moved to London, where he became a sought-after painter of the aristocracy (*'Blue Boy'*, 1770). He also created the genre known as landscape portrait (*'Heneage Lloyd and his Sister'*, c. 1750).

1775: Birth in London of the painter *William Turner* (d.1851), a master of English landscape painting and forerunner of Impressionism.

The Horse Guards

1775–80: *Bedford Square* designed and built.

1776–86: The architect *Sir William Chambers* built *Somerset House* in the style of Palladian classicism, on the site of an incomplete 16C palace.

1788–1827: *Sir John Soane*, the master of monumental classicism, built the *Bank of England*.

1790: *Great Central Synagogue* built by the Jewish community.

1791–5: The Austrian composer *Franz Joseph Haydn* (1732–1809) wrote the twelve London Symphonies during concert tours in England. Birth in London of the poet *John Keats*, (d.1821), the Romantic poet ('Hyperion', 1821).

1801: First official *census* put the population of London at 860,035 inhabitants.

1802–12: Masterpieces of sculpture brought to London by *Lord Elgin* ('Elgin Marbles') from the Parthenon on the Acropolis in Athens, the temple of Apollo at Bassae and the Mausoleum in Halicarnassus.

1802–28: New *docks* built (*West India Docks*, 1802; *London Dock*, 1805; *East India Docks*, 1806; *St Katharine Docks*, 1828) making London the largest harbour in England.

1806: Trade through London docks deleteriously affected by *Napoleon I's continental blockade*.

1807–14: *Gas lighting* introduced in the streets of London.

1811: *Royal Mint* built by *Johnson* and *Smirke*.

1812: *Bethlehem Hospital*, founded in 1247, rebuilt.

1812–25: *John Nash* dominated Regency town planning. *Regent's Park* landscaped, with *Cumberland Terrace* and *Park Crescent*.

1813: *Grand Lodge of England* founded by

English Freemasons. Foundation of the *London Philharmonic Society*.

1819: Birth in London of the artist, writer and social reformer *John Ruskin* (d.1900), the most important art critic of the Victorian era.

1823–55: *Sir Robert Smirke*, of the *'Greek Revival'* movement, builds the *British Museum*.

1824: *National Gallery* founded from the estate of the rich merchant and collector *John Julius Angerstein*. Foundation of the first *Animal Protection Society*.

1824–43: *Isambard Kingdom Brunel*'s *Thames Tunnel* built in the London Docks.

1825–31: The *Rennie Brothers* build the new *London Bridge*.

1827–9: *St.James Palace* (hospital before 1190, palace from 1532) redesigned by Nash.

1828: *London University* founded.

1829: Foundation of the *Metropolitan Police Force* and introduction of *horse buses*.

1830: *Greek independence* guaranteed in London.

1831–9: *Belgian independence and neutrality* guaranteed in London.

1832–8: *National Gallery* built by *William Wilkins* on the N. side of *Trafalgar Square*.

1834: Palace and Westminster where parliament meets burnt down.

1836: First London *railway* ran between *London Bridge* and *Greenwich*. Euston Station, London's first railway station, opened.

1837: Death in London of the painter *John Constable* (b.1776), principal representative of English realistic landscape painting.

1837–9: *'Oliver Twist'* one of the principal works of novelist *Charles Dickens*, who lived and worked in London, published during this period.

From 1837: The natural historian *Charles Darwin* (1809–82), propounder of the theory of evolution, lived in London for several years (principal work *'On the Origin of Species by Natural Selection'*, 1859).

1837–1901: Reign of *Queen Victoria*, who made Buckingham Palace the principal residence of the English monarchy on her accession. The *Victorian style* dominated art and architecture, and in politics the period is referred to as the *Victorian Age*. London expanded enormously as Victorian suburbs sprang up, well served by the newly established railway, which enabled the inhabitants to reach their places of work in the centre of town with speed and ease.

1840–52: *Charles Barry* and *A.W.N.Pugin* built the neo-Gothic *Houses of Parliament*. The famous tower housing the bell 'Big Ben', with its characteristic chimes, became the symbol of London.

1841: *Dardanelles Convention* in London.

1842: *Stock Exchange* completed.

1843: Consecration of *Nelson's Column* by *William Railton* and *Bailey* in *Trafalgar Square* in memory of the *Battle of Trafalgar* of 1805, in which *Admiral Lord Nelson* fell victorious.

1846: Foundation of the *'Evangelical Alliance'*, an international grouping of evangelical Christians.

1847&8: Political refugees from Germany, including *Karl Marx* and *Friedrich Engels* founded the *Communist League* and wrote the *Communist Manifesto*, with its cry: 'Workers of the world, unite!'.

1850–2: *Protocols* on *Denmark* and *Schleswig-Holstein* respectively.

1851: *Great Exhibition* in London. The architect and landscape gardener *Joseph Paxton* (1801–65) created the epoch-making *Crystal Palace* for this purpose. The hall housing the Exhibition covered an area of 63,000 square yards, and was built like an enormous greenhouse, in prefabricated glass and cast iron sections.

1851&2: *King's Cross Station* built, the first London station constructed of iron.

1852: *Marine Aquarium* opened. Foundation of the *Museum of Ornamental Art* in

Detail of Victoria Memorial outside Buckingham Palace

South Kensington (now *Victoria and Albert Museum*).

1853: First *pneumatic postal system* initiated in London.

1858: *E.M.Barry* built the *Royal Opera House, Covent Garden*.

1862: Second World Exhibition in London, in which Japanese wood carvings were among the more striking exhibits.

1863: Opening of the first *underground railway* from *Bishop's Road* to *Farringdon*.

1863–72: *Sir George Gilbert Scott* rebuilt the *Albert Memorial* erected on the occasion of the Great Exhibition of 1851.

1864: *Karl Marx* founded the 'First Internationale', which he led until 1872. The Internationale finally collapsed as a result of internal disagreements between Marxists and anarchists in 1872.

1867: *Treaty of London* on the subject of *Luxembourg*.

1868: Last *public execution* in London.

1868–71: *St. Thomas's Hospital* built.

1868–74: *William Ewart Gladstone*, the liberal politician, opponent of Disraeli over imperialistic foreign and naval policy, was Prime Minister (again 1880–5, 1886 and 1892–4).

1868–82: *Law Courts* built by *G.E.Street*.

1870: First *telegraph* between *London* and *Calcutta*.

1871: *Pontus conference*.

1873: The French Emperor *Napoleon III* (b.1808) died in exile in Chislehurst, near London.

1873–80: *Alfred Waterhouse* built the *Natural History Museum* in neo-Romanesque style.

1875: The Conservative politician *Benjamin Disraeli* (1804–81), Prime Minister 1866 and 1874–80, secured influence for Great Britain over the *Suez Canal* by the acquisition of shares.

1878: *William Booth* (1829–1912) founded the *Salvation Army* in London, a successor of the *'Christian Mission'* (1861), which he also founded.

1881: Death in London of the Scottish author and critic *Thomas Carlyle* (b.1795; 'History of Frederick the Great', 6 vols. 1857–65).

1884: Foundation of the *Fabian Society* by *Sidney* and *Beatrice Webb*, with the aim of creating a socialist society without class struggle and revolution (movement of bourgeois-radical intellectuals).

No.10 Downing Street, Margaret Thatcher receiving Egyptian President Mubarak

1886–94: *Horace Jones* and *John Wolfe-Barry* built Tower Bridge with a lower part which can be raised in two sections and a fixed upper part.

1888&9: Introduction of the *London County Council* for the administration of Greater London; the Lord Mayor and City retained their rights.

1892: Foundation of the *Independent Labour Party*, predecessor of the social-democratic Labour Party.

1895: Foundation of the *London School of Economics and Political Science*, which became a centre of the social sciences. The *Webbs*, the founders of Fabianism, were instrumental in the foundation. Sidney Webb ('Socialism in England', 1890) was also Minister of Trade (1924) and Minister for the Colonies (1929–31).

1895–1903: *John Francis Bentley* builds *Westminster Cathedral* in early-Christian Byzantine style. It is the most important Roman-Catholic place of worship in Great Britain.

1896: *Second Internationale* meets in London, founded in Paris in 1889. Death in London of the author and architect *William Morris* (b.1834). The socialist critic and theoretician associated with the pre-Raphaelite group. He prepared the way for art nouveau and reformed applied arts by the foundation of his own workshops.

1897: Opening of *Sidney R. J. Smith's Tate Gallery*. *Charles Harrison Townsend* built the art nouveau *Whitechapel Art Gallery*. *Lady Wallace* founded the *Wallace Collection*.

1899: *International Publishing Congress* held in London. *Greater London* formed from the 28 boroughs.

1900: Foundation of the British *Labour Party*. *Pan African Conference* held in London. The Russian politician and revolutionary *Vladimir Ilyich Lenin* (1870–1924) spent time in London during his first period of emigration.

House of Saxe-Coburg (1901–10)

1902: The Russian socialist *Leon Trotsky* (1879–1940) fled to London from East Siberia. *Claude Monet* (1840–1926), the French Impressionist painter, painted Waterloo Bridge.

1903: Russian socialists at the *Second Party Congress of the Russian Socialist*

Guildhall

Kings and Queens of England

Anglo-Saxon Kings

Edwin	955–959
(Ruler of Wessex only from 957)	
Edgar	959–975
Edward the Martyr	975–978
(Wessex only)	
Ethelred II	978/9–1013
Sven Forkbeard of Denmark	1013–1014
Knut I	1016–1035
Edmund Ironside	1016
(with Knut from April–November)	
Harold I Hare Foot	1035/6–1040
Hardknut	1040–42
Edward the Confessor	1042–1066
Harold II Godwinson	1066
(Jan–Oct)	
(Edgar II Atheling)	(1066)

Norman Kings

William I, the Conqueror	1066–1087
William II Rufus	1087–1100
Henry I Beauclerc	1100–1135
Stephen I of Blois	1135–1154

House of Plantagenet

Henry II	1154–1189
Richard I Lionheart	1189–1199
John Lackland	1199–1216
Henry III	1216–1272
Edward I	1272–1307
Edward II	1307–1327
Edward III	1327–1377
Richard II	1377–1399

House of Lancaster

Henry IV	1399–1413
Henry V	1413–1422
Henry VI	1422–1461

House of York

Edward IV	1461–1483
(in captivity and exile	1469–71)

Edward V	1483
Richard III	1483–1485

House of Tudor

Henry VII	1485–1509
Henry VIII	1509–1547
Edward VI	1547–1558
Mary I	1553–1558
Elizabeth I	1558–1603

House of Stuart

James I	1603–1625
Charles I	1625–1649

Commonwealth and Protectorate

Oliver Cromwell	1653–1658
(Protector)	
Richard Cromwell	1658–1659
(Protector)	

House of Stuart

Charles II	1660–1685
James II	1685–1688
Mary II and William III	1689–1702
(of Orange)	
Anne	1702–1714

House of Hanover

George I	1714–1727
George II	1727–1760
George III	1760–1820
George IV	1820–1830
William IV	1830–1837
Victoria	1837–1901

House of Saxe-Coburg

Edward VII	1901–1910

House of Windsor

George V	1910–1936
Edward VIII	1936
George VI	1936–1952
Elizabeth II	1952–

Westminster Abbey, Tomb of the Unknown Soldier and choir screen [

Democratic Workers' Party split into the majority party of *Bolsheviks* under Lenin and the minority of *Mensheviks* under Plechanov. Death in London of the American painter *James Whistler* (b.1834), who had lived and worked in London and Paris since 1859 and from 1875, approached Impressionism in style.

1904: Meeting in London of the *World Federation for Women's Suffrage*. The painter *Frank Brangwyn* painted monumental works for the London *Skinners' Hall* and for the *Stock Exchange*.

1906: Concept of *'Genetics'* introduced at the *Third International Congress of Plant Breeding*.

1907: The German physicist *Arthur Korn* (1870–1945) established a link between *Munich and London* by *pictorial telegraphy*.

1908: *Fourth Olympic Games* of the modern age take place in London, featuring 21 sports. First International *Congress of Morals*.

1908&9: *Conference* and *Declaration on Marine Law*.

1909: Opening of the *Victoria and Albert Museum*, built in neo-Gothic style by *Aston Webb*. Permanent waves invented in London.

House of Windsor (from 1910)

1910: Accession of *George V*, first king from the House of Windsor. Death in London of *Florence Nightingale*, the famous nurse from the Crimean War.

1911: London had 7 million inhabitants. *Webb* built *Admiralty Arch* in memory of Queen Victoria.

1913: *Titanic Conference* on the safety of shipping. *First Balkan War* concluded by the Peace of London.

1914: Death of the liberal-conservative statesman *Joseph Chamberlain* (b.1836) in London. He was Colonial Minister 1895–1903. The *Treaty of London* allied the Entente powers against the Central powers. Death in London of *Sir Hubert Herkomer*, (b.1849), the portrait-painter. *Ralph Vaughan-Williams* (1872–1958) composed his *London Symphony*.

1915–18: German *airships* attacked London during the *First World War*, causing the loss of more than 2,000 lives.

1921: London *Reparations Ultimatum* accepted by the German Reichstag.

Windsor Castle, Changing of the Guard

1922: *Port of London Authority* built on *Tower Hill.*

1926: The German painter *Lesser Ury* (1861–1931) painted *'Pictures from London'* in Impressionist style.

1930–1: *Broadcasting House* built.

1931: *Mahatma Gandhi* (1869–1948) at the London Conference.

1932: The conductor *Sir Thomas Beecham* (1879–1961) founded the *London Symphony Orchestra.* Author and social critic *John Galsworthy* (1867–1933) awarded the Nobel Prize. He died in London in 1933. Principal work *'The Forsyte Saga'* (trilogy, 1906–21).

From 1933: *Senate House* of *London University* built. Sociologist *Karl Mannheim* (1893–1947) worked at the London School of Economics. Principal work *'Man and society in the age of change'.*

1936: Britain, France and the USA agreed to restrictions on naval armament at the *London Naval Disarmament Conference* (revised 1938). London protocol regulating submarine warfare. Death in London of the Anglo-Indian author and journalist *Rudyard Kipling* (b.1865). Principal works *'The Jungle Book'* (two volumes 1894&5),

'Kim', 1901. Awarded the Nobel Prize in 1907.

1938&9: *Sigmund Freud* (1856–1939), the Austrian Jewish psychiatrist and founder of psychoanalysis fled from the Nazis to London, where he died. Posthumous publication *'The man Moses and monotheistic religion'.*

1940–5: The 'Blitz' (1940) marked the beginning of numerous *German air-raids* on London. Approximately 30,000 people died in night attacks and a third of the buildings in central London were destroyed. *Winston Churchill* was Prime Minister and Minister of Defence, but had to resign during the Potsdam Conference (1945) because of his party's electoral defeat. During the Second World War London was the seat of various *governments in exile* from Fascist terror.

1944: *'Plan for Greater London'* with the intention of shifting industry out of the centre.

1945: *Agreement for the establishment of an international military tribunal* for the judgment of Axis war crimes.

After 1945: *Rebuilding,* slum clearance in the *East End* and *new towns.*

Eton College, Windsor

1948: *XIV Olympic Games* of the modern era held in London, with more than 5,000 sportsmen and women taking part.

1950: *House of Commons* rebuilt and re-opened after destruction in an air raid.

1951: *Festival of Britain* in London with large-scale cultural and technical exhibitions. *Robert Matthew* and *J.L.Martin* built the *Royal Festival Hall*. The *'Dome of Discovery'* had the then largest aluminium dome, 361 ft. in diameter.

1951–5: *Churchill* Prime Minister again.

1952: The *London Conference of Foreign Ministers* approved the *European Defence Union.* Accession of *Queen Elizabeth II.*

1952&3: Measures to counteract increasing *smog problems.*

1953: *Churchill* awarded the *Nobel Prize for Literature.* Coronation of *Queen Elizabeth II* in Westminster Abbey.

1954: *London Nine-Power Conference* agreed to the acceptance of Italy and Germany to membership of the Brussels Pact of 1948. *Temple of Mithras* discovered in the City of London.

1956: *Suez Conference* in London.

1958: Architects *J.Stirling* and *J.Gowan* built houses in the brutalist style at *Ham Common* (London).

1959: Architect Denys Lasdun built the *Cluster Block* in Bethnal Green (London).

1960: Finnish-American architect *Bero Saarinen* (1910–1961) built the *American Embassy* in London.

1961–3: *Hilton Hotel* built.

1963–8: *Hayward Gallery* built.

1965: Greater London Council replaced the London County Council. Death of *Sir Winston Churchill,* twice Prime Minister, in London. Principal work *'Second World War',* (6 volumes, 1949–54).

1966: 621 ft. high *Post Office Tower* built.

1967: Architect *Mies van der Rohe* proposed the *Mansion House Square* project for London.

1968: London traffic and trade brought almost to a standstill by the *strike of factory, port and dock workers.*

1973: *Local government reform.*

1977: *Twenty-fifth jubilee* of the accession of Queen Elizabeth II.

1979: *Rhodesia-Zimabawe Conference* in London, the final act in the transformation of the British Empire into the Commonwealth.

1982: Thousands of people demonstrate in London against the *military conflict* for the *Falkland Islands.* Heir to the throne *Prince Charles* married *Lady Diana Spencer.* Rising *unemployment* caused *race riots* and *tension.*

1986: *Greater London Council* dissolved. *Prince Andrew,* the Queen's second son, married *Miss Sarah Ferguson.*

Ecclesiastical buildings

All Hallows by the Tower (Byward Sreet, EC3): This church is near the Tower, and probably also somewhat in its shade. It was built in 675, damaged in the Second World War and rebuilt in the 1950s by Lord Mottistone; the architecture is of various different periods. The original massive square brick tower has survived (mid 17C), a rare specimen of Cromwellian architecture. The spire, soaring and elaborately wrought, is a later addition; it is said that Pepys watched the horrors of the Great Fire from here in 1666. The *museum* in the 14C crypt with Roman mosaic floor is also worth a visit (by appointment only). Exhibits include historic items from Saxon and Roman London, a faithful model of 'Londinium', the Crusader King Richard I's portable altar and the old church register, with an entry recording the baptism in 1644 of William Penn, the founder of the American Quaker State of Pennsylvania.

All Hallows by the Wall (London Wall, EC2): This building's predecessor, dating from the 12&13C, was built on a bastion of the Roman town walls, but it no longer exists. The present church was built in 1765–8 by George Dance the Younger.

St.Paul's Cathedral ▷

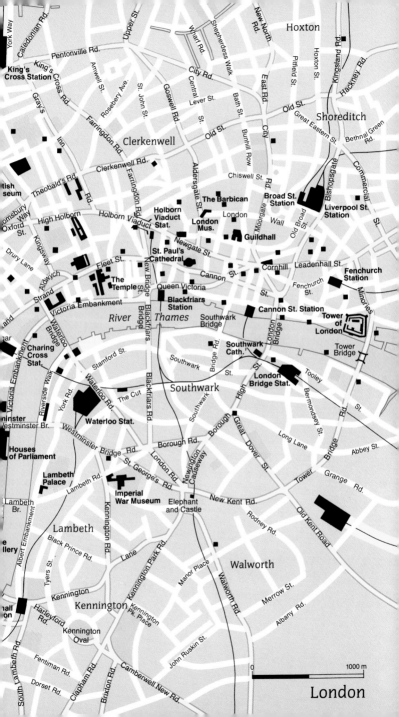

London

UNDERGROUND

Chelsea Old Church, interior

Tunnel vaulting supported by Ionic columns spans the plain, charming interior lit by high lunette windows. The elegantly decorated coffered ceiling is an exact copy of the original destroyed in the Second World War.

All Saints (Margaret Street, W1): This building in black, red and white brick with one brick and one slate tower was completed in 1859 by William Butterfield, and is considered to be among the finest examples of Gothic Revival style. The comparatively sober exterior contrasts strikingly with the gloomy, solemn interior, in which patterns in coloured brick, glass, precious materials such as marble and alabaster, frescos and mosaics combine to make a harmonious overall picture.

All Souls (Langham Place W1): John Nash completed this unusual building, designed to complete the visual line of Regent Street, in 1824. A round portico with Corinthian columns, supports a similarly designed soaring spire—a combination of neoclassical and Gothic elements which did not meet with universal approval. The interior has been modernized.

Brompton Oratory (Brompton Road SW1): The official name of this impressive church in an Italian Renaissance style unusual for its period is *'Church of the London Oratory'*. It is the church of the Order of the Oratorians, a world congregation of priests founded in 1575 by the Florentine priest Filippo Neri, established in Britain by Cardinal J.H.Newman (1801–90). H.Cribble completed the building in 1884; the dome was added about ten years later. Decorative features of the interior with its marble and gilded ornaments are

Mazzuoli's marble Apostle statues of 1680, formerly in Siena cathedral. The Lady Chapel (1693) altar is also from Italy. Church concerts in the Oratory are highly recommended.

Chapel of St.John see *Tower*.

Chelsea Old Church (Chelsea Embankment SW3): Chelsea's *All Saints Church* dates originally from the 13&14C; the apparently modern exterior is the result of restoration after the Second World War, but large parts of the building are original. The *devotional chapel* for *Thomas More* rebuilt in 1528 was scarcely damaged; it contains two early Renaissance capitals said to be the work of More's friend Holbein. Whether the statesman and philosopher is buried with the ladies of his family in the More tomb is as uncertain as the assertion that Henry VIII secretly married Anne Seymour in the church in 1536. Specially noteworthy among the contents and tombs dating mainly from the 17&18C are Bernini's monument to *Lady Cheyne*, the monument to *Sarah Colville*, showing the dead woman in her shroud, monuments to *Thomas Hungerford, Lord Dacre* and *Sir Hans Sloane*, and a plaque to the American writer *Henry James*.

Christ Church (Newgate Street EC1): Only fragments of walls and a tall, slender square tower, one of Sir Christopher Wren's masterpieces, have survived of this late-17C church.

Christ Church Spitalfields (Commercial Street E1): This church with a baroque W. façade reached by an open flight of steps was built by Nicholas Hawksmoor *c.* 1720. The massive building with tunnel-vaulted porch is a harmonious composition of interlinked triumphal arches, culminating in an imposing stone tower. In the lavish interior aisles and choir are separated by Corinthian columns with ornate capitals

All Hallows-by-the-Tower, façade

and high bases. The W. gallery with carved organ front is extremely striking.

Grosvenor Chapel (South Audley Street W1): This church built in Colonial style in 1730 has a façade with central square tower topped with a small spire, and a columned portico in front of it; the church was refurbished in 1912&13. The tombs of the nobility are no longer accessible to the public.

Holy Trinity Church (Brompton Road SW7): This church consecrated in 1829 is in Gothic Revival style, and forms a strong contrast with the nearby *Brompton Oratory*. It is known particularly for its excellent choir.

Holy Trinity Church (Sloane Street, SW1): This church, one of the most striking products of the 'Arts and Crafts Movement' was completed by J.D.Sedding in 1890. The interior is lavishly decorated, including coloured marble, and has a fine E. window, glass by William Morris to designs by the pre-Raphaelite artist Burne-Jones.

London Mosque (Hanover Gate, NW1): The round mosque with a slender minaret built by Sir Frederick Gibberd in 1978&9 is the religious meeting-place of London's Muslims.

Notre-Dame de France (Leicester Place WC2): This litle church refurbished in the 1950s is worth a visit for a French Aubusson carpet and a wall painting by the French artist Jean Cocteau.

Methodist Chapel (Fournier Street, E1): This church built in 1743 with its austere gallery on Tuscan columns served for a time as a synagogue and is now a mosque.

Queen's Chapel at St.James's (Marlborough Road, SW1): This is a masterpiece by Inigo Jones, in his typically severe classical manner, built for Queen Henrietta Maria and dating from 1623–7. The interior was refurbished in the manner of the period *c.* 1660. The finest features of the interior, accessible only by arrangement or on a tour of *Marlborough House* are the white and gold coffered ceiling, the Venetian window which occupies the entire E. wall and Grinling Gibbons' sensitive carving.

Queen's Chapel of the Savoy (Savoy Hill, WC2):Built in the early 16C in Tudor style and radically altered in the 19C, the church contains a fine 13&14C stained-glass window and a magnificent royal stall.

St.Alban (Brooke Street, EC1): Church built in the mid 19C by William Butterfield has been entirely refurbished. It contains a wall painting by H.Feinbusch.

St.Alban (Wood Street, EC2): Only a tower designed by Sir Christopher Wren has survived.

St.Andrew (Holborn Circus, EC1): Wren built this, the largest of his parish

Notre Dame-de-France, wall painting by Jean Cocteau

churches, in 1686 on the site of an earlier building; he used the old foundations for the tower, not completed until 1704. The church had to be completely rebuilt after the Second World War. The furnishings in the somewhat cool interior are from the *Foundling Hospital* founded by Thomas Coram (d.1751); they include Coram's tomb, the pulpit, the font and the organ, a present from the baroque composer Georg Friedrich Händel. The statues of two children above the door (1696) are from a nearby school.

St.Andrew by the Wardrobe (Queen Victoria Street EC4): This church built by Wren in 1696 was restored with a modern interior after the Second World War.

St.Andrew Undershaft (Leadenhall Street EC3): This 16C church was once under a maypole (removed by the moralistic Puritans): 'under the may(shaft)', and the present name is a reminder of this. Fine features of the interior are the wrought-iron altar rail by the French artist

Tijou and Nicholas Stone's font. This sculptor was also responsible for the memorial to *John Stow*, the historian whose 'Survey of London' contains valuable information about the town before the Great Fire of 1666. The Lord Mayor replaces the quill pen in the chronicler's stone hand each year in April in a traditional ceremony.

St.Anne (Dean Street, W1): This 17C Wren church was destroyed in air-raids in the Second World War. Cockerell's tower (1805) has survived, now surrounded by the cemetery, which has been turned into a park.

St.Anne and St.Agnes (Gresham Street E2): This austere red-brick church dating from 1677–80 is another architectural masterpiece by Wren, notable above all for its use of space and ground plan. A square with a dome is surrounded by a cross with tunnel-vaulted arms and groin vaulting at the point of intersection, supported by Corinthian columns. The small tower was added in the early 17C. The furnishings

St.Andrew-by-the-Wardrobe, window

St.Andrew Undershaft, John Stow monument

St.Bartholomew-the-Great, arcades (left), cloister (right)

have been replaced, but the carved reredos is original.

St.Anne Limehouse (Three Colt Street, EC2): This church dating from 1714–24 is the work of Hawksmoor, who managed to transform Perpendicular into classical design in the tower. P.C.Hardwick restored the interior in 1853.

St.Bartholomew the Great (West Smithfield, EC1): Thomas Rahere, a Norman nobleman and courtier of Henry I fell ill with yellow fever on a pilgrimage to Rome, and vowed that he would build a church and a monastery if he were to recover and see his home again. He kept this vow in 1123; at the same time he became the first Prior of the Augustinian monastery, to which the church and *St.Bartholomew's Hospital* belonged. The monastery was dissolved in the Reforma-

tion and the nave of the church destroyed. The remains of the church, which had been used as a warehouse, for accommodation, and as a workshop were not restored until the reign of Queen Victoria by Aston Webb, after Benjamin Franklin had worked here for a short period at a printing press.

The present church includes one bay, choir, transepts and the *Lady Chapel* (early 14C) of the original building and is thus the oldest church in London, after *St.John's Chapel*. A Romanesque stone portal under a half-timbered house in the Tudor style leads across the cemetery, once the S. aisle, to the surviving aisle bay, which now seems like a small entrance portico. Above this is the square tower (1628) with battlements and a decorative lantern. All the outer walls were re-rendered in the 19C. The interior gives an impression of the former size of the

St.Bartholomew-the-Great, interior

church, which originally consisted of the choir only. The massive round piers, the horseshoe-shaped arches framed with austere ornamental stone bands, the galleries above them and the ambulatory with groin vaulting are probably the finest specimens of Norman architecture in London. The clerestory, as can be seen from its design, was added at the point of transition from the 14C to the 15C. The oriel window on the S. side of the choir bears the coat of arms of Bolton, the last prior of the monastery, who added it. The finest features of the furnishings are the early-15C font, *Rahere's tomb*, completed *c.* 1500 and with a 12C statue of the founder of the church in Augustinian habit, the Renaissance tomb of *Sir Walter Mildmay*, one of Elizabeth I's chancellors, the tombs of *Sir R.Chamberlayne* (1615) and *J.Rivers* (1641), and the monument to *Edward Cooke* (1652), whose statue does indeed 'weep' when the weather is wet, as the inscription suggests.

St.Bartholomew the Less (West Smithfield, EC1): The chapel of *St.Bartholomew's Hospital* was built with the hospital in the 12C and rebuilt in the 15C, as tower and sacristy show.

St.Benet (Upper Thomas Street, EC4): It would be difficult to tell from the plain exterior of this church, built by Wren 1677–85, with its brick walls broken up by stone ornaments, tower and elegant lead dome, what treasures are to be found in the interior, one of the best-preserved of all Wren's creations. The gallery is supported by Corinthian columns, and its fine carvings vie with those on the pews, choir stalls, pulpit, altar-table, the rear wall of the communion rail and a door frame on the W. side.

St.Botolph Aldersgate (Aldersgate EC1): This church, built in the 13C and dedicated to the patron saint of English travellers was rebuilt *c.* 1790 and slightly altered again in 1831.

St.Botolph Aldgate (Aldgate High Street EC3): George Dance the Elder built this church *c.* 1744, and John Francis Bentley made alterations, largely in the interior, in 1889; additional alterations followed in the 20C. The organ has a fine housing by Harris (*c.* 1675) and there are numerous outstanding tombs.

St.Botolph Bishopsgate (Bishopsgate EC2): This church built by J.Gould in 1729 and surrounded by an extensive cemetery has a baroque tower; the poet John Keats is said to have been baptized here.

St.Bride (Fleet Street, EC4): The 'journalists'' church', as this work of Wren's has long been known because of its position, was destroyed in the Second World War. Only the spire has survived; at 230 ft. it is Wren's tallest, and its unusual shape inspired a nearby baker to produce his famous wedding cakes: the top of the spire consists of four well-proportioned octagons, decreasing in size as they rise, and pierced with decorative arches. The interior of the church, rebuilt in the fifties, is modern. There is a small *museum* in the little crypt, showing traces and parts of seven earlier buildings from Anglo-Saxon times onwards, and a Roman mosaic floor.

St.Clement Danes (Strand EC2): This new church was built by Wren *c.* 1680 on the site of an earlier place of worship destroyed in 1666, itself probably built for a group of Danish settlers. The new church burned down in the Second World War with the exception of the outer walls and the tall, slender tower by James Gibbs (1719). The existing building was based as closely as possible on Wren's plans and is now the principal *church of the Royal Air Force*: the walls are decorated with the badges of individual units, and tablets commemorate individuals who died for their country. There is a fine stucco ceiling, and the pulpit, which has survived

St.Bartholomew-the-Great, Rahere monument

+ hic jacet Raherus Primus Canonicus et Primus Prior hujus Ecclesie

in its original form, is said to be the work of Gibbons. The bells are also famous, and play the nursery rhyme 'Oranges and Lemons' every three hours. Every year in March the 'Oranges and Lemons Service' is held here, in the course of which all the children present are given an orange and a lemon.

St.Clement Eastcheap (Clements Lane, EC4): The interior of this church built by Wren in 1687 was restored by Butterfield in the 19C. There is some fine carving, for example the font and the pulpit; the late-17C organ is also well known.

St.Cyprian (Clarence Gate, NW1): The plain exterior of this church built by Ninian Comper in 1903 conceals an interior which has survived intact and is one of the architect's masterpieces, bringing the solemn church architecture of the Middle Ages back to new life. Font lid, stained glass, hangings and the exquisitely pierced rood screen were all designed by Comper.

St.Dunstan in the East (St.Dunstan's Hill, EC3): Only the picturesque tower with flying buttresses and tall spire have survived of this church built by Wren *c.* 1700. The tower is now surrounded by a garden.

St.Dunstan in the West (Fleet Street, EC4): This church on the site of an earlier one was completed by John Shaw in Early Victorian style in 1833; like *All Souls* in York it is on an octagonal ground plan. It survived the Great Fire of 1666, but needed considerable restoration. The clock was endowed in 1671 in thanksgiving for the church's survival in the Great Fire; two mythological giants strike the quarter hours. There are two interesting statues which originally decorated the *Ludgate*, the main W. gate of the town, which survived until the mid 18C. They are figures of the legendary King Lud and his two sons, and a statue of Elizabeth I created in 1586, and considered one of the best contemporary likenesses as well as one of the best portraits of a monarch in the country. Most of the monuments in the interior came from the old church, the stellar vaulting has been restored. The

St.Bride, nave

St.Clement Danes, crypt

iconostasis in the chapel used by orthodox Christians is 19C work from the Antim Monastery in Bucharest.

St.Edmund the King (Lombard Street EC2): This church, built in the late 17C by Wren on the site of an earlier building, is dedicated to an English king who died as a martyr at the hand of the Danes. The harmonious building contains some fine carving.

St.Ethelburga (Bishopsgate EC2): This small church with a tower, decorated with a lantern, dates from the Middle Ages; it is dedicated to a Saxon queen. The interior, with paintings including one by H.Feibusch, was considerably rebuilt by Comper. The church is now one of the 14 churches of the London City Guilds.

St.Etheldreda (Ely Place, EC1): Despite later restoration this church built *c.* 1300 is still a fine, indeed striking, example of the Decorated style. It is dedicated to the founder of *Ely Abbey*. Formerly it was the chapel of the abbey bishops; they had a palace nearby; in 1880 it returned to the

Catholic church, in the possession of which it remains.

St.George (Bloomsbury Way, WC1): This church completed by Hawksmoor in 1731 was restored in the 19C. The exterior with its portico supported by six massive Corinthian columns is surmounted by a steeple copied from the mausoleum of Halikarnassos with a statue of George I, the monarch at the time, as the Knight St.George. The flood of light, massive columns and lavish stucco give the square interior a solemn appearance. The most striking features are the altar wall and the ceiling decoration in nave and E. apse.

St.George (Hanover Square, W1): This church with square tower, columned bell chamber and lantern was completed by John James, a pupil of Wren, in 1724, and restored by Arthur Blomfield in the 19C. The entrance in St.George's Street has a massive portico with Corinthian columns; the triangular pediment was intended to carry a statue of George I. The two 20C bronze hounds are impressive. The interior is very light, and divided into nave

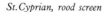

St.Cyprian, rood screen

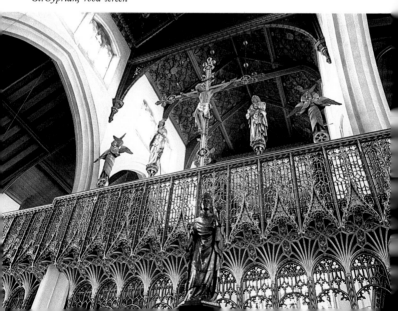

and aisles with side galleries. Distinguished features of the furnishings are the
pew of the composer Händel, who lived
in the parish, the wonderful window in
glowing Flemish stained glass on the E.
wall and the 'Last Supper' attributed to
Kent. In the last century St.George's was
a fashionable church for weddings, including those of Shelley, George Eliot,
Disraeli, Asquith and even Theodore
Roosevelt, who was to achieve distinction
in the New World.

St.Giles Cripplegate (Fore Street, EC2):
This 16C church seems small and unassuming alongside the *Barbican Centre*.
It is surrounded by remains of the city
walls, and is said to stand on the site of
their oldest gate, which led to a secret
passage. The interior of the church, which
has a tower dating from the 15C in its
lower sections and the 17C in its upper
ones, was restored in the 1950s. Oliver
Cromwell was married here, and a slab in
front of the altar marks the tomb of the
poet *John Milton* (d.1674).

St.Giles in the Fields (St.Giles High

Street, WC2): There are numerous tombs
in the solemn interior of this church built
1731–3 by Henry Flitcroft and restored
in the 1950s.

St.Helen Bishopsgate (Great
St.Helen's, EC3): This church dates from
the 13C, and was slightly altered over the
centuries; the square tower with lantern
is 17C. It is dedicated to the Empress
Helena, the mother of Constantine the
Great; she is credited with finding the
Cross of Christ. The plain but imposing
entrance façade with battlements indicates
one of the unusual features of this church:
it consists of two naves of equal size, the
N. of which was reserved for the nuns of
the adjacent Benedictine nunnery, the
other served as parish church. On the N.
wall of the nuns' nave the steps leading
to the nuns' cells are still to be seen; in
the choir is a holy sepulchre built at the
same time as the 'peepholes' used by the
nuns. Striking features other than the fine
Jacobean pulpit are the tombs and grave
slabs: for *John Crosby* (d.1476), the builder
of Crosby Hall, *Hugh Pemberton* and his
wife, (d.*c.* 1500), *Sir William Pickering,*

St.George Bloomsbury, tower

St.Helen Bishopsgate, interior

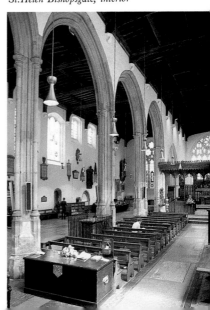

ambassador to Spain under Elizabeth I, *Sir Thomas Gresham* (d.1579), the founder of the Royal Exchange, *Sir John Spencer* (d.1605), Lord Mayor of London in 1594 and his wife, the judge *Sir Julius Caesar* (d.1636) and *Martin Bond* (d.1643), whose tomb shows the dead man in his army tent.

St.James (Clerkenwell Gardens, EC1): This impressive stone building with a massive tower dates from the last decade of the 18C; it was restored in the late 19C.

St.James Garlickhythe (Garlick Hill, EC4): This is another Wren church, built 1674–87 on the site of an earlier building. The tower dates from 1713; it has a stone lantern and three little temples which decrease in size as the height of the tower increases, an unusual feature. Fine aspects of the interior are iron sword rests and the carving on pulpit, W. gallery, rear choir stalls and organ front.

St.James (Piccadilly, W1): This brick church with stone filling was completed by Wren in this ambitious and elegant residential area in 1684. The austere,

sparsely-furnished interior with simple galleries and almost undecorated ceiling vaulting can house 2,000 worshippers; it was lovingly restored after the Second World War. William Pitt the Elder was among the prominent figures baptized in Grinling Gibbons' white marble font, decorated with a relief of Adam and Eve and the Three Wise Men and lavish floral carving. Gibbons was also responsible for the gilded figures on the organ front, brought here from Whitehall in the 17C, and the fine altar wall.

St.James (Sussex Gardens, W2): This severe-looking building was built *c.* 1880 in late Victorian style.

St.James the Less (Thorndyke Street/Vauxhall Bridge Road, SW1): G.E.Street built this red and black brick church in 1860&1; it is one of his more unusual works and one of the most interesting creations of the period. The massive tower, dominating the portico, is separated from the church itself. The multi-coloured bricks in the walls and red granite columns with foliate capitals give

St.Helen Bishopsgate, monument to Sir John Spencer

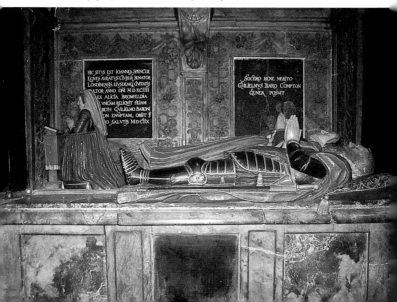

a friendly, relaxed feel to the interior; the church is lit by colourful stained-glass windows. The fresco of the Last Judgement over the choir arch is the work of G.F.Watts. The lavishly decorated pulpit and massive font complete the picture.

St.John (Smith Square, SW1): Thomas Archer worked on this church, one of the finest baroque buildings in London, from 1714–28. The exterior is somewhat disparagingly compared to an up-turned footstool by local people. The vestibules opening on to the N. and S. sections of the church square with their imaginatively decorated gables are surrounded by four elegant corner towers; these were arranged in such a way as to support the building, which is set on marshy land. The spacious interior with four massive Corinthian columns supporting a powerful cornice burned down completely in 1941 and is now used as a concert hall. Art exhibitions are held in the former *crypt*, in which there is also a buffet.

St.John (Waterloo Road, SE1): This early-19C neoclassical church with columned portico with triangular pediment and square three-storey tower with spire is not unlike St.Martin in the Fields. After the church burned down completely in the Second World War only the exterior was restored.

St.John Clerkenwell (St.John's Square, EC1): Along with *St.John's Gate* this church is all that survives of the monastery of the Order of St.John dissolved in 1540 by Henry VIII's reforms. Only the rib-vaulted crypt and parts of the walls have survived. The church was completely rebuilt after the Second World War. In the crypt the impressive tomb of the Spanish nobleman *Juan Ruyz de Vergara* (d.1575), showing the knight in full armour with a page, points to the greatness of the area's past.

St.Katherine Cree (Leadenhall Street, EC3): The most striking interior feature of this church completed in Gothic style in 1631 and subsequently much altered is the great E. rose window, in a square frame. The window, known as the 'catherine wheel', is supposed to symbolize

St.James, Piccadilly, font (left), nave (right)

St.John, Smithsquare, façade

the instrument of torture on which the patron saint died a martyr's death. The fields of the Gothic ceiling in the nave are decorated with the arms of the London Guilds. The organ front and alabaster font date from the 17C; the memorial to the father-in-law of the explorer Sir Walter Raleigh was erected in the late 16C.

St.Lawrence Jewry (Gresham Street, EC2): This church completed by Wren in 1687 has been completely restored with the exception of a few sections of wall.

St.Luke (Sydney Street, SW3): This church was built in 1820 by John Savage in the style of the Gothic Revival. Charles Dickens (1812–70), who painted such a masterly and authentic portrait of 19C London and its inhabitants in his novels, was married here.

St.Magnus the Martyr (Lower Thames Street, EC3): This church with a square tower topped by a spire over 160 ft. high and dating from 1705 is also the work of Wren (1685). The baroque interior, one of the finest in the City, is decorated with wood-carvings of the highest artistic quality, including the altar wall, door frames, pulpit, W. Gallery and organ front, the latter works by Jordan dating from 1712. The wrought-iron communion rail and sword rests dating from 1708 also show high artistic quality.

St.Margaret (Lothbury, EC2): This church with an imposing spire was completed in 1695, and is also the work of Wren. The good, pleasingly-arranged furnishings were largely brought here from other Wren churches, since pulled down. For example, the pulpit, reredos and altar rails and font attributed to

St.John, Waterloo Road

St.Magnus the Martyr, choir

Gibbons are from St.Olave's Jewry. The fine choir screen is based on a design by Wren.

St.Margaret Pattens (Eastcheap EC3): This church with its tall, slender spire is also the work of Wren. It is still not clear whether it was named after the pattens— shoes with iron rings in the soles—made in the area; whether it was or not, there are some on display in the church. It also possesses some interesting canopied pews and masterly carving (e.g. reredos, communion rail and W. wall with royal coat of arms).

St.Margaret Westminster (Parliament Square SW1): Built in the early 16C as a parish church with 18C tower by John James and radically rebuilt in the 19C in Gothic Revivalist style, this church makes a modest, unassuming impression in the shadow of the mighty Westminster Abbey. It has been the parish church of the House of Commons for centuries, and many important weddings have taken place here, such as that of John Milton (1608–74) and Sir Winston Churchill (1874–1965). The E. window, a masterpiece of Flemish stained glass, also has an interesting history. It was a gift of Their Spanish Majesties Ferdinand and Isabella on the occasion of the wedding of their daughter Catherine of Aragon to Arthur, heir to the English throne, and came to London in the early 16C. The unfortunate prince died, however, and in 1509 Catherine became the first of the six wives of Henry VIII. The valuable window passed through various places on its way to St.Margaret's. Among the numerous tombs from the period of Elizabeth I and James I an illuminated memorial tablet for *Sir Walter Raleigh* is particularly striking;

St.Margaret Pattens, sword holder

an ancient temple with massive Corinthian portico topped by a pediment decorated with a coat of arms. Directly beyond the portico with fine Corinthian portal the square tower rises, reminiscent of a Wren tower with two cubic storeys with cornices and intermediate storey topped with the pointed, temple-like lantern.

The interior seems broad, light and spacious. Side chapels and galleries are separated from the nave by large, but not excessively massive columns. The tasteful stucco decoration on the vaulted coffered ceiling is the work of the Italians Artari and Bagutti, working under the direction of Gibbs.

The church is both the parish church of the ruling house (unused as such), and of the admiralty, as the coats of arms near the altar remind us. Traditionally the church was a refuge for the poor and homeless, who used to shelter under its arches. Today free concerts are held here, often given by folk groups.

the explorer and writer, founder of Virginia and favourite of Elizabeth I, was executed by James I in 1618 accused of high treason and is said to have been buried in this church.

St.Martin in the Fields (Trafalgar Square WC2): There was a church on this site as early as 1222, which Henry VIII had rebuilt in 1544; relics from the earlier buildings are on display in the fine crypt. In 1722–6 the Scottish architect James Gibbs, a pupil of Wren and the Italian C.Fontana, created the present building, which unites baroque and neoclassical elements, suspected and criticized at first, but then often copied throughout the English-speaking world, particularly in the USA. The building did not make its full impact until Trafalgar Square was laid out in its present form in the early years of the last century. The church itself is like

St.Martin Ludgate (Ludgate Hill, EC4): This church on the site of a medieval predecessor was completed by Wren *c.* 1685; it includes sections of the old town walls (the *Lud Gate* was nearby) and is dominated by a tall spire. The church is known above all for its original 17C wood carvings, such as the pulpit, backs of the choir stalls, altar rails and door frames, of which some are attributed to Grinling Gibbons.

St.Mary Abchurch (Abchurch Lane, EC4): The unassuming exterior of this brick church built by Wren 1681–6 with its tall, slender spire conceals a splendid, broad, sparsely-decorated interior, with a dome supported by three powerful arches. The baroque dome fresco of 1708 is attributed to W.Snow. Lavish ornamentation makes W.Gray's wooden pulpit of 1685 with its massive sounding board into one of the finest features of the church.

St.Martin-in-the-Fields, pulpit

The marble font with lid date from about the same period. Gibbons' baroque wooden reredos (1686) was restored in a masterly fashion after the Second World War.

St.Mary Aldermary (Queen Victoria Street EC4): The present church was built by Wren in 1681&2 on the site of the earlier medieval church of which only the foundation walls of the tower survived the Great Fire of 1666. The top of the tower, dating from 1702–4, is most unusual: four massive corner buttresses rise to turrets decorated with delicately chamfered cornices. Wren was stimulated by the medieval original in designing the interior, hence the interesting and elegant fan-vaulted ceiling, with fields and shallow domes decorated with lavish tracery. The interior was much altered in the mid 19C; the finely-carved wooden pulpit, a sword rest and a door frame survive from the time at which the church was built.

St.Mary at Hill (Great Tower Street, EC3): Once more it was Wren who on 1676 replaced a medieval predecessor destroyed in the Great Fire; his church was thoroughly and sensitively restored in the mid 19C. After finding one's way through the numerous little alleyways around the building into the church the breadth and spaciousness of the square interior with its vaulting supported on four columns are surprising. The contrast between the fine stucco of 1787&8 and the masterly, dark wood carving gives the church a suitable solemnity. The gilded and enamelled sword rests are among the finest in the City. Formerly fish of all kinds were sold near the church in *Billingsgate Market*, and the *Fishermen's Harvest Festival* on the second Sunday in October is a reminder of this.

St.Mary-le-Bow (Cheapside, EC2): A Norman chapel stood on this site in the early 11C, and forms the crypt of the present church, built by Wren 1670–7 above the massive arches ('bows'). It had to be almost entirely rebuilt after the Second World War. The modern interior with delicately coloured stained glass in decorated in white, gold and blue, and makes an elegant impression.

St.Martin Ludgate, sanctuary

The spire, over 23O ft. high, was also painstakingly restored. Its neoclassical temple anticipates the Victorian style; detractors consider it to be Wren's most tasteless work, but its admirers place it among his finest. Anyone born within the sound of the bells of this church ('Bow Bells') is considered to be a genuine Cockney.

St.Mary-le-Strand (Strand WC2): This little baroque church stands on an island surrounded by a never-ending stream of traffic. Queen Mary commissioned it from James Gibbs, who built it 1714–17. The exterior demonstrates clearly that he was still under the influence of his stay in Italy: the façade, in two storeys articulated with Corinthian columns and pilasters and topped with a balustrade, is decorative but not pompous; there is a semicircular columned portico in front of it, decorated with an urn rather than the projected statue of the royal patroness. Behind this is the tower, reminiscent of Wren, but rather more baroque; it consists of two storeys, one rather broader than the other, each with a cornice decorated with urns,

and at the top the lantern. The interior with double rows of columns has a fine coffered ceiling. The massive, lavishly carved pulpit is a striking feature.

St.Marylebone Parish Church (Marylebone Road, NW1): The present church with portico and tower was built on the site of a much-altered predecessor in the early 19C. The spacious interior is in gold and blue. The *'Browning Room'* is a memorial to the poet Robert Browning (1812–89) and his wife Elizabeth Barrett-Browning (1806–61), known above all for her sonnets. They were married in this church in secret.

St.Mary Woolnoth (King William Street, EC3): Nicholas Hawksmoor's monumental, unusual façade makes a particular impact because of its corner position. The windows are surrounded by heavy bosses, which also form the decoration for the massive double tower. The interior, centrally supported by four groups of tripartite Corinthian columns, has a lavishly carved stucco ceiling and makes a broad and spacious impression.

St.Margaret Westminster, E. window

St.Mary Aldermary, ceiling

St.Mary-le-Bow, view of sanctuary

Most of the fine original wood carving has survived, outstanding examples are the reredos and the lavish casing of Father Smith's organ.

St.Michael Cornhill (Cornhill, EC3): Wren built the church and Hawksmoor added the tower in 1721. The exterior is still the original, but the interior was incongruously refurbished in the Victorian style by George Gilbert Scott in the mid 19C. Font, altar table and a fine 18C pelican in carved wood have survived of the original furnishings.

St.Michael Paternoster Royal (College Street EC4): Dick Whittington, Lord Mayor of London on numerous occasions, commissioned this church on the site of a predecessor in the 15C; it and his tomb perished in the Great Fire. Wren, of course, was responsible for rebuilding. His church fell victim to the air raids of the Second World War and was not rebuilt until after it; the fine wooden pulpit and reredos have survived, however.

St.Nicholas Cole Abbey (Queen Victoria Street, EC4): This church renewed by Wren after the Great Fire also had to be restored after the Second World War. The trumpet-shaped tower was a particularly sensitive and successful achievement. Some fine 17C woodwork has survived in the interior.

St.Olave (Hart Street EC3): The elegant 15C church had a cemetery reached by a door with death's heads and used principally for victims of the plague. It survived the Great Fire but had to be restored after 1945. One of the most important tombs is that of *Elizabeth Pepys*, the wife of the diarist.

St.Marylebone, façade

St.Mary Woolnoth, guild sign

St.Pancras Old Church (Pancras Road, NW1): This little church with free-standing square tower dates from the Norman period, as its exterior shows; the foundations go back even further, to the 4&5C. The present building is a faithful 19C copy. The nearby *Old Cemetery* is now a park, but still contains numerous old gravestones.

St.Pancras Parish Church (Upper Woburn Place, WC1): William and Henry William Inwood created this fine example of Greek Revivalist architecture 1819–22. The Ionic temple façade and flanking sacristy buildings with their somewhat inelegant caryatids are based on the Erechtheion on the Acropolis in Athens, while the octagonal tower is reminiscent of the 'Tower of the Winds' in Athens. The interior is surrounded by a gallery supported on columns with lotus-flower capitals. The pleasing furnishings also fit in with their classical Greek surroundings; some items are more modern.

St.Paul (Covent Garden): This church was rebuilt after a fire in 1795, and is based on a design made by Inigo Jones in 1638. At that time the Covent Garden building project was nearing completion, and the King's purse was running low. For this reason great economy was urged on the architect from the highest quarters: he was told to build 'something like a barn'. The project did not work out particularly cheaply, however, and turned out as an antique temple with overhanging gutters and a 'blind' Tuscan portico (the actual entrance, a modest door, is on the other side). St.Paul's is the actors' church; numerous plaques commemorate great figures of the theatre. Also a wreath carved by Grinling Gibbons indicates that

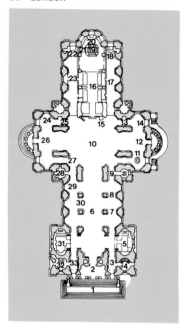

St.Paul's Cathedral 1 W. portico **2** Large W. portal **3** SW portal **4** Dean's Staircase **5** Chapel of St.Michael and St.George **6** Nave **7** S. aisle **8** 'The Light of the World' **9** Stairs up to Library, Whispering Gallery and Dome **10** Dome **11** Font **12** S. transept **13** Entrance to crypt **14** Dean's Vestry **15** Pulpit **16** Choir **17** S. side aisle of choir **18** Lady Chapel **19** High altar **20** Jesus Chapel, also American Memorial Chapel **21** Tijou railing **22** Chapel of Anglican Martyrs **23** N. side aisle of choir **24** N. sacristy **25** Samuel Johnson monument **26** N. transept **27** Joshua Reynolds monument **28** Lord Mayor's Vestry **29** N. aisle **30** Wellington monument **31** St.Dunstan's Chapel **32** All Souls' Chapel **33** NW portal

the great sculptor (1648–1721) and his wife are buried here.

St.Paul's Cathedral (EC4): Sir Christopher Wren's masterpiece, based on St.Peter's in Rome, stands at the heart of the City of London, now the home principally of shops and offices, amidst modern high-rise buildings. After the Great Fire of 1666, (which destroyed four

fifths of the City in only five days the 2–7 September) Wren was instr tal in designing the new City, and all its churches. St.Paul's is today t of the Bishop of London and church of the Commonwealth.

History: While the foundations cathedral were being dug, traces found which suggested that there church on the site as early as 604. T the end of the 11C the N conquerors started work on St. church, which was extended and pa rebuilt in the 14&15C. This churc over 580 ft. long and the tower almc ft. high, making it one of the fine richest in Christendom. In the earl the magnificent building had beco run down, partially as a result confusions of history, that in 1634 Jones was commissioned to resto once majestic Gothic cathedral. We a great W. portico, but the revolut activities of the Civil War affect work deleteriously, and building cou be properly continued until Charles fully reasserted his power afte Restoration. A few days before the Fire, Wren submitted plans for crossing dome. As the fire damag devastating, however, it was deci rebuild the church completely, after vain attempts at repair. Wren set abc designs immediately, but many of were rejected. The foundation sto the present cathedral was finally 1675, however, but the original c was much altered by the architect building. The imposing building, long and 365 ft. high, was comple 1711, but it did not please all V contemporaries. Many thought th church was too 'foreign' and 'mo Subsequent generations and art hist have held rather more favourable opi St.Paul's is now considered the fir the 55 churches built by Wren aft Great Fire, of which 23 are still sta

St.Paul's Cathedral,

St.Paul's Cathedral, seen from Fleet Street

and is also one of London's chief attractions and among the finest churches of its kind in Europe.

Building: Wren based his church on the traditional English (Gothic) cathedral: the ground plan is in the form of a Latin Cross; nave and aisles have a clerestory and buttressed vaulting, the transepts have ambulatories, and the choir and two W. towers are also part of the cross plan. The architect replaced the crossing tower with a massive drum dome; this made it necessary to revise the design of the building to retain its proportions, and also unity of style. Wren made the outer walls as high as the nave, almost like dividing walls with balustrades; they thus conceal the roofs of the aisles, and above all the buttresses, which did not fit in with Wren's classic baroque plan. The entire building is therefore a unified two-storey complex articulated with Corinthian pilasters and

opening into round-arched windows in the lower section and in the upper section windows framed in columned aedicules with triangular pediments. The protruding, massive transept arms are similar in design to the W. façade. A frivolous, unfitting addition is the three-storey, square tower with balustrade, pointed corner turrets and delicate open lantern at the E. end, complementing the towers on other Wren churches.

The 'show side' of St.Paul's is the W. façade. The portico with its six pairs of Corinthian columns is approached by a broad flight of steps. Immediately above the massive cornice of an ancient temple façade rises the second level of the façade, with four pairs of Corinthian columns supporting the triangular pediment. This is decorated with a relief showing the conversion of the Rabbi Saul, who subsequently spread the gospel of Christ as

St.Paul's Cathedral, arch towards side aisle (left), mosaics in vault spandrel (right)

the Apostle Paul. There is also a statue of the church patron on the point of the pediment. This, like the Apostle statues on the pediment bases, is the work of Francis Bird.

The design of the two side axes, which are articulated with Corinthian columns, is consistent with that of the rest of the building. They form the lower sections of the W. towers, which rise above a base decorated with a massive frieze and groups of statues. The towers are identical, and are considered to be the most clearly baroque of all Wren's creations in this vein. The temple-like intermediate section with Corinthian columns and powerful cornice with friezes and topped with urns, grows out of the level containing the clock, with round arches and cornice likewise decorated with urns. Above this is the ornate, artful lantern, consisting of several stages with round-arched openings.

Between the towers is the dome, the second-largest (after St.Peter's in Rome) on any European church. It is supported by Corinthian columns on a plain base with eight supporting buttresses placed behind every fourth column. This level is topped with a balustrade, behind which, set inwards a little, is the pavilion-like hemispherical dome, supported on a circular drum with rectangular windows. The whole is topped by a gold cross on a lantern which resembles the upper parts of the towers. The 'inner life' of this simple-looking construction is, as one might suspect, rather more complex than the exterior suggests. If one looks up into the dome from inside the church one sees a stone domed section beginning a little below the outer storey of columns, the vault of which scarcely reaches the base of the outer dome. The space between the inner and the outer dome is occupied by

a massive cone of stone supporting the lead-clad timbers of the' outer dome as well as the stone lantern; this idea is a piece of constructional genius; the Dôme des Invalides in Paris was built on the same basic principle at almost exactly the same time.

Interior: The visitor can absorb the full majesty of the baroque interior right through to the altar from the W. side, above which is Father Smith's organ with case by Grinling Gibbons. The decoration, consisting of geometrical patterns and foliage, is restricted to the arches and inner sides of the round-arched arcades and the capitals of the Corinthian pilasters. The dark ornamental frames of the shallow domes and the ornamentation of the galleries form an attractive contrast with the light stone. The ground plan is the best guide to the individual sights of the church. The *Dean's steps* (4), an elegant spiral staircase by W.Kempster with an artful, plain wrought-iron rail by J.Tijou is not open to the public, and therefore only visible from below. The *chapel* (5) dedicated to St.Michael and St.George with a high baroque altar crowned with urns and statues and dome decorated with geometrical patterns has since 1906 been the chapel of the Order of the same name, founded in 1818 and awarded for services to foreign and colonial policy. The picture *'The Light of the World'* (8) in a fine gold frame shows Christ with a lantern; he is wearing a golden crown interwoven with the crown of thorns, now bearing leaves, and is knocking on a door symbolizing the soul of Man. The picture is a variation on his own work, to be found in its original form at Keble College, Oxford, by William Holman Hunt. The version in St.Paul's was painted in 1909. A staircase (9) leads up to the *library*, which has fine wooden panelling and beautiful old bookcases. The same staircase leads to the *Golden Gallery* above and the *Stone Gallery*, which provides a wonderful view

◁ *St.Paul's, the Prophet Ezekiel*

of London, and also to the *Whispering Gallery*. The latter is an echo chamber in which a whispered word can be heard almost 100 ft. away. If one looks upward to the beautifully designed *dome* (10) the stone cone supporting the lantern can be seen through the circular opening at the apex. Under this are the so-called *Thornhill cartoons*, framed in *trompe-l'oeil* architecture; six scenes from the life of the Apostle Paul created 1716–19 by Sir James Thornhill. Below these is the whispering gallery, mentioned above, and lit by rectangular windows with Corinthian pilasters and eight niches containing statues between them. The *frescos* in the dome spandrels under another geometrically ornamented gallery date from the 19C. The goblet-shaped *marble font* (11) with lid was completed by F.Bird in 1727. In the S. transept (12) are several monuments, including one to Lord Nelson (1818) with a realistic picture of the admiral by Flexner, and one to *General Abercromby* (1801). The S. choir aisle (17) is the monument to *John Donne* (d.1631), the poet and former Dean of St.Paul's. The statue was rescued from Old St.Paul's, and shows the poet in his shroud. The newly-furnished *Lady Chapel* (18) contains a white statue of the Madonna in a plain wooden frame with two recumbent angels. The fine *wooden pulpit* (15) with curved sounding board decorated with garlands and angels is of more recent date (20C). The *choir* has decorations on the inside of the arches and cornice which are painted or gilded in a similar fashion to the decorative work in the nave. The golden decoration of the ceiling and the ceiling paintings in warm colours were repainted in the 20C after the originals. The modern *high altar* (19) in white Sicilian marble was consecrated in 1958. The fine wooden baldacchino, crowned by Christ Triumphant and four angels is supported by twisted, vertically fluted wooden Corinthian columns.

St.Paul's, John Donne monument ▷

St. Paul's, view from choir into nave

Grinling Gibbons' lavishly-carved *choir stalls* have survived, and so have Tijou's masterly, playfully elegant *wrought-iron gates* (21). Behind the altar is the *Jesus Chapel* (20), which since 1958 has served as a memorial for American soldiers who fell in the Second World War. Their names are listed on a Roll of Honour in a glass case. A gilded eagle, the armorial bird of the USA, tops the English oak reredos, gilded in subtle patterns. The scenes from the Life of Christ in the windows symbolize service, sacrifice and glorification. The marble crucifix in the *Chapel of Anglican Martyrs* (22) is from the former high altar. At the end of the *N. aisle of the choir* (23) is a memorial (25) to *Samuel Johnson* (1709–84). In the *N. aisle* (29) are the tombs of *Lord Leighton* (1830–96) and *General Charles G. Gordon*, killed in 1885 during the Mahdi revolt in the Sudan. The marble *Wellington Memorial* (30) makes a rather more pompous impression. It dates from 1877 and has a bronze sarcophagus and baldacchino supported by Corinthian 'temple porticos'. The baldacchino reaches its pinnacle in a kind of altar table, on which stands a bronze equestrian statue of the Duke. The other bronze statues symbolize virtue, cowardice, truth and lies. *St. Dunstan's Chapel* (31) has a magnificent dome ornamented in gold, a picture of the Resurrection and grisaille angels, and is reserved for private prayer. In the *All Souls Chapel* (32), which has a plain Pietà on the altar, is the white marble memorial to *Lord Kitchener* (1850–1916). Not to be missed is the *Trophy Room* above the NW chapel, in which Wren's various church models and historical documents about the old church are exhibited. The *crypt* (13) is well worth seeing; it occupies the whole of the lower

St. Paul's, crypt, Admiral Nelson's sarcophagus (left), bishop's statue in cathedral treasure (right)

storey, and is said to be the largest in Europe, if not in the world. It contains the diocesan treasure. The collection of tombs, monuments and plaques is dominated by the sarcophagus on a high pedestal of *Admiral Lord Nelson*, who died in the course of his victory over the French at Trafalgar, and aroused gossip before this by his affair with Lady Hamilton. The black marble sarcophagus, on which lies a coronet on a cushion, is directly under the dome; it was made by the Italian B.da Rovezzano for Cardinal Wolsey in 1524, confiscated by Henry VIII, and finally received Nelson's mortal remains in 1805. Opposite is a bust in memory of *Thomas Edward Lawrence* (1888–1935), the author and archaeologist who became famous as 'Lawrence of Arabia' as a result of his support of the Arab uprising against the Turks.

The mortal remains of the *Duke of Wellington* (1769–1852), victor along with the Prussian Field Marshall Blücher over Napoleon at Waterloo, are in a plain porphyry sarcophagus on a granite base decorated with lions' heads. The gun carriage which is also on display was cast by G.Semper in 1852 from cannon-balls used in the Duke's battles. In the so-called 'Painters' Corner' are a bust and the death-mask of *Sir Christopher Wren*, and also his plain tombstone. At the E. end of the chapel is the *Chapel of the Order of the British Empire*; the order dates from 1917, and is awarded to British nationals and allies who have given notable service at home and in the dominions. The chapel was decorated in pink and grey by Lord Mottistone 1957–63, and is divided into a military and a civilian section. The windows are decorated with emblems of the order. Also noteworthy are the wrought-iron work and grisaille pictures of the founders and patrons of the order.

St.Peter (Vere Street, WC1): This dark-brick building with stone corner posts was completed by James Gibbs in 1724. The ceiling is in stucco, the work of the Italian artists Artari and Bagutti; it is supported by Corinthian columns on high bases. Other fine features are the stained-glass windows dating from 1871–89 and Barbara Jones' altar painting. Parts of the church are now used as an office by a Christian association.

St.Peter ad Vincula see *Tower*

St.Peter upon Cornhill (Bishopsgate, EC3): This Wren church dating from 1687 stands at the highest point of the City, on the site said once to have been occupied by the oldest church in London. The domed tower is topped by an obelisk. The font has survived from the time of building of the church, together with some fine wood carving, for example on the door frames, organ case, rear of the choir stalls

and above all on the choir screen which crosses the nave and both aisles, designed by Wren and possibly also his daughter. Medieval mystery plays and concerts of Elizabethan music are performed in the church.

St.Sepulchre (Holborn Viaduct, EC1): Wren was involved in redesigning the interior of the largest parish church in the City after the Great Fire, but the Gothic exterior has been preserved, thanks to thorough restoration, most recently in the 19C. Some items of the original furnishings have survived, including the 17C font lid, the wooden gallery and the case enclosing the Harris organ. Today St.Sepulchre is the musicians' church, and the stained-glass windows in particular are a reminder of this. The ashes of *Sir Henry Wood*, the founder of the Promenade Concerts, are also kept here. The building also has less pleasant associations: the bell was always rung when inmates from nearby Newgate Gaol were taken on tumbrils to the place of execution, after the warden had indicated their fate to them by ringing a little bell which is also kept

St.Paul's, Duke of Wellington's sarcophagus

here. The students of the nearby St.Bartholomew's medical school used to help themselves to bodies from the cemetery as aids to their studies so often that a watchman's hut had to be built specially to prevent this.

St.Stephen (Walbrook, EC4): Wren completed this parish church in 1679, and the interior is considered to be one of his masterpieces. The dome is coffered in the interior, and the rest of the building is square with a protruding section to the W., making it to some extent a dress rehearsal for St.Paul's Cathedral. The dome is supported by beams borne by groups of Corinthian columns. The interior has recently been restored, and it and the magnificent wood carving on the pulpit, organ gallery and case, and font now shine in their former splendour.

St.Stephen's Chapel see *Houses of Parliament*

St.Vedast (Foster Lane EC2): The most interesting feature of this church built 1670–3 by Wren on medieval foundations

is the elegant bell tower, which shows Italian influence in its alternate concave and convex levels. The furnishings (17&18C) in the interior with its stucco ceiling were assembled from other Wren churches which have since been destroyed.

Southwark Cathedral (Borough High Street, SE1): A church and the convent of *St.Mary Overie ('Over the river')* stood on this site in the 7C; the convent passed to the Augustinians in the early 12C. At this time a Norman church was also built, but little of this has survived; the sections that did were incorporated in the existing church, built after a fire in the early 13C and extended and rebuilt in the 14&15C. After the dissolution of the monasteries in the mid 16C the church was a parish church of *St.Saviour* until it became a cathedral in 1905. Like many other London churches it was so neglected over the centuries that thorough restoration was necessary in the late 19C; this was carried out by Sir Arthur Blomfield from 1890, with great skill and sensitivity. Thus the church, with its massive square crossing tower with chequerboard battlements and

St.Sepulchre, tower

Southwark Cathedral, tower

Southwark Cathedral, tomb monument

Southwark Cathedral, tomb

pointed corner turrets is, after *Westminster Abbey* one of the finest Gothic churches in London.

The austere yet spacious interior, beautifully rebuilt to the original design by Blomfield, is imbued with all the serene majesty of Gothic.

Original Norman and Gothic sections were integrated in the SW behind the font and the crossing. The restored altar screen dates from the early 16C; the figures were placed in the niches in the early 20C, to replace the originals, which had disappeared. The cathedral contains numerous fine tombs, including that of *John Gower* (*c.* 1330–1408); it shows the poet, who was the favourite of two kings and a friend of Chaucer, known above all for his 'Confessio amantis' (*c.* 1390), his head pillowed on three of his best-known works. The tomb of *Joyce Austin, Lady Clarke* (W. wall, 1633) is attributed to Nicholas Stone, and shows an agricultural allegory. The monument to *Lionel Lockyer* on the N. wall dates from 1672; he was a miraculous healer who enjoyed a certain notoriety. In the N. Choir aisle is a wooden effigy of a knight, good late-13C work, and valuable above all because it is one of the few surviving pieces of its kind. Opposite is the tomb of of the London Councillor *Richard Humble* (early 17C) and his two wives. The figures on the *Trehearne Monument*, representing the court official who died in 1618 and his family, give a good impression of court dress in the early 17C. In the S. choir aisle is the tomb of *Bishop Lancelot Andrewes*. The *alabaster memorial* of 1912 and the *Shakespeare Window* (1954), showing figures from the plays, are a reminder that England's greatest dramatist, *Shakespeare*, lived in the area. Edmund, the dramatist's younger brother, is said to have been buried here in 1607; a plaque in the floor commemorates this. There is a marvellous Elizabethan chest in the retro choir, and a fascinating but horrible mask of a hungry

Southwark Cathedral, nave

demon devouring a child in the S. aisle. Among the chapels the *Harvard Chapel* is particularly worth mentioning. It was built in 1907 by Blomfield with money from Harvard, Massachusetts and is a memorial to *John Harvard*, who was baptized here in 1608, and founded the famous American university 30 years later.

Spanish and Portuguese Synagogue (Bevis Marks, EC3): This is the oldest synagogue in London and indeed in the country; it dates from 1701 and is similar in style to other ecclesiastical buildings of the period. The fine, and in some cases very valuable, original wood carvings have survived. The ten brass chandeliers still shine out with all their old beauty on special occasions.

Temple Church (Inner Temple, EC4): This former church of the Order of St.John is hidden away behind the *Temple* buildings. The round nave (known as *The Round*) was built in the Norman style between 1160 and 1185 on the model of the Church of the Sepulchre in Jerusalem, and is one of the few surviving examples

of this sort of architecture in the country. From the outside it looks like a rotunda, articulated with pilasters and pierced with arched windows, with a narrower 'upper storey' reminiscent of a battlemented medieval round tower. A Norman doorway with squat arch leads into the nave, where the elegant pointed arches are supported on slender piers of Purbeck marble. The chancel (*The Oblong*) in Early English style was added in 1240. The church was restored to the original design after the Second World War, and is a fine example of the transition from Norman to Gothic style. Wren was involved in the restoration of the reredos in 1692. Particularly interesting are the numerous Purbeck marble *tombs* of knights of the Order of St.John, most of which have been reconstructed, however, with the exception of that of *Robert de Ros* (d.1227).

Wesley's Chapel (City Road, EC1): This chapel was built in 1778 by the theologian and founder of Methodism *John Wesley* (1703–91), which was rebuilt about 100 years later near his house (see *Wesley's*

Southwark Cathedral, reredos

House). There is a memorial statue to him in the churchyard, and some items of the original furnishings have survived in the chapel itself.

Westminster Abbey (Broad Sanctuary, SW1): The majestic Gothic cathedral of Westminster stands near the Thames not far from the Houses of Parliament. Its official name is *Collegiate Church of St.Peter in Westminster*. Elizabeth I placed it under an independent Dean and Chapter, who are still the competent authority. Since 1066 almost all the kings and queens of England have been crowned here, and until the 18C were also buried here. It has also been the scene of many royal weddings. The fact that many public figures are buried or commemorated here sometimes makes the visitor feel that he is in a museum and not a church.

History: The site of the cathedral was settled in Roman times. The date of the monastery's foundation is unknown, but it is certain that there was a church here in the 7&8C. *Edward the Confessor*, the pious Anglo-Saxon king from the House of Wessex (*c.* 1003–1066), canonized in 1161, commissioned the rebuilding of monastery and church in 1050, but did not survive to see the work completed. His successor Harold II Godwinson was defeated by the Norman King William at the momentous Battle of Hastings on 14 October 1066; William's claim to the throne was based on kinship and a promise made by Edward. William was the first king to be crowned in the still incomplete abbey on 25 December 1066.

The history of the present church began in 1245, when King Henry II (1207–1272) decided to create a worthy burial place for Edward and all the subsequent Kings of England. Henry of Reyns, his architect, who worked on the church until 1253, based his designs on the cathedrals of Amiens and Reims, magnificent examples of French Gothic. Within ten years transepts, choir and part of the nave had been built; the nave continued to grow rapidly until the end of the century. Building continued in the mid 14C, and the W. section of the nave was completed under Henry Yvele, who followed the original plans in minute detail, and was also responsible for the

Wesley's Chapel, stained-glass window

Westminster and Westminster Abbey

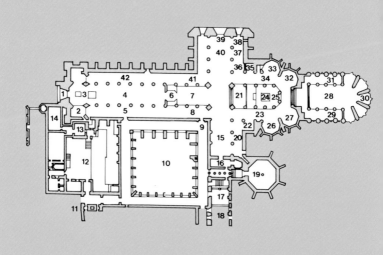

Westminster Abbey 1 W. portal **2** St.George's Chapel **3** Churchill memorial plaque and Tomb of the Unknown Warrior **4** Nave **5** S. aisle **6** Organ loft **7** Choir and choir screen **8** S. side aisle of choir **9** Gate to cloister **10** Cloister **11** Deanery courtyard **12** Deanery (not accessible) **13** Jericho Parlour (not accessible) **14** Jerusalem Chamber (not accessible) **15** S. transept **16** St.Faith's Chapel **17** Chapel of the Pyx **18** Crypt museum **19** Chapterhouse **20** Poets' Corner **21** Sanctuary **22** St.Benedict's Chapel **23** S. covered walk **24** St.Edward's Chapel **25** Henry V Chapel **26** St.Edmund's Chapel **27** St.Nicholas' Chapel **28** Henry VII Chapel **29** Tomb of Mary Queen of Scots **30** Royal Air Force Chapel **31** Tomb of Elizabeth I and her sister Queen Mary **32** St.Paul's Chapel **33** Chapel of St.John the Baptist **34** N. covered walk **35** Islip Chapel **36** Chapel of St.John the Evangelist **37** St.Michael's Chapel **38** St.Andrew's Chapel **39** N. portal **40** N. transept (Statesmen's Aisle) **41** N. side aisle of choir **42** N. aisle

demolition of the Norman sections of the building. The old Lady Chapel was replaced by the *Chapel of Henry VII* from 1503. The monastery was dissolved and the church raised to the status of cathedral in the course of the subsequent religious turmoil which started with the separation of the English Church from Rome under Henry VIII. Queen Mary restored the old status in 1556. The monastery was finally secularized by her successor Elizabeth I, who also conferred its present status upon the church. The building itself was hardly damaged during this period: indeed, work continued. The great Sir Christopher Wren was involved in designing the façade at a later date, and the two towers were added by Nicholas Hawksmoor in the mid 18C. Much of the original exterior detail was lost in the course of 19C restoration, but the interior retained its original furnishings, majesty and beauty.

The buildings: It is not just its imposing dimensions which make the abbey 'great' (it is almost 500 ft. long, 200 ft. wide and over 100 ft. high). The W. façade, neo-Gothic in appearance, rises massive and undecorated behind a small portico with

Westminster Abbey, Henry VII Chapel

battlements and pointed windows. There are no statues in the pointed niches with crockets intended for them, contrary to Gothic cathedral tradition, and the trefoil and quatrefoil friezes make an essentially flat and sober effect. The 'classic' rose window is replaced by a plain mullioned Gothic window extending through several storeys and decorated with delicate trefoil friezes. The portal seems squat, and is again undecorated. The tower storey gives the impression of having been stuck on the top, which is in fact the case. It has a central pediment pierced by a window with pointed arches, and the pierced balustrade and pointed turrets which top them are more like confectionery than true Gothic architecture, a typical feature of the neo-Gothic style. The stylistic discrepancy caused by the different building periods shows clearly in the N. section of the nave, where lavish Gothic tracery (13C) is placed side by side with undecorated and only lightly articulated walls. The *chapter house*, dating from 1245–50, the oldest part of the building, with a 19C pyramidic roof is articulated with massive flying buttresses. The outer walls of the Chapel of Henry VII are also most attractive, with flying buttresses rising to the height of the turrets topped with delicate crocketed Tudor domes. The buttresses are decorated with numerous realistic and phantastic creatures in carved stone, between them are windows set in a zig-zag pattern.

Interior: The first thing to strike the visitor is the lightness and breadth of the church, an impression enhanced by its height and length: the Abbey possesses the largest Gothic nave in the land. The next impression is of the unity and harmony of the building, despite the fact that it dates from so many different periods. The

Westminster Abbey, monuments to Georg Friedrich Handel (left) and William Shakespeare (right)

pointed arches are built in greenish Purbeck marble of a slightly lighter shade than that of the elegant rounded piers. The same restrained elegance is continued in the pointed, trefoil-patterned arches of the triforium. A fan vault with lavish hanging decoration spans the aisles and chapels, which are set in a stellar pattern. The design of nave and apse is particularly interesting and unusual: pairs of fans with powerful ribs meet at a central seam formed from a chain of adjacent, and elegant keystones. The individual monuments in the Abbey are listed on the ground plan, but they are so numerous that the list cannot claim to be complete. The relatively small *W. portal* (1) is framed by a monument to *William Pitt the Younger* in the form of an altarpiece, with statues by Richard Westmacott (1806). The great *W. window* (1735) above it is

decorated with statues of prophets. On the second SW pillar is a *portrait of Richard II* dating from 1389, the earliest contemporary portrait of an English monarch. *St. George's Chapel* (2), the actual baptistery, is now dedicated to the memory of the dead of the First World War. *Sir Winston Churchill* (1874–1965) is commemorated by a plain marble slab set in the floor. In front of this, equally plain but always lovingly tended, is the *Tomb of the Unknown Soldier* (3), an English victim of the First World War, buried in Flanders earth. In the *nave* (4) are numerous memorials, including those of the African explorer *David Livingstone* (1813–73) the architects *Sir Charles Barry* and *Sir Gilbert Scott*, the engineer *Robert Stephenson* (d.1848), the politician *Neville Chamberlain* (1869–1940) and other distinguished personalities. On the N. side

Westminster Abbey, Edward the Confessor's shrine (left), Coronation Throne (right)

the eight *windows by Ninian Comper* each show a king and a contemporary Abbot of Westminster. The S. wall of the *S. aisle* (5) is decorated with wall paintings of St.Christopher and Doubting Thomas, dating from the 13C. Important among the monuments here are that to the novelist *Thomas Hardy*, (1860–1928), that to the distinguished Dean *Joseph Wilcocks* (1756), who was concerned that the façade should be completed, and that of *General Hargrave*, considered to be one of Louis Roubiliac's finest works, and of course the first Renaissance tomb in the country, splendidly built by Pietro Torrigiani in 1513 for *Lady Margaret Beaufort*. In the nave is the *organ* (6), lavishly cased in gold. The *choir* is separated from the nave by a splendid screen gilded by Edward Blore (1834); it is similar to a Gothic triptych and decorated with colourful figures of the saints. In the 'side wings' under lavish

tracery are monuments for *James Earl of Stanhope* and *Sir Isaac Newton* (1642–1727), created by Kent and Rysbrack in the 18C. The choir aisles are lined with gilded canopies with lavish tracery. The stalls are by Blore, 1847. In the *S. choir aisle* (8) is the *door* (9) into the *cloisters* (10), of which the N. and NE sections are 13C, the remainder 14C. One door arch has a set of figures depicting the Stem of Jesse. The memorial to *Jane Lister* is a moving expression of grief for the dead child. At the end of the E. section of the cloister is the '*Dark Cloister*', low and undecorated. In the *S. transept* (15) are more monuments, including Kent's to *William Shakespeare* (1713) and that of a great Shakespearean actor, *David Garrick* (1717–19), taking a last bow before the curtain. There are also memorials to the historian *Thomas B.Macaulay* (1800–59), *John Duke of Argyll*, whose monument is

Westminster Abbey, Stone of Scone under the Coronation Chair

an excellent piece of work by Roubiliac (*c.* 1750), the baroque composer *Georg Friedrich Händel* (1685–1759), commemorated by a Roubiliac monument and a grave slab, the writers *Charles Dickens* (1812–70) and *Rudyard Kipling* (1865–1936), also the 'Swedish Nightingale', *Jenny Lind* (1820–87). The glass in the rose window is an early-20C addition. In *St. Faith's Chapel* (16) are a portrait of the patron saint and two splendid 16C Brussels tapestries. In the *Chapel of the Pyx* (17), the sacristy at the time of Edward, is the oldest stone altar in the church, dating from the 13C. The 'pyx' used to be kept here, a chest containing the gold and silver test plates used as standards for the purity of the coins of the realm. The *chapter house* dates from 1253, restored in 1855. It is an octagonal room, with rib vaulting supported by a single pier with several elegantly decorated column shafts. The paintings under the trefoil arches along the walls are somewhat faded. In the entrance tympanum is Christ with angels, surrounded by a quatrefoil. The trefoils in the corners above the elegantly designed arches are occupied by statues of the saints, and there are also flanking statues of the saints in trefoil niches. This room, with its fine original floor, was the former meeting place for members of the House of Commons. *Poets' Corner* (20) contains the monument to Geoffrey Chaucer ((*c.* 1340–1400), the creator of the 'Canterbury Tales', who was buried in a much more austere tomb in the Abbey itself. The following are also commemorated by busts, plaques and statues: *Robert Browning* (1812–69), *Alfred Lord Tennyson* (1809–92), *Henry Wadsworth Longfellow* (1807–82), *John Dryden* (1631–1700), *Wystan Hugh Auden* (1907–73), *Dylan*

Westminster Abbey, tomb of Arthur Penrhyn Stanley (left), Henry VII Chapel (right)

Thomas (1914–53), *Lewis Carroll* (1832–98), *Thomas Stearns Eliot* (1888–1965) and *Ben Jonson* (1573–1637) with a monument by Gibbs and Rysbrack. English monarchs are still crowned in the *sanctuary* (21). The lavishly ornamented, gilded reredos with statues of the Evangelists in lavish tracery niches is the work of Sir Gilbert Scott (1867). The frieze shows scenes from the Life of Christ. Above the altar is a modern *mosaic* by Salvati depicting the Last Supper. The *marble floor* is 13C Italian work. The 13C sedilia (seats for the clergy), each with a bishop's head on the base, are placed under pointed trefoil arches in front of two surviving larger-than-life-size *portraits of kings* (Henry III and Edward I?). On the N. side are the masterly 13&14C Gothic tombs of *Edmund Crouchback, Earl of Lancaster* (d.1296), the brother of Edward

I and his consort *Aveline* (d.1272) and that of *Aymer de Valence* (d.1327), a cousin of Edward I. Each of the sarcophagi is lavishly decorated with tracery and statues, and has a recumbent figure of the person commemorated. The tombs are surmounted by pointed Gothic baldacchinos, those for the two men being the most lavishly decorated. *St.Benedict's Chapel* (22) contains the alabaster tomb of *Simon Langham*, Archbishop of Canterbury (d.1376). In the *S. ambulatory* (23) is a 13C retable decorated with statues of Christ and saints and elegant stellar wainscotting. The *Chapel of Henry V* (25)has numerous 15C sculptures and a picture of the king's coronation; it spans the ambulatory to link up with *St.Edward's Chapel* (24). This chapel dedicated to Edward the Confessor is the heart of the abbey. The king's *tomb*, which

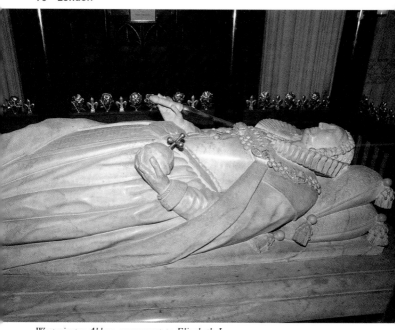

Westminster Abbey, monument to Elizabeth I

Westminster Abbey, Innocents' Corner, tombs of Sophia and Mary

Westminster Abbey, tomb of Eleanor of Castile

Westminster Abbey, tomb of Richard II

has suffered greatly from the ravages of history, carries today only hints of its former beauty; it was commissioned by Henry III in 1241 and completed in 1270. Above the stone lower section, decorated with geometrical patterns and pierced with trefoil arches is a two-tier wooden section with columns in brown and gold. This replaces the lid, decorated with valuable jewels, which was stolen by thieves. As well as Edward other rulers of the House of Plantagenet are buried in the chapel. *Edward I* (d.1307) lies in a plain, undecorated coffin in black Purbeck marble. The magnificent gilded recumbent figure of his consort Eleanor of Castile (d.1290) on her marble sarcophagus is the sensitive work of W.Torel. The same artist is responsible for the image of *Henry III*. The two-tier sarcophagus of *Edward III* , lavishly decorated with coats of arms, tracery and sculpture, upon which lies the gilded bronze effigy of the ruler, with long hair and beard, was the work of Henry Yvele. The realistic marble figure of his queen *Philippa of Hainault* (d.1369) is the work of Hennequin de Liège. *Richard II* and his queen *Anne of Bohemia* are in a double tomb with coffins by Yevele and Steven Lot (1395): the two recumbent figures are the work of N.Broker and G.Prest.

The wooden *Coronation Chair*, supported by four lions and with a pointed back-rest stands in front of a 13C stone wall decorated with a frieze showing scenes from the life of St.Edward. The paintings on the venerable but uncomfortable-looking seat, on which all English monarchs have been crowned, have now faded to some extent. The chair was made *c.* 1300 by Walter of Durham. Under the seat is the *'Stone of Scone'*, a reddish-grey block of sandstone. Until 1296 all the kings of Scotland sat on it for their coronation; then it was seized by Edward I, who then commissioned the chair as a sort of shrine, and brought to London. Since then it has symbolized the unity of the two countries. Outstanding among the numerous tombs in *St.Edmund's Chapel* (26) is that of *William de Valence* (d.1296), a half-brother of Henry III. The splendid enamelled recumbent figure is said to be from Limoges. The *St.Nicholas Chapel* (27) contains the marble tomb of *Sir John*

Westminster Abbey, tomb of William de Valence, detail

Villiers (d.1606) and the tomb of *Elizabeth of Northumberland* (d.1676), a masterpiece by Robert Adam and Nicholas Read. A jewel of the Perpendicular style is the *Chapel of Henry VII* (28), in which the tracery and statues are a veritable feast for the eye. The Renaissance tomb of the founder and his consort *Elizabeth of York* in black marble is decorated with gilded ornaments, cherubim bearing coats of arms, recumbent figures of the royal pair and two lions; it is masterly work by the Italian Pietro Torrigiani dating from 1518. The surrounding bronze rail is the work of Thomas Ducheman. Since 1725 this has been the chapel of the *Most Honourable Order of the Bath*, the banners of which hang on the walls.

Cornelius Cure created the tomb of *Mary, Queen of Scots* (29), with a beautiful effigy of the Scottish queen. James I had the mortal remains of his mother, executed in 1587 at Fotheringay on the orders of Elizabeth I, brought to the abbey. In 1947 a small chapel with gilded tracery and sculpture was dedicated as the *RAF Chapel* (30), in memory of the men victorious in the Battle of Britain in 1940. Hugh

Easton's *Memorial Window* is decorated with the badges of the squadrons involved; in the central section Crucifixion and Resurrection symbolize sacrifice and victory. *Viscount Trenchard*, the 'father' of the Royal Air Force, was buried here in 1956. In front of the chapel is a reminder that *Oliver Cromwell* was once buried here. Maximilian Colt created the tomb of *Elizabeth I* (1533–1603) in 1606: four lions couchant support a realistic recumbent figure of the 'Virgin Queen'. The tomb is canopied by a pompous baldacchino lavishly decorated with coats of arms and statues and supported by black marble columns with gilded Corinthian capitals on a high plinth. Next to Elizabeth is her half-sister *Mary I* (1516–58), who from 1553 tried to make England Catholic again in a brutal fahion which earned her the name 'Bloody Mary'. Opposite, in 'Innocents' Corner', lie *Sophia* and *Mary*, the two daughters of James I who died in infancy. Their tombs are decorated with touching figures of children. *St.Paul's Chapel* (32) contains tombs of dignitaries from the periods of Henry V and Charles I. The *N. ambulatory* (34) leads to the *Islip*

Westminster Abbey, tomb of Mary Queen of Scots

Chapel (35), dedicated to the abbot and church architect of the same name, who was buried here in 1532.

In the chapel of *St. John the Baptist* (33) is the marble tomb of *Thomas Cecil, Earl of Exeter* (d.1623) and his wife. The other *side chapels* (36,37,38) also contain notable tombs. The *N. transept* (40) contains the tombs of many distinguished statesmen. Outstanding among the tombs in the *N. aisle* (42) are: the marble tomb, attributed to Colt, commemorating *Sir Francis Vere* (1609), who is represented in full armour, supported by four kneeling knights. Westmacott's tomb, completed in 1815, for *Charles James Fox*, a devotee of the ideals of the French Revolution, supporter of the rights of the American colonies and campaigner for the abolition of slavery; for these reasons the tomb is decorated with allegories of peace and freedom and a coloured man at prayer. Finally the touching *Nightingale Monument* by Roubiliac (1761): James Nightingale seeks desperately to turn aside the deadly lance which is threatening his young wife. The *Deanery* (12), the *Jericho Parlour* (13) and the *Jerusalem Chamber* (14), in which Henry IV is said to have died, are not open to the public.

The *undercroft museum* (18) is also worth a visit. It is entered via the 'dark' or Norman cloister. Funeral effigies and statues of rulers and other eminent personalities and various exhibits are displayed under low Norman arches.

Westminster Cathedral (Ashley Place, SW1): Not to be confused with Westminster Abbey is the Roman Catholic Cathedral, seat of the Archbishop of Westminster. It is a basilica with four shallow domes on a rectangular ground plan built 1895–1903 by John Francis Bentley on the model of Hagia Sophia in Istanbul, and Italian basilicas. There is a splendid view of London from the campanile, 284 ft. high, and based on the campanile of Sienna cathedral.

The plain red-brick outer walls with white stone bands enclose an interior with nave and two aisles which makes a strangely alien, solemn and perhaps slightly mysterious effect because of the diffused lighting, the use of various shades of marble from white to black, the statues and decorative mosaics, in gold and glowing colours, entirely Byzantine in style, and like the marble cladding still incomplete. The spacious *nave*, 149 ft. wide including the aisles and side chapels, is the widest in England. The aisles are separated by rounded arches above which runs a gallery. The dark green marble of the columns is said to have come from the same Greek quarries as that used for Hagia Sophia. None of the beautifully carved capitals in Carrara marble is exactly like the others. The walls are clad in marble shaded from grey to black. The baldacchino over the high altar is supported on two columns, and made of particularly luminous material. The light marble pulpit is also a masterpiece of the stonemason's art. Outstanding among the furnishings, dating largely from the 1930s, are the reliefs on the main piers depicting the Stations of the Cross, carved by Eric Gill from 1913–18. The *chapels* show the same exotic Romanticism as the nave, gleaming with marble and luminous mosaics; most of them contain tombs or monuments. The *crypt* is also worth a visit. It houses a collection of relics, some of which are very valuable.

Secular buildings

Albany (Piccadilly, W1): Built in the late 18C for Lord Melbourne, it was sold in the early 19C, extended, and converted into exclusive apartments for gentlemen; former occupants included Gladstone, and at the time of writing Edward Heath lives here.

Apothecaries' Hall (Blackfriars Lane,

Westminster Abbey, tomb of Henry VII and Elizabeth of York

EC4): The Guild of Apothecaries was founded in 1617, and for a long time held a monopoly over the sale of medicaments in the City. The present building was erected by the Guild on the foundations of the former *Blackfriars monastery* in 1684, and was radically altered about a century later. The coat of arms of the guild can be seen above the entrance; the interior is not usually open to the public, but contains fine paintings and other notable furnishings.

Apsley House see *Wellington Museum*.

Athenaeum Club (Waterloo Place, W1): All members of this highly exclusive gentlemen's club founded in the early years of the last century are noted for their services to the arts. The façade is decorated with a statue of Pallas Athene, the patroness of the arts and science in ancient Greece, and the entire building, which is of course not open to the public, is Greek in style. Only club members are allowed to use the library with its valuable collection of books and manuscripts. The two stone blocks outside the building were placed there to make it easier for venerable club members to alight from their carriages.

Oversea-Chinese Banking Corporation (Cannon Street): The 'London Stone', is built into a niche in the S. wall. It used to be in the middle of the road, and served as a milestone for the military roads leading out of Roman Londinium.

Bank of England (Threadneedle Street, EC2): The guardian of the British currency was founded as a private company in 1694 and was nationalized in 1946. The building, affectionately known as 'The Old Lady of Threadneedle Street' was built by Sir John Soane from 1788. As the influence of the bank increased and its sphere of business widened, so the need for personnel grew; the mountains of documentation grew at the same rate, so that an extension was needed, completed by Sir Herbert Baker 1924–39. Soane's impressive façade with balcony supported on eight Corinthian columns remained untouched. Above this is a massive rusticated storey with statues supporting

Apothecaries Hall (left). Banqueting House, Rubens ceiling in banqueting hall (right)

a further storey like an ancient temple portico with triangular pediment with a statue resting on six pairs of columns. The rest of the building now includes seven storeys above ground level and three below, in which the national gold reserves are stored. Only the entrance hall is open to the public; it contains an exhibition of coins and banknotes.

Banqueting House (Whitehall SW1): This building articulated by Corinthian columns and topped with a balustrade is all that remains of the old palace of *Whitehall*, which burned down in 1698; it was the town residence of the monarch until that time. It was completed in 1622 and is considered a masterpiece of the architect Inigo Jones. Jones had studied and come to admire buildings and theoretical writings by Andrea Palladio (1508–80) in the course of an Italian journey, and subsequently introduced the Palladian style to England.

The most magnificent feature is the double-cube *Banqueting Hall*, in which gala occasions are still held. Tall slender Corinthian columns with discreetly gilded capitals separate the windows of the lower storey, while the walls of the upper storey are enlivened by pilasters with more lavish Corinthian capitals. The underside of the gallery balcony, topped with balustrades, is decorated with delicately gilded helixes derived from the capitals. The coffered ceiling is a masterpiece commissioned by Charles I from Peter Paul Rubens in 1630; Rubens received a knighthood for the work. A large and four small ovals and two rectangular and one square painting, lavishly framed in curlicued gold, are allegories, of greatness, wisdom, goodness, the victories of the Stuarts and the unification of England and Scotland. Charles was to meet his end shortly after this, and indeed at the very place where he had set so magnificent a monument to himself and his line: on 30 January 1649 the king, who through his absolutism had sparked off the Puritan Revolution, stepped through this very room to the scaffold which Cromwell had set up for him in front of the building. A bust of the unhappy monarch marks the place from which he stepped through the window to his execution. It was also in this room that

Banqueting House, banqueting hall, detail of ceiling paintings by Rubens

Cromwell later refused the crown and Charles II swore his oath of allegiance to Parliament in 1660, after the restoration. William and Mary offered the Crown here.

Billingsgate Market (Lower Thames Street, EC3): The typical 19C buildings of the old fish market, which moved further E. in 1982, are now the property of a bank.

Blackfriars Inn (Queen Victoria Street, EC4): This pub is hardly a historic building, but an appealing, highly typical late-Victorian corner house (1897), with a well-fed monk inviting in passers-by with a welcoming smile. The ceiling is decorated with gold leaf, and the comfortable room has open fires and an unusual bar; engravings on the wall show the monks at work. The pub took its name from a 13C monastery which used to stand nearby.

Buckingham Palace (The Mall SW1): The Duke of Buckingham commissioned

a fairly plain brick building under the mulberry trees which then grew in the area in 1703; this was *Buckingham House*. George III bought the land for his wife Charlotte in 1762, and it was known from that time on as 'Queen's House'. It became a palace in 1826–30 under George IV, who commissioned his architect John Nash to change the plain building into a larger complex fit for a king. The enterprise swallowed so much money, however, that it became a source of scandal. Queen Victoria finally declared Buckingham Palace to be the official town residence of the monarch in 1837, and it has remained so to this day: the hoisting of the royal standard above the palace confirms the presence of the monarch. A visitor approaching from *The Mall* sees the E. façade, the most recent section of the building, behind the railings decorated with the royal coat of arms and supported between posts of carved stone. The two-storey façade, designed in neoclassical style by Sir Aston Webb in 1913, is topped by a balustrade, articulated with Corinthian pilasters and supported on a massive,

Banqueting House, ceiling paintings, detail

Blackfriars Inn

rusticated lower storey. The central and side sections are in the form of ancient temples, each with four Corinthian half columns and triangular pediment decorated with coats of arms and friezes. The palace is closed to the public, with the exception of the *Queen's Gallery* and the *Royal Mews*. Visitors invited to the Queen's garden parties pass into the grounds through the *Bow Room*.

Carlton House Terrace (SW1): Nash completed this charming complex articulated by squat and slender columns in 1832; it takes its name from *Carlton House*, the residence of the Prince Regent, which used to stand on this site. A gigantic bronze statue by Richard Westmacott (1834) commemorates *Frederick Duke of York*, the extravagant son of King George III.

Carlyle's House (Cheyne Row, SW3): *Thomas Carlyle*, the Scottish essayist and historian (b.1795) moved into *No. 24*, a plain house, typical of its period (1708) in 1834 with his wife Jane, with whom he is said to have had a stormy marriage.

He lived here until his death in 1881. A plaque near the entrance commemorates the 'Sage of Chelsea', as he became known. The interior was left essentially as his wife had planned it. This is also confirmed by the picture 'A Chelsea Interior', in which only the former owners and occupiers do not fit in with the present interior. The writing materials exhibited for visitors in the attic study still seem to be waiting for their master.

Central Criminal Court see *Old Bailey*.

The Charterhouse (Charterhouse Square, EC1): Sir Walter Manny founded a Carthusian monastery here in 1371. It was dissolved under Henry VIII and passed into the possession of various noblemen. It later accommodated a famous boys' boarding school, now in Surrey. The bachelor or widower pensioners have remained, however; rigid conditions have to be fulfilled to qualify for accommodation. The building is entered through the restored 15C *gatehouse*. Many sections of the original building have survived in the *Master's*

Buckingham Palace

Court, and also in the *Wash-House Court*, which dates back to the 14&15C. The stones of the former *monastery church* were used to build the *Great Hall*. The tomb, dating from 1615, of the founder of both boarding school and hospital, *Thomas Sutton*, is in the pleasantly decorated chapel.

Chelsea Royal Hospital (Royal Hospital Road, SW3): In 1682 Charles II, prompted by the foundation of the Hôtel des Invalides in Paris and by the essayist and diarist John Evelyn, commissioned Christopher Wren to build a refuge for old and disabled soldiers. Work was completed in 1692. 400 pensioners still live here, easy to recognise by their uniforms dating from the 18C (blue coat in winter, red in summer). After extension in the 18C the building, which is open to the Thames on the S., was completed by Sir John Soane in neoclassical style in 1819. Entrance to the building is through a Tuscan portico with triangular pediment. The building is in brick, enlivened with tile patterns, and topped with a square tower with lantern. A small *museum* deals with the history of the hospital. Grinling Gibbons' bronze statue of Charles II stands in the *Figure Court*. The walls of the *Great Hall*, in which Wellington lay in state, are decorated with portraits of kings, including an allegorical one by Verrio of Charles II, and flags which are the spoils of war. Wren's fine chapel has survived in its original state, with panelled walls and fine contemporary furnishings, including Sebastiano Ricci's outstanding picture of the Resurrection, which is in the rectory. The annual *Chelsea Flower Show* takes place in the gardens which run down to the Thames. The annual *Founder's Day Parade* on 29 May may be attended by invitation only.

Chiswick House (Burlington Lane, W4): The first Earl of Burlington acquired a Jacobean house surrounded by a splendid park towards the end of the 17C. One of his successors, the third Earl of Burlington, a devotee of Palladio, had a villa designed by himself added on to the old house; it is one of the finest country houses in England in this style. In front of the low, undecorated, square lower

Buckingham Palace, gate

storey is a columned portico approached by two double flights of steps. The house has an octagonal dome. The summer garden at the E. end forms a connection with the old house. The rooms in the lower storey once served as a library, and still contain documentation on the history of the villa. William Kent was responsible for the decoration of the upper rooms, which are reached by a spiral staircase. The dome over the main hall has a fine coffered ceiling, and the white and gold gallery is decorated with fine ceiling frescos. The adjacent rooms in red and green are hung with costly wallpaper, and also contain fine and sometimes valuable furnishings.

Clarence House (The Mall SW1): John Nash built this painted and stuccoed two-storey house adjacent to the W. of *St. James Palace* in 1825 for the Duke of Clarence, later King William IV. It is now the town house of the Queen Mother.

College of Arms (Queen Victoria Street EC4): This society, founded in the 15C and accommodated in this building, some-times also known as the *Heralds' Office* is the authority on heraldry in the United Kingdom, but also deals with the maintenance of tradition on official occasions. They are the authority on ancestral matters, and responsible for the design of new coats of arms. Queen Mary presented the society with a building on this site in 1555, but it was subsequently destroyed in the Great Fire. The present building, truncated by the extension of *Victoria Street*, was completed in 1688. The lower storey is rusticated, and the upper storey has pilasters with lavish stone capitals, a reminder of the former beauty of the building. The beautiful wrought-iron railings are also worthy of attention. Only the entrance hall is open to the public.

County Hall (Belvedere Road, SE1): There is a particularly fine view from the Thames of the seat of London's former governing body. The building was completed in 1956. The heart of the neo-Renaissance façade, over 650 ft. long, is the entrance hall, curving inwards, articulated with Corinthian pilasters, flanked by aedicules and topped by a broad frieze.

Chelsea Royal Hospital

College of Arms, entrance

Crewe House (Curzon Street, W1): This town house in the Georgian style with columned portico and triangular pediment over a rusticated storey dates from 1730.

Cromwell House (Highgate Hill, N6): This red-brick town house reputed to have been occupied by army commander, statesman and Lord Protector *Oliver Cromwell* (1599–1658) was built in 1640 after Dutch models.

Crosby Hall (Cheyne Walk, SW3): Wool merchant *Sir John Crosby* commissioned a town residence which was built 1466–75, and was soon among the finest in the City. After his death the house was occupied by the future *King Richard III* and owned by the statesman and humanist *Sir Thomas More* (c. 1478–1535). The entire house with exception of the hall was destroyed by fire in the mid 17C. To save

it from ultimate destruction it was moved stone by stone in 1910 to its present site, once part of More's garden. Naturally parts of the building had to be replaced, and they stand out clearly from the older sections. The finest features are the oriel window extending through three storeys and the beautifully gilded timber ceiling. The picture of Sir Thomas More and his family is a copy of the original painted by Holbein.

Custom House (Lower Thames Street, EC3): This large building is the custom house for the London docks. It was built 1817–25; the neoclassical façade was designed by Sir Robert Smirke, and there is a particularly good view of it from *London Bridge*.

Dickens' House (Doughty Street, WC1): *Charles Dickens* (1812–70), one of the

County Hall, façade towards Thames

great 19C writers, not only succeeded in his novels in in drawing an exact, affectionate and sometimes fairly ironic picture of London as it was during his lifetime; he also created numerous lifelike characters who have stamped themselves on the imagination of his readers. This house, in which he lived with his family from 1837–9, is the only residence of the many he occupied in London to have survived. Here he completed the *'Pickwick Papers'*, which established his fame as a writer; he also wrote the novels *'Oliver Twist'* and *'Nicholas Nickleby'* in this little study. The rooms in this house, of which the kitchen described in 'Pickwick Papers' is the most striking, have been restored without exception. Personal possessions of the writer, furniture, manuscripts, family portraits and contemporary illustrations from his books are on display, as well as an important Dickens library.

Fishmongers' Hall (London Bridge, EC3): The Guild of Fishmongers was founded in the 13C, and still controls the sale of fish in the City. Their Hall was completed in 1834, though later restored and refurbished; the neoclassical façade is still very impressive when seen from the Thames. The interior is not normally open to the public. It contains the statue of the important guild master *Sir William Walworth* (14C) and two excellent portraits of the present Queen and her husband by Annigoni.

George Inn (Borough High Street, SE1): The Romantic medieval coaching inn was destroyed by fire in 1677, but it has been rebuilt to the original design. The inner courtyard will certainly seem familiar to lovers of the novels of Charles Dickens.

Gray's Inn (Holborn High Street, WC1):

Gray's Inn Place, house No. 1/2

Guildhall, Great Hall, window

The mass of buildings in various styles which house one of London's four law schools are set in a beautiful garden with splendid old trees. Only the 17C *gatehouse* is original. A bronze statue in the court-yard commemorates the philosopher, author and politician *Sir Francis Bacon* (1561–1626), probably the most prominent member of the school, who lived and worked here almost all his life. The 16C Great Hall can be visited with special permission; it has been restored to the original design. It saw the first performance of Shakespeare's 'Comedy of Errors' in 1594. The fine late-17C chapel has been splendidly restored.

Guildhall (Cheapside/King Street, EC2): The City's *town hall* dates from 1411. Wren was involved in restoration work after the Great Fire of 1666. Bombing in the Second World War caused such

devastation that only the *Great Hall* and *crypt* could be restored in their original form. The hall with its delicate square tower and crocketed spire is for this reason set between modern buildings. The gable façade with a Gothic arch and windows is topped by another delicate tower with a trefoil at its tip. The façade is flanked by octagonal towers with spires; the slant-roofed buttresses which articulate the side façade spring from their lower level. The 'confectionery' façade in the S., neo-Gothic with with round arches and turrets, is the work of George Dance the Younger, dating from 1788. The problems of the town were discussed in the adjacent hall by members of the council in their historic livery. The *Sheriff* is chosen here annually in a magnificent ceremony, and the *Lord Mayor* takes up his office in June. The walls with stone decoration have survived in their original form, and the ceiling was

Guildhall, Great Hall

restored to its original splendour by Sir Giles Gilbert Scott after the Second World War. The hall is decorated with the splendid coats of arms and banners of the City Guilds. There is also a series of statues of important personalities. Giant statues of the mythical *Gog* and *Magog* flank the entrance, reproductions of the 18C originals. Along the walls surrounded by galleries with fine oak balustrades are statues of *Sir Winston Churchill*, *Lord Nelson*, the *Duke of Wellington* and the two *Pitts*. On the right by the *Royal Fusiliers' memorial* are the only surviving 15C windows. The City sword and sceptre are contained in a fine oak chest. The 15C *crypt* under the hall is the largest of its kind in London. The Purbeck marble columns at the E. end are original. The groin vaulting and other parts of the room have been restored. The *Guildhall Library* has more than 150,000 documents on the history of the City, a map of London dating from 1593, valuable folios of Shakespearean plays and a certificate of purchase of a London house signed by the poet himself. The building also houses the *Clockmakers' Company Museum* and the *Guildhall Art Gallery*.

Guy's Hospital (St. Thomas Street SE1): The London bookseller and merchant *Thomas Guy* founded the hospital in 1721; he is commemorated by a bronze statue (1733) by Scheemaker in the courtyard. The building was completed towards the end of the 18C. It is in three sections; the central portico with six slender Doric columns supporting a triangular pediment with carved frieze rises above a rusticated storey. Although it has been much restored the original appearance has been retained. *John Keats* studied at the medical school, opened in 1769, from 1814–16.

Guildhall, E. crypt

Henry VIII's Wine Cellar (Whitehall SW1): This is the only surviving part of Cardinal Wolsey's house, now below ground level and absorbed into the *Ministry of Defence* building.

Hogarth's House (Hogarth Lane, W4): The painter and engraver *William Hogarth* (1697–1764) lived in this 17C town house, then on a somewhat rowdy street, from 1749–64. The building has been restored to the original design, and houses an exhibition of personal effects, furniture, sketches and completed works by the artist.

Horse Guards (Whitehall SW1): This building in Italian Renaissance style dating from 1753 was designed by William Kent, but he was unable to execute the plans himself. Behind the façade with rusticated lower storey and two square towers is a tower with lantern. The building originally protected the palace of *Whitehall*, which no longer exists; it now houses government offices.

House of St.Barnabas (Greek Street W1): The plain outer walls of this town house built in the Georgian style in 1745 conceal rooms with lavish, masterly rococo stucco and fine carving. The building belongs to a charitable organization, and is thus only open to the public at certain times.

Houses of Parliament (Parliament Square SW1): The best views of the Houses of Parliament are to be obtained from the opposite bank of the Thames, the *Albert Embankment*, or from *Westminster Bridge*.
History: The building is frequently called the Palace of Westminster, reminding us

Houses of Parliament with Parliament Square

that it was once the monarch's town residence. Edward the Confessor built a palace in Norman style on the site, but it was not impressive enough for his successor William the Conqueror, who had it extended and redesigned. His son, William Rufus, added *Westminster Hall* in 1097; this is said to be the largest Gothic hall ever built in Europe. The massive ceiling was added in the course of rebuilding by Richard II towards the end of the 14C. *St.Stephen's Chapel* and the *Crypt* were built in the same century, and they and the hall survived a fire which caused extensive damage to the rest of the buildings. After Henry VIII had moved to *Whitehall* in 1529, Parliament moved to Westminster in 1567. The *House of Lords* selected a chamber at the S. end of the building, and the *House of Commons* assembled in St.Stephen's Chapel. On 5 November 1605 Guy Fawkes and his fellow Catholic conspirators tried to blow up the venerable building, the members of Parliament and King James I, who was attending the opening of Parliament. From that day onwards the building has been searched for concealed explosives a few hours before the monarch's arrival for the State Opening of Parliament in late October or early November. The Houses of Parliament were again seriously damaged by fire in 1834. Once more Westminster Hall and the crypt survived, together with a few other parts of the building. The task of rebuilding the complex in either Gothic or Elizabethan style fell to the architect Sir Charles Barry, who built the present building from 1840–60. Damage by bombing in the Second World War has been expertly repaired, and the building appears in its former glory.

Visitors wishing to attend debates in either

Houses of Parliament, Robing Room, Queen Victoria's Chair

House of Lords Chamber

house must obtain tickets in good time at *St.Stephen's Gate*. The magnificent interior can only be visited when Parliament is not sitting. There are usually guided tours on Saturdays.

The buildings: The neo-Gothic Houses of Parliament are essentially a series of well planned rooms, galleries and corridors grouped around *Central Hall* and a series of courtyards along the Thames. Examination from close quarters shows the phenomenal architectural skill of Barry, his builders and the restorers simply in the execution of the decorative detail of the exterior of the building, with its many pinnacles, friezes, crockets, tracery, canopies, decorative railings, statues and coats of arms. The long Thames façade is topped by pairs of low, square corner towers crowned with balustrade and battlements; these shapes and details recur in the two inner towers. Between these, by two small towers with lanterns, is the central tower (over the central hall), lavishly designed and topped with a open lantern with pointed spire. The design is reminiscent of masterpieces by Wren. The S. wing of the building is dominated by the massive square *Victoria Tower*, dating from 1858. It is similar to the towers of nearby Westminster Abbey, but is much more richly articulated, with traceried mullioned pointed windows, and also friezes and canopies. The battlemented corner towers, each with tips in the form of a crown, grow out of its rounded corners. From the flagpole, which towers from a lavishly designed base, a flag flies to indicate that Parliament is in session. Opposite this splendid piece of neo-Gothic design, on the N. wing of the building is the *bell and clocktower*, architecturally somewhat inapposite, more reminiscent of an Italian campanile or the tower of a Romanesque basilica. The cubic lower section, with longitudinal friezes, supports the clock storey, which protrudes to a certain extent. The next level is

Houses of Parliament, Richard I

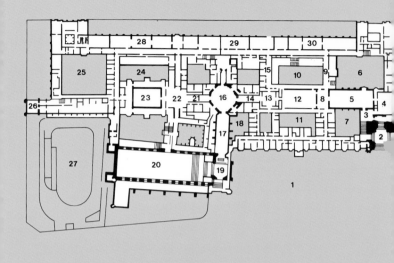

Houses of Parliament 1 Old Palace Yard with statue of Richard I **2** Victoria Tower with Royal Porch **3** Norman Porch **4** Royal Robing Room **5** Royal Gallery **6** Royal Court **7** Chancellor's Court **8** Prince's Chamber **9** Bishop's Corridor **10** Peers' Court **11** State Officer's Court **12** House of Lords **13** Peers' Lobby **14** Peers' Corridor **15** Law Lords' Corridor **16** Central Hall **17** St.Stephen's Hall **18** St.Stephen's Court **19** St.Stephen's Entrance and Porch **20** Westminster Hall, with the crypt and baptistery underneath **21** Commons' Corridor **22** Commons' Lobby **23** House of Commons **24** Commons' Court **25** Speaker's Court **26** Big Ben **27** New Palace Yard **28** Commons Library **29** Refreshment rooms **30** Peers' Library

slightly inset, with pointed arches, and supports the hipped roof with roof lights, and above this again is the lantern with its pointed spire and arched lower section. A light in the tower shows when the Commons are sitting at night. The name 'Big Ben', familiar throughout the world, is properly applied to the bell, rather than the tower, named after Sir Benjamin Hall, First Commissioner of Works when it was

hung. The sound of the bell has become world-famous because of its use by the BBC. The minute hands of the clock are similar in length to a double-decker bus. The staff responsible for the clock have numerous tricks to ensure that it maintains its reputation for timekeeping.

Interior: This description again follows the ground plan. Entrance to the building for peers, the chancellor and visitors is via *Old Palace Yard* (1). The *Royal Entrance* is in the *Victoria Tower* (2), used by the monarch on the occasion of the State Opening of Parliament after a magnificent procession down The Mall and Whitehall in the Irish State Coach. In the Gothic *Norman Porch* (3) are splendid stained-glass windows, excellent wood carvings by Augustus W.Pugin, coat-of-arms keystones in the vaulting, and also busts of Wellington and two former prime ministers. The *Royal Staircase* leads from

Houses of Parliament, Robing Room, coffer-work ceiling

here to the *Robing Room* (4) in which the monarch dons and doffs robe and crown before and after the State Opening of Parliament. The room has a magnificent wooden ceiling, and a fine marble fireplace by Pugin. The carved wooden panelling shows scenes from the lives of various kings, whose arms and symbols also adorn the walls. W. Dyce's frescos deal with scenes from the legend of King Arthur. The throne, originally made for Queen Victoria, stands between two gold-framed pictures of kings in front of a tapestry embroidered with the royal coat of arms. The *Royal Gallery* (5) again has a splendid coffered ceiling, along with portraits of various members of the royal family from the 18C onwards, and two large paintings by Daniel Machise: 'The Death of Nelson' and 'Wellington and Blücher after the Battle of Waterloo'. Beneath the stained-glass windows with the royal arms is a

moulding also decorated with coats of arms and monarchs' symbols. The gallery leads directly into the *Prince's Chamber* (8), now used as an anteroom by peers. The walls are elegantly clad in wood, and decorated with royal coats of arms and portraits of Henry VIII and his wives, and other Tudor monarchs. William Theed's bronze reliefs show scenes from the history of the house of Tudor. The skilfully decorated fireplaces are once more the work of Pugin. John Gibson's statue of the young Queen Victoria on the coronation throne is set before a background decorated in gold. The *House of Lords* (12) is a veritable treasure chest of furnishing and decoration. It was first used as the meeting-place of the Upper House in 1847; the peers' leather benches are in the traditional royal colour of red. Walls and the coffered ceiling are masterly specimens of ornamental wood carving. The panes

Houses of Parliament, Royal Gallery

of the tall tracery windows are decorated with peers' arms from 1360–1900. There are statues of the eighteen barons who wrested Magna Carta from King John Lackland in 1215, set on plinths decorated with their coats of arms, under tracery baldacchinos. The wall niches are similar in design to the windows and contain scenes from the history of the country and allegories of justice, faith and chivalry. The magnificent Gothic canopy behind the throne with arms and crown, similar in design to the coronation throne is Westminster Abbey, is considered to be one of Pugin's masterpieces. The monarch sits here when making the traditional speech at the State Opening of Parliament. It is adorned with lavish Gothic decoration, as well as coats of arms, angels and statues of the national saints. Formerly members of the Privy Council sat on 'woolsacks' in the centre of the chamber;

only one of these seats is still used, by the Lord Chancellor. The wool filling was a sign of the importance of the wool trade in the Middle Ages. The *Peers' Lobby* (13) is the anteroom of the upper house, again magnificently decorated by Pugin in the Gothic style. Like the *Peers' corridor* (14) it has fine encaustic tiles in the floor. The *Central Hall* (16) is placed between the two houses, and also leads to other parts of the building. Furnishings and decoration of this octagonal room with ribbed vaulting with tendril patterns and armorial keystones are again neo-Gothic. Statues of former sovereigns under traceried canopies occupy the arches of doors and windows. The mosaics above the doors show the national saints, and there are statues of the politicians Granville, Gladstone, Iddesleigh and Russell. *St.Stephen's Hall* (17) is a reconstruction by Barry of the old *St.Stephen's Chapel*; it is high and light,

 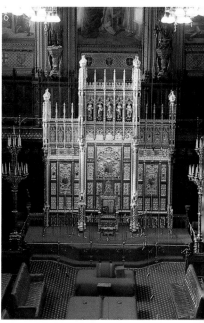

House of Lords Chamber, Pugin wall, monarch's throne (left), overall view (right)

and the rib vaulting is decorated only with imaginative keystones. There are statues of monarchs in the archways, which are also decorated with trefoil friezes, crowns and angels' heads. Large statues placed along the walls commemorate various distinguished statesmen. Mosaics and wall paintings tell the story of the foundation of the chapel: coats of arms in the stained-glass windows. Tickets for visitors wishing to attend parliamentary debates are available at *St. Stephen's Gate* (19). *Westminster Hall* (20), with its massive oak-beamed ceiling, impressive in its noble austerity, dates from 1097, and is the oldest part of the entire complex. Barry added the stained-glass window with coats of arms and the podium in 1840. The statues of monarchs under pointed tracery canopies are originals from the period in which the hall was built. Famous trials have taken place in the hall: Thomas More, Charles I and Guy Fawkes were all condemned to death here. Members of the Royal Family and other distinguished men and women now lie in state here; the hall is also used for conferences. Below the hall are the *crypt* and the *baptistery*. The former was built in the 13C by Edward I as the crypt chapel of *St. Stephen's Chapel*; it was restored by Barry and Pugin after the fire of 1834. The low room with its splendid Gothic stained glass and pictures of saints on the altar wall is now used for services and family occasions involving Members of Parliament. The magnificent vaulting, decorated with tendrils and elegant keystones, has ribs springing from low, smooth, bundled columns and gives the room a romantic feeling. The *baptismal chapel* is a gem of lovingly-executed, detailed decoration, with pictures of Christ enthroned worshipped by angels on the walls. The font, goblet-shaped and with a lid in the shape of a crown supporting a statue of John the Baptist, is now usually used for the baptism of children of Members of Parliament. Westminster Hall and St.Stephen's Hall are connected by an elegant two-tier *cloister* dating from the 16C, with largely original fan vaulting. The *Commons' Lobby* (21) and the *Commons' Corridor* (22) are Gothic rooms in which statues commemorate distinguished 20C statesmen. Sir Giles Gilbert Scott was responsible for redesigning the *House of Commons* (23) after the Second World War. The original Gothic form was retained, but simplified in tune with modern taste, on the one hand giving the chamber a certain specific elegance, and on the other hand showing how magnificent it must once have been. The MPs' leather benches are in green, the traditional Commons colour since the 18C. The focal point of the chamber is the Speaker's chair, under a fine canopy from Australia, decorated with coats of arms and other Gothic-style decoration. To the Speaker's right the Premier and ministers sit on the 'Treasury Bench', with the MPs of the governing party behind them. The Opposition sit to the Speaker's left, so that government and their 'shadows' face each other eye to eye. MPs are not allowed to cross the red lines in front of the benches while Parliament is in session. The Dispatch Boxes, both from New Zealand and handsomely mounted in bronze, contain editions of the Old and New Testaments and the oaths taken by MPs. Beyond *Speaker's Court* (25) is the Speaker's house; he is accompanied from here to his place in the House by a traditional procession bound by rigid rules. The MPs' entrance is in *New Palace Yard* (27). There are separate *libraries* for the *Lords* (30) and *Commons* (28), with fine wooden ceilings and wall panelling and also valuable furnishings, as well as their outstanding collections of books.

Imperial Institute Tower (Prince Consort Road, SW7): T.E.Collcutt built the *Imperial Institute* on the occasion of Queen Victoria's golden jubilee in 1887. Only the bell tower, built in light stone and with a copper roof, has survived.

Houses of Parliament, Westminster Hall

Johnson's House (Gough Square, EC4): The author and journalist *Samuel Johnson* (1709–84) lived and worked in this plain, four-storeyed house from 1748–59. His 'Dictionary of the English Language' (1755), on which he worked with six colleagues for eight years, was produced here. The first edition, personal effects of the author and Johnsonian memorabilia are exhibited here.

Kensington Palace (Kensington Gardens, W8): William III bought this Jacobean town house in 1689 and commissioned Sir Christopher Wren to extend and alter it; this work was completed in 1702. The relatively plain brick building grouped around three courtyards, not at all like a palace, was the monarch's residence until the death of George II. Queen Victoria was born and baptized here, and it was she who opened the *State Apartments* to the public. The rest of the palace is strictly private, even though many a curious visitor would like to risk a peep, as it is the home of the Prince of Wales and his family. The *Queen's Staircase* is by Wren, and dates from 1691. The

Queen's Gallery contains carvings by Grinling Gibbons and fine oak panelling. The rooms used by Queen Anne, Queen Mary and Queen Victoria have displays of their personal effects and furniture. In the *King's Gallery*, also decorated to designs by Wren, are 18&19C paintings of views of London, carving by Gibbons and a cycle of paintings of the Adventures of Odysseus by William Kent. Kent worked alongside Wren on the interior of the house, and designed the *Cupola Room*, among other things. Finally, the *Orangery* is the work of Nicholas Hawksmoor, who also built the S. façade in 1695. The statue of *William III* in front of it was a present from Kaiser Wilhelm II to his uncle Edward VII. There is a statue of *Queen Victoria* in front of the E. wing of the palace.

Lancaster House (Stable Yard, SW1): Benjamin Wyatt was commissioned to build this house in light Bath stone by the Duke of York in 1825. The most striking feature of the façade is the massive portal section: the rusticated lower storey with corner arches supports a balcony portico

Kensington Palace

with Corinthian columns; the triangular pediment is decorated with a coat of arms. Charles Barry was responsible for the design of the interior from 1840. The *staircase*, which mixes elements of rococo and baroque, and the spacious *gallery* with numerous paintings by great masters are particularly fine features. Other rooms are gems of baroque design, including the *drawing room* with ceiling paintings by Veronese, two dining rooms and the *red* and *gold* rooms, so called after the colours predominant in them. Lancaster House is the property of the state, and used above all for official receptions and banquets.

Lambeth Palace (Lambeth Road, SE1): This complex resembles a medieval castle with buildings grouped around an inner courtyard, and is set in a fine park. For more than 700 years Lambeth Palace has been the London residence of the Archbishop of Canterbury and setting for the Conference of Anglican Bishops, held every ten years. The palace, open to the public only to a limited extent, has retained its original appearance despite heavy rebuilding and restoration. The gatehouse, also called *Morton's Tower*, was built in the 15C and has two massive square battlemented towers of unequal size. The *Great Hall* dates from the 17C, and is late Gothic with Renaissance elements. It has a huge roof with wooden beams. The *chapel* dates from 1230; the floor, altar rail and parts of the pews are original but the stained-glass windows are modern. The oldest section to have survived in its original form is the *crypt*, dating from 1200, with fine marble piers. The water tower *(Lollards' Tower)* was used as a prison for a long period. There are valuable documents and books in the *library*.

Lincoln's Inn (Chancery Lane, WC2): Lincoln's Inn is one of the four great London law schools, or Inns of Court, and was first mentioned in documents in 1422. The historic buildings in which men such as Thomas More, Benjamin Disraeli and William Gladstone lived and were initiated into the secrets and mysteries of the law are now used principally to house lawyers' chambers, though some teaching is done.

Kensington Palace, garden

Entrance is via Chancery Lane through a slightly wilful gatehouse dating from 1518. The severe Tudor *Old Buildings* nearby are superb specimens of the architecture of the period, and are more or less contemporary with the gatehouse. The *Old Hall* dates from 1492, was extended in 1624, then rebuilt in 1928 using almost exclusively original materials. Fine features are the largely original beamed roof, a rood screen attributed to Inigo Jones and a far from typical Hogarth painting. The windows bear the arms of successful pupils of the Inn. The attribution of the chapel, built in 1623 in late Gothic style, to Inigo Jones is speculative, but it is quite certain that Wren was responsible for thorough restoration before it was extended towards the end of the previous century. The stained glass has coats of arms and apostle statues said to be Flemish work. Some of the impressive stalls are original. Pulpit and sounding board are fine 18C work. The crypt with its solemn Gothic rib vaulting is open to the public. It was once used as a burial place for members of the Inn, and as a 'dumping ground' for unwanted male offspring, who were then generally taken into the Inn. The *library*, with a fine collection of books and manuscripts, was built 1843–5 by Philip Hardwick, and later restored by G.G.Scott. Hardwick also built the *New Hall*, and designed its interior. The gigantic mural of Justice is by G.F.Watts. To complete the impression the visitor should now look at the buildings in *Old Square* and *New Square*, the late-18C *Stone Buildings* and the archway leading to Carey Street, which is decorated with coats of arms.

Mansion House (Mansion House Street, EC4): This Palladian building has been the official seat and residence of the Lord Mayor of London during his year of office since it was completed by George Dance the Elder in 1753. The principal façade is concomitant with the importance of the building, rising through two storeys articulated with Corinthian pilasters and topped with a frieze, set above a rusticated lower storey with round-arched entrance and windows. The tall, narrow windows of the first floor have alternate triangular

Kensington Gardens, fountain near Lancaster Gate

Lancaster House

and semicircular pediments separated by decorative friezes. The storeys are separated by a cubed frieze. Two short flights of steps lead to an entrance portico with triangular pediment (with an allegory of the power and greatness of the City) on a high base with friezes supported by six massive Corinthian columns. The low top storey with simple pilasters and almost square windows is topped with a roof balustrade. The magnificent interior, quite in keeping with the importance of the building, can only be visited by appointment. Particularly noteworthy are the so-called *Egyptian Room*, actually Roman in style, and used for receptions, and the *Saloon*, with fine Victorian wallpaper and a magnificent chandelier. The mayoral insignia (chain, sword, sceptre) are kept here, and another sign of the importance of his office are the courtroom and some prison cells.

Marlborough House (Pall Mall, SW1): Wren completed this red-brick building, somewhat plain on the street side, in 1710 for *Sarah Duchess of Marlborough*, who enjoyed great influence as lady-in-waiting to Queen Anne. The main façade overlooks the park. Her husband was the famous *John Churchill*, first Earl of Marlborough (1650–1722) and later Duke; he shone in the War of the Spanish Succession (1701–13/14) alongside Prince Eugène as a brilliant general and great winner of battles, thus earning the gratitude of his country: he was relieved of all his offices and functions. The deeds of its former owner are celebrated in the house, which was much altered and extended in the course of the 19C by splendid wall paintings by the French artist Louis Laguerre (early 18C). Probably the finest room in this lavishly furnished building is the drawing room,

Lambeth Palace

also known as the *Blenheim Room*. The ceiling paintings by the Italian painter Gentileschi came from the *Queen's House* in Greenwich; they were brought here by the Duchess Sarah, presumably with the permission of her royal patroness. Marlborough House has been lived in by many crowned and uncrowned heads in the course of its history, is now the Commonwealth conference centre, and therefore not fully open to the public.

Mayflower Inn (Rotherhithe Street, SE16): The *Mayflower*, the famous ship which in 1620 carried the Pilgrim Fathers from Plymouth to Cape Cod, in the modern State of Massachusetts, was berthed at the nearby dock before her great journey. The comfortable interior of the inn which bears her name has retained much of the character of a 17C hostelry.

Michelin House (Fulham Road, SW3): This excellent specimen of art nouveau with its wilful façade showing variations on the theme of classicism dates from 1910. The ceramic pictures show a rally in the infancy of the internal combustion engine, and are not only of interest to fans of motor-sport.

Middlesex Guildhall (Broad Sanctuary, SW1): This courthouse in neo-Renaissance style on the site of the former *sanctuary* of Westminster Abbey was completed in the early years of the present century.

Old Bailey (Newgate Street, EC4): Only the name of the street reminds us of the fearful earlier use of the site of the *Central Criminal Court*, affectionately known as the 'Old Bailey'. Here used to stand *Newgate Prison*, from the Middle Ages the largest, dirtiest and most notorious prison in the town, the horrors of which are described in annals, historical novels and other stories. From 1783 to 1868 public executions were held here. After the prison was pulled down in the early years of this century, the present three-storey court with rusticated walls, Ionic pilasters and columns and roof balustrade including triangular pediments in the main façade was built using some of the materials. The building is dominated by a dome on a tall base with Ionic columns, windows and a lantern which seems to owe a little to that of St.Paul's. On top of the lantern a gilded goddess of Justice with scales and sword stands guard. Anyone wishing to watch a trial in one of the courts must start to queue early at the entrance. Visitors to the courts may be amazed why the austere judges in their historic robes have bunches of fragrant flowers on the desks in front of them. The decoration is traditional, and was probably very necessary in the days when trials were held in a building close to the evil-smelling prison.

Old Curiosity Shop (Portsmouth Street WC2): The history of this little, crooked building, presumably built in the 17C, is more interesting than the antiques and minor works of art which it sells. *'The Old Curiosity Shop'* is the title of a Dickens novel, and the present owners of this shop, which was well out into the country in the author's lifetime, and thought to have sold groceries, assert that it was this very building which Dickens had in mind when he was writing his novel. Scholars, however, maintain that the shop was called after the book, and the model for the novel was somewhere quite different.

Post Office Tower (Maple Street, W1): Like all other major cities London has its communications tower, formerly with viewing platform and revolving restaurant. The building is 619 ft. high, and was completed in 1966.

Royal Albert Hall (Kensington Gore, SW7): The *Royal Albert Hall of Arts and Sciences*, as the building named after Victoria's consort is officially known, was completed in 1871. The low base storey supports a first floor pierced with rectan-

Middlesex Guildhall, portal sculptures

gular windows. The second floor with round-arched windows, pilasters and frieze is topped with a balustrade. The next storey, somewhat less high and with very few windows, is surrounded by a terracotta frieze showing the relationship of man and art throughout the ages. Above this again, the glass dome which covers the entire elliptical building is supported by another inset storey. The entrance doors extend through two storeys and are designed like the façades of classical villas. The auditorium seats over 5,000 people and was once notorious for its less than excellent acoustics, it has been put right now and is a popular venue for concerts of all kinds and other events.

Royal Courts of Justice (Strand WC2): George Edmund Street, one of the best-known Victorian architects, did not survive to see the completion in 1882 of his building in the prevailing Gothic Revival style. The façade on the Strand with its low porch is a gem, or fearful example for some, of Victorian delight in copying. It uses every known neo-Gothic element, from the crocket and pointed

arch to the rosette, but in individual combinations and with remarkably cool and sober attention to design detail. In the interior, where all important civil trials are held, the *Great Hall* is impressive in its dimensions.

Royal Exchange (Threadneedle Street, EC3): Sir Thomas Gresham, a rich, influential merchant and financier, founded what was later to become the Royal Exchange in 1566 as a meeting and trading place for City merchants. A building consecrated by Elizabeth I burned down in 1666, its successor in 1838. The present neoclassical building was completed by Sir William Tite in 1844. The entrance portico, supported by eight tall, slender Corinthian columns, rises behind a statue of Wellington and a war memorial. Westmacott's pediment frieze is an allegory of trade. Traditionally important events such as declarations of war or major peace treaties are announced here. Folk tunes from the English-speaking Commonwealth are played several times per day from the delicate campanile with columned, open sound

Royal Festival Hall, seen from Hungerford Bridge

St.Bartholomew Hospital, entrance

elegant neoclassical façade articulatd with pilasters and statue niches has a portico supported by six Corinthian columns with triangular pediment. It was designed by Edward M.Barry, and completed in 1858. The interior is sumptuously decorated, and performances are always quickly sold out because of the reputation of the house and the calibre of the artists who perform there.

St.Bartholomew's Hospital (West Smithfield, EC1): The hospital was founded in 1123, together with the parish church of *St.Bartholomew the Great*; it is the only London hospital which has remained on its original site. It was handed over to the City of London by Henry VIII in the course of the secularization of ecclesiastical goods and institutions in 1546. James Gibbs was responsible for a new building in the mid 18C, and this was much restored in the 19C. The *Great Hall* was designed by Gibbs, and its stained-glass window commemorates the handing over of the hospital to the City. There are two paintings by Hogarth of Biblical scenes on the staircase.

chamber, and domed lantern. The weather-vane is in the shape of a grass-hopper, the Gresham family crest. The spacious inner courtyard has striking wall frescos of scenes from the history of London and England. Exchange business is no longer transacted here.

Royal Festival Hall (South Bank, SE1): This modern concert hall with much-admired acoustics was built in cool, smooth concrete and glass by architects Martin and Matthew on the occasion of the 'Festival of Britain' in 1951. The Festival Hall, *Queen Elizabeth Hall* and *Purcell Room*, built around a decade later, the *Hayward Gallery* and *National Film Theatre* together form the *South Bank Arts Centre.*

Royal Opera House (Covent Garden, WC2): This famous theatre with its

St.James' Palace (Pall Mall, SW1): In 1532 Henry VIII pulled down the hospital for women with leprosy which stood on this site and commissioned a residence for himself and his then wife Anne Boleyn, the mother of Elizabeth I. The palace was much altered in the course of the centuries, and now forms a unit with *Clarence House* and *Lancaster House*. The complex also includes the *Royal Chapel* and the *Queen's Chapel of the Savoy*. When the Palace of *Whitehall* burned down in 1698 the court moved to St.James' Palace, which remained the royal town residence until Queen Victoria moved to Buckingham Palace in the middle of the last century. St James' Palace, the birth-place and nursery of many monarchs, still has the atmosphere of a comfortable Tudor home. Foreign ambassadors are still accredited to the Court of St.James, and

Queen Alexandra monument, near St.James's Palace

a new sovereign is proclaimed from the balcony of Friary Court. It is now occupied by the Gentlemen and Yeomen-at-Arms, the Lord Chamberlain and contains 'Grace and Favour' apartments. Tourists have to make do with a glimpse of the Tudor gatehouse with its two round, battlemented flanking towers; they must take it on trust that the *Armoury* and *Tapestry* rooms were refurbished in the 19C, and that the skilful hand of Grinling Gibbons was responsible for the wall carving in the Throne Room.

St.John's Gate (St.John's Lane, EC1): This Tudor gatehouse with battlements and two square flanking towers dates from 1504. It is now all that remains of the *Priory of the Knights Hospitallers of St.John of Jerusalem*, founded in 1110 and later dissolved, to which the church of *St.John* also belonged.

Somerset House (Strand WC2): The present building was built in the 1780s by Sir William Chambers on the site of a 16C predecessor. The arched entrance is on the Strand side, but the monumental neoclassical façade with outstanding stone carving faces the Thames. The E. and W. wings are 19C additions. The building, in which many adminstrative institutions work, is open to the public when there are exhibitions in the beautifully restored *'Fine Rooms'* on the first floor.

Staple Inn (Holborn, WC2): There was an inn here in the 14C, used above all by wool merchants for checking, weighing, comparing and selling their goods. The present building with its cool and elegant half-timbered façade and protruding upper storeys dates from the late 16C.

Stock Exchange (Throgmorton Street

Heraldic beast of the City of London with Staple Inn (left), entrance to The Temple (right)

EC2): London had a Stock Exchange in 1773, with a building on this site. The present building is modern. Galley open to public; good explanatory shows.

The Temple (EC4): This delightful area with well-tended lawns and mainly Georgian buildings stretches down to the Thames. It can be reached from Fleet Street. From 1160 it belonged to the Knights Templar, then came to the crown, and then to the Order of St.John, who established a law school here in the 15C. Two of the four Inns of Court are now housed here, the *Inner Temple* and the *Middle Temple*. The red-brick *Middle Temple Gateway* is attributed to Wren, and dates from 1685; it leads to *Middle Temple Lane* and the buildings of the Middle Temple, outstanding among which is *Middle Temple Hall*, the assembly and

dining hall of the Inn. The hall was built in 1565 and restored in a masterly fashion after the Second World War. The massive beamed ceiling is particularly impressive. The rood screen with columns, arches and figures is a masterpiece of Elizabethan wood carving. Some of the fine wall panelling is also original. Coats of arms commemorate famous members of the Inn, including Sir Walter Raleigh, for example. The Inner Temple buildings are reached via the *Fountain* and *Pump Courts*. The *Inner Temple Hall*, assembly hall of the second Inn of Court housed here is a copy of the 18C original. The crypt was built in the 14C. Here too coats of arms commemorate famous pupils of the Inn. After a visit to the fine *Temple Church* the visitor rejoins Fleet Street through the *Inner Temple Gateway*, dating from 1611, and also restored. The half-timbered build-

Temple, Middle Temple Hall

ng contains *Prince Henry's Room*, with a ine coffered ceiling.

Temple of Mithras (Queen Victoria Street, E4): This 2C AD temple was discovered in the course of excavations in 1954. It is a typical Mithraic temple, in the form of an underground shrine. Mithras was worshipped by the soldiers of the Roman Empire as a redeemer-god connected with the sun, and they built shrines to him, mainly in garrison towns outside Italy. The cult of Mithras was reserved exclusively for men, and had secret rites, ceremonies and sacrifices in which only the initiated could take part.

Tower of London (Tower Hill EC3): This is the most famous, most notorious but also best-preserved fortress in the country, woven about with countless stories, anecdotes and legends. It stands defiant and majestic on the bank of the Thames, and although a little away from the centre of things, it is a must for tourists.

History: The Tower dates from the all-important year 1066, when William the Conqueror built a massive wooden fortress here at the E. end of the old Roman city walls. He used it as a residence, with the intention of demonstrating his power and, to the citizens of the town, who had by no means all welcomed him with open arms, the fact that they were now under his protection. There was also an excellent view over the Thames from here, and the monarch was able to keep an eye on activities on the river. Eleven years later, in the year 1077, William started to build a symbol of his power in stone, the *Tower*, which was completed by his son William Rufus. This massive square complex in light and dark stone with battlements, four

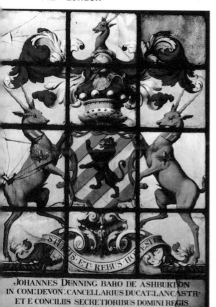

JOHANNES DUNNING BARO DE ASHBURTON
IN COM:DEVON:CANCELLARIUS DUCAT:LANCASTR·
ET E CONCILIIS SECRETIORIBUS DOMINI REGIS
A· VICESIMO SECUNDO GEORG:TERTII

Temple, Middle Temple Hall, heraldic window panes commemorating famous members of the school

corner towers (for which Wren probably provided the lanterns), arched windows and pilaster watched alone on Tower Hill for more than a century. In the late 12C Richard Lionheart (1157–99), who had been on the throne since 1189, started to build fortifications. The Third Crusade had taught him that ingratitude is the currency of the world, and on returning home he had then had to deal with his brother John's treachery. And this had probably taught him that in times like these a king's residence should be well fortified and easy to defend. Henry III and above all Edward I (1239–1307) completed the bastions and fortifications in the next century and gave the Tower the appearance it has retained until today, thanks to intelligent restoration. A legend maintains that the fortress will remain for as long as the ravens stay within its walls. For this reason the great

black birds, by no means everybody's favourite, have not only had their wings clipped, but are also looked after with great care and affection. The ravens, who are seen by many as harbingers of death, are possibly also a symbol of one of the more interesting aspects of the building's past because of the slightly spine-chilling feeling associated with them. London has plenty of royal residences, and the Tower was one until the early 17C, and mints, treasuries, observatories and zoos are also nothing unusual, particularly when stripped of their former dignity. Prisons and places of execution, however, always hold a particular attraction for visitors. Now, there are no gloomy cells and dungeons to be seen in the Tower, but many great personages have here reflected on the fate which cast them from the sunny heights of power and influence into

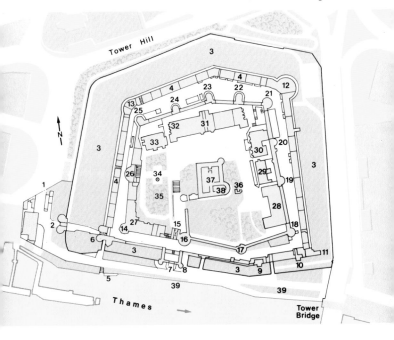

imprisonment and shame. And many others ended their days here with the 'assistance' of the hangman. This began as early as 1100, when the tower was still a residence. Richard II (1387–1400) ruled from 1377–99, and had his opponents, whether from the people or from the nobility, executed here. During the bitter Wars of the Roses (1455–85) Edward IV had his rival Henry VI murdered in the Wakefield Tower, an event still commemorated by a plaque. Edward's brother Richard III (1452–85) is reputed to have had Edward's sons, Edward V and Richard, Duke of York, murdered in the Bloody Tower in 1483, when they were both still innocent children. Henry VIII, notorious anyway, behaved in an even worse fashion. He sent his former Chancellor, Thomas More, to the Tower, when More refused to sign the Act of Supremacy. More's later canonization by

the Roman Catholic church was scant comfort to the beheaded man's descendants. In 1533 Anne Boleyn, Henry's second wife and mother of Elizabeth I was crowned Queen in the Tower amidst much splendour. Only three years later her husband ordered her to be tried for infidelity in the same place, and to be beheaded on Tower Green. As Henry was also displeased with his fourth wife, Anne

Tower, coat-of-arms

of Cleves, he sent his minister Cromwell, who had been responsible for choosing the bride, to the block in the Tower. And in 1542 Anne's successor Catharine Howard, who had only been Queen for two years, went the way of Anne Boleyn. Anyone interested in the dramatic details of these bloody deeds is recommended to refer to Shakespeare's *Henry VI*, parts 1, 2 and 3, *King Richard III* and *King Henry VIII*. Queen Mary I, known to history as 'Bloody Mary' sent the nine-day queen Lady Jane Grey (1537–54) and her husband first to the Tower and then to the block, and also had her sister, Elizabeth I, confined within these gloomy walls. Elizabeth herself later had the seafarer, explorer and writer Sir Walter Raleigh imprisoned for a short time because he had married against her will. Then in 1603 Raleigh was careless enough to allow himself to become entangled in

a plot against King James I, which cost him 13 years in the Bloody Tower, during which he found the time to write his 'History of the World'. After his unfortunate mission to England in 1941 Rudolf Hess began his odyssey through various prisons in the Tower.

The buildings: The details described here and individual buildings open to the public, can easily be identified on the ground plan. Modern visitors enter the Tower via the compulsory *cash-desk* (1) through the *Middle Tower* (2), a battlemented gatehouse dating from the 14C. This is fortified in the first place by *moat* (3), broad on the three town sides and narrower on the Thames side. There follows a circle of *casemates* (4), a second protective ring, including various towers, the *Byward Tower* (6), dating from the 13C, with portcullis and a guardroom containing a 14C religious wall painting.

Traitors' Gate (7) was the entrance used by prisoners and delinquents arriving by boat. The sovereign entered the Tower via the *Queen's Stair* (5), which is also to be found here. *St. Thomas's Tower* (8) contains a memorial chapel to Thomas Becket, the Archbishop of Canterbury murdered in his cathedral in 1170. The Thames side is further fortified by the *Cradle Tower,* (9), *Well Tower* (10) and *Develin Tower* (11). Salutes are fired from *Tower Wharf* (39) on special occasions. *Brass Mount* (12) and *Legge's Mount* (13) are at the NE and NW extremities. In the inner ward are the following towers: *Bell Tower* (14), the prison of Thomas More and Elizabeth I, dating from the 12C, the 13C *Bloody Tower,* as its name suggests not only the scene of the murder of the little princes in 1483, but generally a notorious dungeon. The *Wakefield Tower* (16) has a 13C vaulted room. Next come the *Lanthorn Tower* and the *Salt Tower* (18), in which scratched inscriptions are a reminder of many prisoners. We then pass the *Broad Arrow Tower* (19) and the *Constable Tower* (20) to reach the *Martin Tower* (21) in the NE corner. Here in 1671 Colonel Blood is said to have attempted to steal the crown jewels on behalf of his sovereign Charles II, who was in financial difficulties. Next come the *Brick Tower* and the *Bowyer Tower.* In the torture chamber there is a display of the ancient instruments and tools used to 'encourage' prisoners to confess their deeds by 'painful questioning', before they were executed as a result of their admissions. *Flint Tower* (24) and *Devereux Tower* (25) are further fortifications in these walls. In the *Beauchamp Tower* (26), called after Thomas Beauchamp, imprisoned here in the 14C, inscriptions on the walls tell of notables incarcerated here, including Lady Jane Grey and her husband Guildford Dudley. *Queen's House* (27), a charming 16C half-timbered building, is the residence of the Governor of the Tower, and therefore closed to the public. Adjacent to the N. is the house formerly

Tower, White Tower, armour

occupied by the chief gaoler. The *New Armouries* (28), the former arsenal dating from the 17C, have an interesting collection of 18&19C weapons, and also armour and weapons from Africa, Japan and other Eastern lands. The adjacent building (29) formerly housed the *Hospital.* The *Royal Fusiliers' Museum* (30) contains uniforms and medals of the regiment. *Waterloo Barracks* (31) date from the 19C, and formerly housed this regiment. The *Oriental Gallery* has a display of oriental armour and weapons, including an Indian elephant's armour. The *Heralds' Museum* provides a short history of heraldry.

Probably the most-visited, and also the most closely guarded building of all is the *Jewel House* (32), containing the Crown Jewels. Almost all the items exhibited here were made after 1660, as Oliver Cromwell either sold regalia and other royal possessions during the Revolution, or simply had them melted down. We are prepared for the treasures to come by a collection of fine banqueting plate, swords richly adorned with precious metal and stones, and the magnificent insignia and robes of the various orders of knighthood, and the Coronation Robes. A fine 12C spoon and a 13C phial survived Cromwell's vandalism. *St.Edward's Crown*, in pure gold, and weighing well over four pounds, was made for Charles II in 1660, and is now worn by the sovereign in the coronation ceremony. The *Imperial State Crown* with its countless diamonds was created specially for the coronation of Queen Victoria in 1837. The great glowing ruby is assumed to come from Castile, where it was presented to Edward the Black Prince by Pedro the Cruel in 1367. The pure, sparkling diamond is one of the two 'Stars of Africa' cut from the Cullinan diamond, the largest ever found. Its 'brother' adorns the 17C royal sceptre. This crown is worn today on important occasions such as the State Opening of Parliament. The *Indian Imperial Crown* is decorated with numerous diamonds and a gleaming emerald. The *Crown of Queen Elizabeth* was made for the present Queen Mother in 1937; it contains the Koh-i-noor diamond, an Indian stone acquired by Queen Victoria in the middle of the last century. These are only a few of the wonderful royal crowns and insignia displayed here; they also include the elegant little crown in which Queen Victoria was so often painted. In the *Chapel of St.Peter ad Vincula* (33), built in the 12C and rebuilt in the 16C, delinquents executed in the Tower and buried in unmarked graves were interred here. The *block* (34) on *Tower Green* (35) was the place at which the executioner's axe brought the lives to so many guilty and innocent people to an end. *Wardrobe Tower* (36) marks the line of the old Roman city walls. The *White Tower* (37) is divided into an archive, small arms

room, sword room, armoury, knights' chamber, and mortar and cannon room. The large collection of weapons and armour is based on the arsenal of Henry VIII, whose own enormous suit of armour is a particular attraction. The collection is a vivid demonstration of the development and history of weapons, military equipment and dress until the First World War. An impressive and beautiful manifestation of early Norman architecture is the *Chapel of St.John* (38) dating from 1080, said to be the oldest church in London. It was rebuilt in the 13&14C, and robbed of its ecclesiastical treasures at the time of the Reformation. A particularly unusual feature are the plain, lifelike owls on the column capitals.

Vintners' Hall (Upper Thames Street): The existing building dates from 1671; the Guild of Vintners was founded in the mid 14C. The interior is open to the public only by arrangement. Particularly striking features include fine carving on the staircase, in the reception room and in the hall. The guild is still engaged in the wine trade today, and together with the dyers has the right of owning swans on the Thames. The birds are counted and ringed each year in the famous *Swan Upping* ceremony.

Wesley's House (City Road): The house was completed in 1770 and *John Wesley*, the founder of Methodism, moved in a few years later. His furniture and personal effects are on display here.

Bridges

Albert Bridge (SW3): A suspension bridge in three sections, constructed 1871–3 by R.M.Ordish. The design shows the period's fascination with trying to combine suitability for a purpose with artistic use of materials. The bridge sections are suspended from decorative cast-iron towers on 16 wrought-iron rods. The carriageway was reinforced 1971–3

The Tower's legendary ravens

to accommodate increased traffic volumes. The bridge is one of the three connections between Chelsea and Battersea.

Battersea Bridge (SW11): A wooden bridge over the Thames was built here by Henry Holland in 1771&2 to replace the ferry from Battersea to Chelsea. For a long time it was the only bridge over the river between Westminster Bridge and Putney Bridge. It increased the importance of Chelsea, and introduced the municipal development of this area; its narrow arches proved dangerous to shipping, however. The bridge was demolished in 1881 and replaced by the present bridge with its five cast-iron arches by Sir Joseph Bazalgette from 1886–90.

Blackfriars Bridge (EC4): The first bridge on this site was built 1760–9 to plans by Sir Robert Mylne, and spanned the Thames between Blackfriars and Southwark on nine Portland stone arches. Building was financed largely from fines paid by men who had refused the office of Sheriff of London. A toll was charged until 1785. The present wrought-iron bridge clad in cast iron was built 1860–9 to designs by J.Cubitt and H.Carr.

Chelsea Bridge (SW1): This supension bridge dates from 1851–8, and is another connection between Battersea and Chelsea. Human skeletons and Roman and British weapons were discovered during excavation for the foundations of the cast-iron towers, showing that a battle must have taken place on the site. The bridge was replaced by a new construction designed by architects Rendel, Palmer and Tritton in 1934.

Chiswick Bridge (W4): This concrete

bridge clad in Portland Stone dates from 1933, and connects Chiswick with Mortlake. It marks the end of the annual Oxford and Cambridge Boat Race.

Hammersmith Bridge (W6): This was the first suspension bridge to be built in London, designed by William Tierney Clarke. The central section is 413 ft. long. The original bridgeheads and buttresses were incorporated into his new bridge by Sir Joseph Bazalgette 1883–7.

Hampton Court Bridge (KT8): A wooden bridge in seven sections was built on this site by Samuel Stevens and Benjamin Ludgator in 1753. Despite its wobbly appearance this was a viable road bridge almost twenty ft. wide. It was rebuilt in 1778 and not replaced by an iron bridge until 1865. The present bridge dates from 1933, and is in reinforced concrete, clad in stone and brick.

Holborn Viaduct (EC1): This bridge over the Fleet Valley was built to a design by William Heywood 1863–9, and opened by Queen Victoria at the same time as

Blackfriars Bridge. The four statues on th parapet are allegorical representations c trade and agriculture (N.side) and scienc and the arts (S.side). The structure is ove 450 yards long and 26 yards wide.

Kew Bridge (TW9): A first bridg between Ealing and Kew was buil 1758–9; this wooden structure wa replaced by a stone bridge by James Pain in 1903.

Kingston Bridge (KT1): There has bee a bridge between Hampton Wick an Kingston since the Middle Ages, and it existence is documented from 1219, whe William de Coventry was appointe master of the bridge. The master wa provided with land in return for it upkeep. In 1528 Henry VIII brought hi artillery across the river here, to avoi damaging London Bridge. In 1661 th bridge was replaced by a drawbridge, an the present bridge was built 1852–8 b Edward Lapidge and extended on th upstream side in 1914.

Lambeth Bridge (SE1): Until 1750 on

Albert Bridge by night

of the few ferries carrying coaches and horses crossed the Thames at this point; the ferry service was discontinued after the opening of Westminster Bridge. A suspension bridge providing another connection between Westminster and Lambeth was built here in 1861. In 1929–32 the present bridge on five steel spans was built.

London Bridge (EC4): The first bridge over the Thames at this point was a wooden one constructed during the Roman occupation between AD 100–400. It can also be proved that the medieval bridges were in wood until 1176, in which year the first stone bridge over the river was built under Peter de Colechurch, the priest of St. Mary Colechurch. Houses on the bridge are first documented in 1201. Near the S. end of the bridge was *Nonsuch House*, built completely of wood: the beams were held together with wooden plugs instead of nails. Peter de Colechurch built a St. Thomas Becket chapel, in which he himself was buried, in the middle of the bridge. Pictures of houses up to seven storeys high on the bridge are entirely credible, as St. Thomas Becket was important enough to have two priests and four curates.

The bridge crossed the river on 19 narrow stone arches. At the S. end was a gatehouse, additionally fortified with a drawbridge on the Southwark side. The gatehouse was used for the display of the heads of those executed for high treason or as rebels against the crown. The current under the narrow arches was so strong that it was dangerous to navigate even at low tide. To improve this situation the houses on the bridge were demolished 1758–62 and the two central spans replaced with a single one. The Port of London was generally extended in 1799, and the notion of replacing London Bridge dates from then. In 1823 work began on a stone bridge on five piers only, upstream of the existing bridge. The architect was Sir John Rennie, who realized plans made by his late father. The bridge was opened by King William IV and Queen Adelaide in August 1831. When this bridge was replaced by the present concrete structure in 1967–72 it was demolished and sold, transported to the USA, and rebuilt in Lake Havasu City, Arizona.

Railway bridge with St. Paul's, seen from Blackfriar's Bridge

Chelsea Bridge

Putney Bridge (SW15): When this bridge, sometimes also referred to as *Fulham Bridge*, was built in wood in 1727–9 it was the first W. of London Bridge. After many attempts in the next 150 years to make it compatible with river traffic, it was replaced by the present five-arched granite bridge by Sir Joseph Bazalgette in 1882–6. It has marked the starting point of the Oxford and Cambridge Boat Race since 1845.

Richmond Bridge (TW9): A masonry bridge clad in Portland stone has connected Richmond-upon-Thames with Twickenham here since 1777. It was widened in 1937 to allow for modern traffic.

Southwark Bridge (SE1): The Southwark Bridge Company was founded in 1813, and Sir John Rennie started build-ing the bridge a year later. In 1819 the three-span cast-iron bridge was complete; the central arch had a span of over 239 ft., making it the largest bridge ever constructed in this material until then. It caused Walker's foundry in Rotherham to go bankrupt. The bridge was considered a technical masterpiece at the time. It was replaced by the present steel construction in 1912–21.

Tower Bridge (E1): The only bridge downstream of London Bridge, it connects Tower Hill with Bermondsey. In 1884 John Wolfe-Barry and Sir Horace Jones were contracted to build an opening bridge with a central span of at least 197 ft., and a clearance of at least 131 ft. when open. The towers, which had to be Gothic in style, consist of a steel frame clad with stone to balance the enormous weight of the bascules. The also contain lifts to carry

Lambeth Bridge and Lambeth Palace

passengers to the footbridge between the towers. The access roads to the towers are built on the suspension bridge principle. The bridge was opened by the heir to the throne in a solemn ceremony in 1894. The machinery was electrified in 1976, but the original hydraulic mechanism by Armstrong-Mitchell Ltd was preserved. The bridge is now open to the public and has a fascinating museum.

Twickenham Bridge (TW1): This second connection between Richmond-upon-Thames and Twickenham was built in 1933. It was conceived at the same time as Chiswick Bridge to ease the flow of traffic to and from the centre.

Vauxhall Bridge (SW1): John Rennie started to build another stone bridge between Pimlico and Lambeth here in 1811. However, in 1813 the Vauxhall Bridge Company decided that a cheaper cast iron construction designed by James Walker would be more suitable. This was opened in 1816, and called Regent's Bridge; it was the first iron bridge inside London. It was replaced by the present bridge, designed by Sir Alexander Binnie, in 1895–1906. The allegorical figures on the parapets represent science, arts, local government and education on the downstream side and pottery, engineering, architecture and agriculture on the upstream side; they are the work of F.W.Pomeroy and Alfred Drury.

Wandsworth Bridge (SW18): The first bridge on this site was built 1870–3, and replaced by the present structure in 1936–40.

Waterloo Bridge (WC2): This bridge from Victoria Embankment to Waterloo

Road was started in 1811 as Strand Bridge to designs by John Rennie. In 1816, while building was still in progress, the name was changed to Waterloo Bridge by order of Parliament, because it was felt that so splendid and permanent a structure was suitable to commemorate achievements and success in the struggle against Napoleon. In 1923 two of the piers started to sag noticeably, and traffic had to be diverted on to an auxiliary bridge. Despite much opposition, Rennie's bridge was pulled down in 1936, and replaced by the present bridge 1937–42.

Westminster Bridge (SW1): Early plans to build a bridge from Westminster to Lambeth on this site were mooted in the late 17C, but they were blocked by resistance from Thames boatmen and the City Corporation. In the 18C, however, the growth of Westminster made an improvement in traffic conditions essential. Old ideas were taken up again in the 20s of the 18C, and Colen Campbell provided a design for the bridge. Subsequently competitors submitted plans, including one by Nicholas

Hawksmoor in 1736. Finally Campbell's was chosen, however, and Charles Labelye was given the commission to build in 1738. Thames boatmen and the Archbishop of Canterbury, as owner of the ferry on the site of what was later to become Lambeth Bridge, were awarded compensation, so that building could begin immediately. Despite problems with the foundations for the buttresses in the course of building the bridge was opened with a triumphal procession in November 1750. More recent problems with the foundations led to discussions in Parliament and the award of a contract to James Walker to reinforce the bridge in 1837. This work was scarcely concluded when a decision was taken to commission a new bridge. Sir Charles Barry designed the present cast-iron structure, built 1854–62 by Thomas Page.

Monuments and memorials

Achilles (Park Lane W1): This is the first naked statue to be exhibited in a public place in England. It was set up by 'his countrywomen for Arthur, Duke of

The new London Bridge

Wellington and his comrades-in-arms'. The statue was cast in 1822 after a classical model by Sir Richard Westmacott from captured French cannon.

Albert Memorial (Kensington Gardens, opposite Albert Hall, SW7): In 1862 a committee under William Cubitt, the Lord Mayor at the time, decided to erect a national monument to *Prince Albert*. Queen Victoria was to choose the design, and she and her advisers decided on the one submitted by Sir George Gilbert Scott. The Royal Society of Arts then organized a nationwide appeal to pay for the project. The monument was handed over to the public in 1872, with no particular ceremony. The Queen had visited the site shortly before completion of the work, and Scott was knighted as a result. The statue of Prince Albert was not put in place until 1876; it was finished late by John Foley because the original sculptor Baron Marochetti died while working on the project.

The statue of Prince Albert is over 13 ft. high, and the whole memorial over 180 ft. high. It is surrounded by four marble

groups representing Africa, America, Asia and Europe. There are life-size representations of 169 artists on the base of the monument: painters on the E. side, musicians and poets to the S., sculptors in the W. and architects in the N. This frieze was the work of H.H.Armstead and J.B.Philip. These two artists and J.Redfern were also responsible for the allegorical figures on the various levels of the canopy, which resembles a Gothic tabernacle; they represent individual branches of science and the cardinal virtues. The allegorical mosaics of the arts on the pediments are the work of Salvati, and correspond with the base frieze. The statue of the Prince holds the catalogue of the Great Exhibition in his hand, and the surrounding statues of trade, industry, agriculture and engineering echo the pose.

Prince Albert (on the steps of the Albert Hall, SW7): Joseph Durham originally created this monument in 1863, to commmemorate the Great Exhibition in the Royal Horticultural Society's gardens. The prince is surrounded by representa-

Tower Bridge by night

Tower Pier

tions of Europe, Asia, Africa and America. The monument was transferred to its present site in 1899.

Sir Francis Bacon (South Square, Gray's Inn, WC1): Bacon is represented in the official robes of the Lord Chancellor. The bronze statue was created by F.W.Pomeroy in 1912 and erected to commmemorate the 300th anniversary of Bacon's taking over the treasurership of Gray's Inn.

General Lord Baden-Powell (Queen's Gate, SW7): Built in memory of the founder of the Boy Scouts in front of the movement's headquarters. The monument is in granite, and was carved by Donald Potter in 1961.

Sir Joseph Bazalgette (Victoria Embankment, WC2): Bronze bust by George Simonds to commemorate Bazalgette as builder of the *Embankment* and the London sewerage system. Bazalgette was also responsible for the construction of numerous 19C Thames bridges.

Simon Bolivar (Belgrave Square SW1): This bronze statue by Hugo Daini, erected in 1974, commmemorates Bolivar as the liberator of Latin America.

General William Booth (Mile End Road, E1): Bronze bust by G.E.Wade erected in 1927 to mark the spot at which the founder of the Salvation Army held his first open-air service.

Queen Boudicca or **Boadicea** (Victoria Embankment, SW1): The legendary queen who led a revolt against the Romans *c.* AD 61 is a symbol of the British national consciousness. This bronze by Thomas Thornycroft was cast in the 1850s and shows the queen in a chariot with her daughters; horses from Prince Albert's mews are said to have been the models.

The Brontë sisters (32 Cornhill EC3): Reliefs of the three authoresses Charlotte, Emily and Anne Brontë in conversation with the author *William M. Thackeray*, carved in mahogany by Walter Gilbert in 1939.

John Bunyan (Baptist Church House, Southampton Row, WC1): Richard Garbe's statue dating from 1901 is in a niche on the first floor; the inscription quotes the opening lines of *'Pilgrim's Progress'*.

Burghers of Calais (Victoria Tower Gardens, SW1): A copy of the famous sculpture by Auguste Rodin was placed here in 1915. The French sculptor created the work in 1895 for the Place Richelieu in Calais in memory of the heroism showed by the the six burghers of Calais towards the victorious Edward III in 1347.

Buxton Memorial Fountain (Victoria Tower Gardens, SW1): Until 1957 this fountain was on the NW corner of Parliament Square. It is a monument to *Sir Thomas Fowell Buxton* the leader of the Anti-Slavery Party, donated by his son in 1865. The representations of British monarchs around the fountain are fibreglass copies dating from 1960, when the originals were stolen.

Cadiz Memorial (Horse Guards Parade, SW1): The French mortar mounted on a Chinese dragon here was presented to the Prince Regent, later George IV, by the Spanish nation in commemoration of the Duke of Wellington's victory over French troops near Salamanca (on 22 July 1812). This defeat of the French led to the relief of Cadiz.

Albert Memorial

Thomas Carlyle (Chelsea Embankment and 24 Cheyne Row, SW3): There is a bronze representation of the famous historian by Sir Joseph Boehm on the Embankment, and in Cheyne Row a Portland stone medallion on his house, now a memorial museum.

Cenotaph (Whitehall SW1): The national memorial *'To the Glorious Dead'* was designed by Sir Edwin Lutyens and executed in Portland stone 1919&20. The 'empty coffin' is a memorial to the dead of both world wars. A service of commemoration in which the Queen and leading politicians take part is held here each year on the Sunday nearest to the 11 November.

King Charles I (Trafalgar Square, SW1): Bronze equestrian statue by Hubert le Sueur dating from 1633. John Rivett was

Trafalgar Square, Charles I

Cleopatra's Needle

asked to destroy the statue in 1649, after the King had been executed by Oliver Cromwell, but buried it in his garden instead, and it later came into the possession of Charles II. It was erectd in Trafalgar Square between 1665 and 1667, on a plinth designed by Sir Christopher Wren.

King Charles II (South Court/Chelsea Hospital, Royal Hospital Road, SW3): The monument was erected here in 1692 and shows the king as a Roman. The bronze was cast by Grinling Gibbons in 1676. On 26 May the statue is wreathed in oak leaves to commemorate Charles' birthday and his escape by hiding in a tree after the Battle of Worcester.

Queen Charlotte (Queen Square, WC1): Lead statue by an unknown artist said to represent the consort of George III.

Cleopatra's Needle (Victoria Embankment, WC2): Obelisk over 65 ft. high, hewn in the quarries of Aswan in 1475 BC. It was apparently erected in Heliopolis under Thothmes III; the engraved names of Rameses III and Cleopatra are later additions. The Roman Emperor Augustus was probably responsible for transporting the obelisk to Alexandria. The Turkish viceroy of Egypt presented the block of stone, which had fallen over in the meantime, to Britain in 1819, but no-one dared to transport it across the sea until 1877. The obelisk arrived in London in 1878, and was placed upon its present site. The subsoil outside the Houses of Parliament, where it was intended to stand, proved too soft for the column, which weighs 190 tonnes. Documents walled up in the foundations include photographs of the 'twelve most beautiful Englishwomen of the day'. A

Eros in Piccadilly Circus

counterpart of the obelisk was taken to New York three years later, and set up in Central Park.

Captain James Cook (The Mall, SW1): This bronze of the explorer of the Pacific was completed by Sir Thomas Brock in 1914, honouring Cook as a great seafarer and founder of the British Empire in Australia and New Zealand.

Oliver Cromwell (in front of Westminster Hall, SW1): The victorious leader of the Parliamentary troops against Charles is immortalized here with sword and Bible. The bronze statue was created by Sir Hamo Thornycroft in 1899, but Parliament refused, out of consideration for the Irish Party, to pay for the work from public funds.

Bartolomeu Diaz (South Africa House, Trafalgar Square, SW1): Monumental stone statue of the Portuguese seafarer dating from 1934.

Charles Dickens (Ferguson House, Marylebone High Street, W1): The famous novelist lived in a house on this site for a time. Eastcourt J.Clark's sculptural frieze of 1960 shows Dickens surrounded by some of the characters from his novels.

Duke of York Column (Waterloo Place, SW1): Sir Richard Westmacott's bronze statue of the Duke dating from 1834 stands on a column designed by Benjamin Wyatt. The height of the column, almost 115 ft., was popularly considered adequate to set Frederick, the second son of King George III, out of reach of his creditors.

King Edward VII (Mile End Road, E1):

This memorial column dominated by a winged angel opposite the London Hospital was donated by the Jews of East London in 1911. The sculptor was W.S.Frith. The column is surrounded by fountains and allegorical representations of justice and freedom.

Eleanor Cross (Charing Cross Station Yard, SW1): When King Edward I had his Queen Eleanor brought to burial in Westminster Abbey, he ordered that twelve crosses should be set up at the points at which the procession rested. The last of these crosses, dating from 1290, stood in Charing Cross, the present Trafalgar Square. The original cross was destroyed; the present copy in granite was designed by E.M.Barry and executed by Thomas Earp in 1863.

Queen Elizabeth I (St.Dunstan in the West, Fleet Street, EC4): When the Ludgate was demolished, the stone statue of the last Tudor Queen by William Kerwin (1586) was rescued and brought to its present site above the sacristy porch of St.Dunstan's.

The Monument, relief on its base

Eros (Piccadilly Circus, W1): The *Shaftesbury Avenue Memorial Fountain* was unveiled by the Duke of Westminster in 1893. The monument was conceived as a drinking-water fountain, and the figure of an angel was the first aluminium statue in London. The figure, incidentally, does not represent Eros, but the Christian virtue of charity, in memory of the Earl of Shaftesbury's philanthropic works. Alfred Gilbert, who was responsible for the design, refused to attend the unveiling ceremony because the proportions of his work had been radically altered. For fifty years now the statue has been protected from revellers on New Year's Eve and other occasions of public merrymaking.

William Edward Forster (Victoria Embankment Gardens, WC2): Bronze statue in memory of the founder of the primary school system, designed by H.R.Pinker in 1890.

Sir John Franklin (Waterloo Place, SW1): Bronze statue of the arctic explorer and discoverer of the Northwest Passage, created by Matthew Noble in 1866. The relief on the front of the plinth shows Sir John's burial.

Mahatma Gandhi (Tavistock Square, WC1): India's leader into independence, shown in meditation. The statue is by Fredda Brilliant, 1968, and was unveiled by Prime Minister Harold Wilson.

King George IV (Trafalgar Square, SW1): George IV commissioned this statue, intended for Marble Arch, himself, but died before Sir Francis Chantrey completed the bronze equestrian statue in 1834. For this reason the statue was placed in Trafalgar Square 'temporarily'.

William E.Gladstone (Strand, W. of St.Clement Danes, WC2): This monument, showing the Victorian politician surrounded by allegorical female figures symbolizing his reforming ideals of education, courage, striving and brotherly love, was completed by Sir Hamo Thornycroft in 1905.

Guards Crimea Memorial (Waterloo Place, SW1): Memorial to the dead of the three regiments of guards involved in the Crimean War. A particular feature is that as well as honouring the soldiers, the philanthropic achievements of *Florence Nightingale* and her patron *Lord Sidney Herbert* are recognized. Their statues are to be found on the S. side of the monument.

Sir Henry Irving (Charing Cross Road/St.Martin's Place, WC2): This bronze statue of the first actor knight was commissioned from Thomas Brock by colleagues in 1910, and is thus also a monument to public recognition of the acting profession.

Dr.Samuel Johnson (Strand, E. of St.Clement Danes): St.Clement Danes was the church attended by Johnson on Sundays. He was one of the most impressive 18C personalities, and his first English dictionary is in itself a memorial which will endure.

Katyn (Gunnersbury Park, W3): Controversial memorial to 14,500 Polish prisoners of war who disappeared without trace in 1940. After the war 4,500 of them were identified in a mass grave in Katyn, near Smolensk. The black granite obelisk was erected here in 1976.

Abraham Lincoln (Parliament Square, SW1): Copy of a statue of the American President made by Augustus Saint-Gaudens for Chicago.

Margaret Macdonald (Lincoln's Inn Fields, N. side, WC2): The turn-of-the-century social worker is portrayed holding out her hands to nine small children. From 1896–1911 she lived with her husband Ramsay Macdonald at *No.3 Lincoln's Inn Fields.*

Mercantile Marine (Trinity Square, EC3): Pavilion designed by Sir Edwin Lutyens in the little park dedicated to the memory of the men of the mercantile marine and the fishing fleet who 'gave their lives for their country and have no other grave than the sea'.

John Stuart Mill (Victoria Embankment Gardens, WC2): Thomas Woolner completed this seated statue of the celebrated economist and philosopher in 1878.

Sir John Everett Millais (Millbank, SW1): 1904 bronze statue by Sir Thomas Brock of the pre-Raphaelite artist, seen here with palette and paintbrush, in the courtyard of the Tate Gallery.

John Milton (City of London School, Victoria Embankment, EC4): Statue of the poet placed on the first-floor outer wall of the school on the Blackfriars Bridge side in 1882.

Nelson's Column and National Gallery

Monument (Monument Street/Fish Street Hill, EC2): After the Great Fire of London, Parliament decided that a permanent memorial to this catastrophe should be erected, and the City of London was to be responsible for its design and upkeep. A Doric column was erected in 1671–7, topped by a flaming gilded urn. It was designed by Sir Christopher Wren and his friend Robert Hooke. A spiral staircase with 311 steps leads to the viewing platform below the urn. The column is said to stand 202 ft. feet from the point at which the Great Fire, which destroyed almost all of the town as it then was, broke out on 2 September 1666. The column is 202 ft. high, possibly the tallest free-standing stone column in the world.

Sir Thomas More (Carey Street/Serle Street, WC2): More was a member of *Lincoln's Inn*, which stands N. of the monument. The plinth of the stone statue, by Robert Smith, 1866, bears the inscription: 'The true servant of both his God and his King. He died a martyr's death on 5 July 1535'.

Sir Thomas More (Chelsea Embankment, SW3): This seated bronze figure was erected by L.Cubitt Bevis in 1969 opposite Chelsea Old Church, his parish church. It shows Sir Thomas More with shining gold face and hands.

Sir Thomas More (City of London School, Victoria Embankment, EC4): Another stone statue of Henry VIII's Chancellor, erected in 1882.

Nelson's Column (Trafalgar Square, WC2): The central monument in the square which commemorates Lord Nelson's last great victory at Trafalgar (1805) was designed by William Railton. The Corinthian column in Devonshire granite was erected 1839–42, and E.H.Baily's stone statue of Nelson was placed on top of it in the following year. The bronze reliefs at the foot of the column, which represent Nelsons battles and death, were made of metal melted down from captured French cannons. The monument was not completed until 1867 by the addition of Sir Edwin Landseer's bronze lions, cast by Baron Marochetti

Sir Isaac Newton (City of London School, Victoria Embankment, EC4): This statue of the important physicist and philosopher is between the second-floor windows on the Blackfriars Bridge side

Norwegian Stones (Serpentine, Hyde Park, SW1): A large granite block resting on three smaller ones, set up here in 1978 by the Royal Norwegian Navy and the Norwegian Merchant Navy in gratitude to the British people for their friendly reception during the Second World War

Dame Christabel Pankhurst and Emmeline Pankhurst (Victoria Tower Gardens, SW1): Monument to the co-founders of the Women's Social Political Union. A.G.Walker's bronze statue of Emmeline Pankhurst. the leader of the militant suffragettes, was erected here first in 1930. The bronze medallion of her daughter Dame Christabel was the work of Peter Hills, and it was added to the existing monument in 1959.

George Peabody (Royal Exchange, EC2): The Massachusetts-born American was so shocked by the living conditions of craftsmen and workmen in his adoptive home town, London, that in 1862 he established a fund to provide 'cheap, clean, dry and healthy homes for the poor'. By 1890, 5,000 such homes had been built all over the city, the so-called 'Peabody Buildings'. As the matter was later taken over by the public purse, the foundation has a more general charitable range today George Peabody is the only American buried in Westminster Abbey. His statue at the Royal Exchange is by W.W.Story

City of London coat-of-arm

and was set up here in the year of Peabody's death (1869).

Postman's Park (near Little Britain and the General Post Office, EC1): This little open space consists of the former cemeteries of surrounding churches, and was opened in 1880. The painter and sculptor George Frederick Watts had the idea of establishing a national memorial for heroic men and women here. A wall in the park was dedicated to this purpose in 1900, and this is now covered with countless little plaques telling of the heroism of simple people in their everyday lives.

Protestant Martyrs (St.Bartholomew's Hospital, EC1): A granite plaque on the hospital wall commemorates the Protestants burned in Smithfield in the years 1555–7.

Sir Walter Raleigh (Whitehall, SW1): This bronze, the work of William Macmillan, showing the Elizabethan courtier in contemporary clothes, was unveiled in 1959.

Baron Julius Reuter (behind the Royal Exchange, EC2): Granite column surmounted with the head of the founder of Reuters, the international news agency, designed by Michael Black in 1976.

Sir Joshua Reynolds (Leicester Square, WC2): The famous painter lived at *No.47*, which no longer exists. The stone bust is the work of Henry Weekes (1874).

Sir Joshua Reynolds (Burlington House, W1): Alfred Drury created this bronze statue of the painter with paintbrush and palette for the Royal Academy in 1931.

Richard Lionheart (Old Palace Yard, SW1): Bronze copy of Carlo Marochetti's statue for the Great Exhibition of 1851.

Rima (Hyde Park, W2): This relief of Rima, a character from the novel *'Green Mansions'* by William Henry Hudson (1841–1922) was the work of Jacob Epstein. This monument ot the naturalist Hudson is suitably placed in the bird sanctuary in the NW part of the park. Its unveiling provoked a scandal in 1925, as the treatment was considered obscene.

Dante Gabriel Rosetti (Cheyne Walk, SW3): Fountain designed by J.P.Seddon, featuring a bronze medallion of Rossetti by Ford Madox Brown, one of his fellow pre-Raphaelites.

Bertrand Russell (Red Lion Square, WC1): Bronze bust of the mathematician and philosopher by Marcelle Quinton (1980).

Captain Robert Falcon Scott (Waterloo Place, SW1): Bronze statue of the explorer fully equipped for his Arctic expedition erected by officers of the Royal Navy, a work by his wife, Lady Scott, dating from 1915.

William Shakespeare (City of London School, Victoria Embankment, EC4): Stone statue between the second floor windows on the Blackfriars Bridge side.

William Shakespeare (Cemetery of St.Mary, Aldermanbury, EC2): Memorial designed by Charles J.Allen (1895) with bust of the dramatist.

William Shakespeare (Shakespeare's Head, Great Marlborough Street, W1): The name of the pub is most likely to come from the brothers *John* and *Thomas Shakespeare*, who ran it from 1735–44. A bust on the building shows the dramatist as if he were leaning out of a window.

Sir Hans Sloane (Apothecaries' Garden, Royal Hospital Road, SW3): Sloane established this Apothecaries' Guild garden for botanical research, and the guild commissioned a marble memorial for their benefactor from John Rysbrack in 1732.

Sir Arthur Sullivan (Victoria Embankment Gardens, WC2): Bronze bust of the composer, with allegory of Music weeping on the plinth, created in 1903 by W.Goscombe John.

William Makepeace Thackeray see *the Brontë Sisters*.

Trade Unionists (TUC Building, 23–28 Great Russell Street, WC1): Sculpture by Sir Jacob Epstein carved from a block of stone.

Joseph Mallord William Turner (23 Queen Anne Street, W1): Stone medallion placed here in 1937 to mark the site of Turner's house.

William Tyndale (Victoria Embankment Gardens, WC2): A bronze statue by Sir Joseph Boehm was placed here in 1884 in memory of the reformer who started to translate the Bible into English.

Queen Victoria (New Bridge Street, EC4): Bronze figure of the Queen with orb and sceptre by C.B.Birch (1896).

Queen Victoria Memorial (SW end of The Mall, SW1): Intended as the core of Aston Webb's new design for *The Mall*, the group is over 80 ft. high, and was handed over to the nation by George V in 1911, who knighted the artist responsible, Thomas Brock, on the spot. The seated figure of the Queen looks down The Mall. She is surrounded by a large number of allegorical figures. The entire group used over 2,300 tonnes of marble. The *Queen Victoria gardens*, which surround the statue, were added by Webb at a later date, using parts of *St.James' Park* and *Green Park*.

Edgar Wallace (Ludgate Circus/Fleet Street, EC4): Bronze medallion by F.Doyle-Jones (1934) commemorating the great journalist and world-famous crime writer.

Duke of Wellington (Hyde Park Corner, SW1): Equestrian statue of the *Duke of*

Westminster School

Wellington in uniform on his favourite horse Copenhagen, by J.E.Boehm, 1888.

Duke of Wellington (Royal Exchange, EC2): The City of London decided to erect an equestrian statue of the Duke in gratitude for his support of the rebuilding of London Bridge. Sir Francis Chantrey's design was completed after his death by Henry Weekes in 1844. The Duke was present himself at the unveiling of the statue. He is the only person commemorated by two equestrian statues inside London.

John Wesley (Wesley's Chapel, City Road, EC1): Bronze statue by John Adams-Acton of the founder of Methodism erected by his supporters in 1891.

Westminster School (Broad Sanctuary, SW1): Sir George Gilbert Scott built this column in red granite 1859–61 in memory of the former pupils of Westminster School killed in the Russian and Indian Wars between 1854 and 1859. The figure shows St.George with the dragon, and

around the column are statues of Edward the Confessor, Henry III, Elizabeth I and Queen Victoria by J.R.Clayton.

King William III (St.James Square, SW1): The statue dates from 1808, and shows the king as a Roman general. Beneath the horse is a representation of the molehill which caused his fatal fall in Hampton Court. The monument was designed by John Bacon the Elder, and cast in bronze by his son John Bacon the Younger.

Districts, streets and squares

Adelphi (WC2): In the late 18C the Scottish brothers (hence the name, from the Greek *'adelphoi'*=brothers) John, Robert, James and William Adam started an ambitious slum-clearance project NE of the present Charing Cross Station. They began in 1768 by reinforcing and levelling the banks of the river S. of the Strand. Then in 1772 they built 24 spacious terraced houses above the warehouse vaults which they had created, after

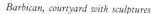
Barbican, courtyard with sculptures

parliament had granted permission for the Thames embankment, to which the City had been opposed. The heart of the complex was the *Royal Terrace* directly above the bank of the Thames. When the Victoria Embankment was built 100 years later the buildings lost much of their attraction, and the Royal Terrace was pulled down 1936–8. Only a few houses of the formerly impressive complex have survived, among them *No. 7 Adam Street*.

Barbican (E. of Aldersgate Street, EC2): Originally a small fortress outside London Wall, a fashionable area in the 16&17C; the Spanish Ambassador to the court of Elizabeth I rented a house here, for example. Later it became a centre of the clothing and textile trades. The section closest to the City Wall was almost completely reduced to rubble in the Second World War. To ensure that the Barbican should remain a residential area with all the necessary social institutions the City of London and London County Council bought the entire tract of land in 1958 and established a large-scale rebuild-ing programme. One of the most attrac-tive features is the inclusion of important cultural projects such as the *Museum of London, Guildhall School of Music and Drama* amd the *Barbican Centre for Arts and Conferences*. As with the *Centre Pompidou* in Paris and other monumen-tal works of modern architecture, opinions are divided about the appearance and practicality of the 'monster', in which not only strangers are prone to get lost. The building was opened in 1982, and contains two auditoria of the *Royal Shakespeare Company*, a concert hall for the *London Symphony Orchestra*, an exhibition hall and numerous flats, shops, galleries and cafés.

Belgravia (SW1): One of the most distinguished and expensive residential districts since the mid 19C. The name comes from the country seat of the Grosvenor family in Belgrave, near Leicester; the family is still the largest landowner in the region. Until the 18C there was nothing here but fields, and some market gardens producing

Barbican, courtyard with sculptures, detail

Barbican, courtyard with sculptures

Barbican Art Gallery, Cecil Beaton exhibition

vegetables. In the daytime it was popular for trips out of town, but the area was notorious for its nocturnal dangers. A row of houses was built in the mid 18C around Grosvenor Place, because of its proximity to Buckingham House, but the area was not really developed until the 1820s, when Lord Grosvenor commissioned Thomas Cubitt to build on his land, and the present district grew up around Belgrave Square. It has remained an area for the well-to-do, interspersed with diplomatic offices.

Billingsgate Market (Lower Thames Street, EC3): Until 1982 the largest fish market in the City. The first customs document for this market dates from 1016. Originally the fish market in *Queenshithe*, between Blackfriars and Southwark Bridge, was more important, but Peter de Colechurch's London Bridge brought advantages for Billingsgate, because the boatmen were only too glad to avoid the navigational problems posed by the new bridge. From the 13C salt and corn were landed here, and fruit and vegetables from the reign of Elizabeth I at the latest. Until 1850 trade took place in the street and from the market stalls. The market hall built in this year swiftly proved inadequate, and the present hall was built 1874–7. Sir Horace Jones, the architect of the City, designed a purely functional hall, the exterior of which resembles a building in French Renaissance style; it is now protected as an ancient monument. The market itself moved to the *Isle of Dogs* in 1982.

Bloomsbury (WC1): The area took its name from William Blemond, who bought the manor, mentioned in the Domesday Book, in the early 13C (then *'Blemondis-*

bery'). In the late 14C it was given to the Carthusians of Charterhouse by Edward III. After the Dissolution of the Monasteries, Henry VIII gave it to Thomas Wriothesley, later Earl of Southampton, in whose family it remained until the late 17C. They also started to establish it as a residential area. Bloomsbury includes the area between *Oxford Street* and *Theobald Street* and *Euston Road* to the N., bordered by *Gray's Inn Road* and *Tottenham Court Road*. In 1660 the Southamptons built an impressive house on the N. side of the present Bloomsbury Square to replace the Manor House. This became a model for the development of the area, not along the streets but around the various squares. Until the late 19C these squares and the little streets associated with them were closed off by gates, and so each had a strikingly singular life of its own. In the late 17C ownership of the land passed to the Russell family, the Earls and later Dukes of Bedford.

Apart from the society events in the great town houses, a mark was made on the district by scientists, artists and writers, and also barristers and judges, attracted by proximity to the Inns of Court. In the 20C it has become less attractive as a residential area, as the dominant features are now the *British Museum*, the *University*, and various hospitals. Recently, however, residents' associations have resisted the encroachment of these institutions: they prevented an extension of the *British Library* within the confines of Bloomsbury, for example.

Bond Street (W1): This famous London shopping street celebrated its 300th jubilee in 1986. It was named after *Sir Thomas Bond* in 1686, and he was the great patron of its development. The N. section, *New Bond Street*, was built in the 1820s. Although Bond Street is narrow and unglamorous in comparison with the great boulevards and promenades of other European cities, it was from the very first a street which attracted saunterers who

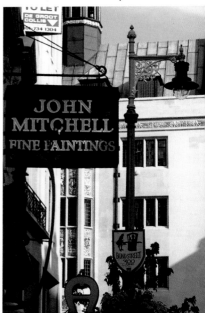

Bond Street

wished to see and to be seen. Even today world-famous houses lie behind the relatively narrow shop fronts. The auction house *Sotheby's*, on the entrance to which an Egyptian sculpture more than 3,500 years old was placed in 1917, is only one among many.

Burlington Gardens (W1): There are two particularly striking buildings here. *No.7*, which houses the *Royal Bank of Scotland*, dates essentially from the mid 18C. Designed by Giacomo Leoni, it was originally the house of the Dukes of Queensberry. In 1785 it was bought by the Earl of Uxbridge, and extended. John Vardy the Younger's stone façade with its 9 massive piers dates from this period. Diagonally opposite is the *Museum of Mankind*, the ethnographic department of the British Museum. This building, designed in the Italian style by Sir James

Pennethorne, was built in 1866&7 as the central administrative building of London University in the gardens of Burlington House (hence the name of the street).

Chancery Lane (WC2): Originally *New Street*, renamed *Chancellors' Lane* under Edward III, who handed over the building, which existed there for Jews converted to Christianity, to the Keeper of the Rolls of Chancery, the archivist of the documents for the Lord Chancellor's Office in 1377. The building was demolished in 1896, and the site taken over by the *Public Record Office*, where all official documents, diplomatic correspondence and other papers of public interest are kept; more recent material is now stored in an extension at Kew. Certain lengths of time have to elapse before the documents can be used for academic purposes, particularly in the case of government papers. A new monarch's accession to the throne is always proclaimed by heralds in an ancient ceremony in Chancery Lane. The main entrance to *Lincoln's Inn* is on the W. side of the road.

Cheapside (EC2): The name is derived from *'chepe'* the Old English word for market. This was the site of the City's great medieval market, sometimes called the *Westcheap*, to distinguish it from the meat market in *Eastcheap*, which was N. of Gracechurch Street, but which disappeared completely when the area was restructured and King William Street extended. The names of the streets adjacent to Cheapside are still a reminder of the parts of the town occupied by the various traders who plied their wares in the market. The town stocks were also in the market place, and executions occurred here from time to time. In the 14C tournaments were held on an open space to the N., and it was as a reminder of this that Wren incorporated a spectators' gallery in the exterior of *St.Mary-le-Bow* when rebuilding that church.

Chelsea Embankment (SW3): This broad embankment road was completed between 1871 and 1874 to Sir Joseph Bazalgette's design. He was at the same time responsible for the sewerage system for the area, which ran beneath it. Once the stretch of bank, formerly marshy, was reinforced, fine residences were built behind attractive gardens.

Clerkenwell (EC1): In the Middle Ages this was a tiny hamlet within the sphere of influence of the monastic foundations in the N. of the town. The name is derived from the drinking-water spring at the convent of St.Mary. *St.Mary* and *St.John of Jerusalem* were founded in the 12C, *Charterhouse* in the 14C. After the dissolution of the monasteries under Henry VIII their possessions passed to the new Tudor aristocracy, who built country houses here. In 1611 Charterhouse was finally turned into a home for impoverished gentlemen and a school by Thomas Sutton. The school is one of the country's most famous public schools. In the 17C the West became more interesting for the nobility because of the court, and rich merchants and craftsmen moved into Clerkenwell. Huguenot refugees from France and other Protestant refugees from the continent moved into the area as it was outside the City, where the guilds were closed to them. It was thus easy for them to establish themselves as craftsmen here. The air was fresh in this hilly area, and there were also springs with a reputation for curative powers since the Middle Ages, and this led to the development of spas and baths, as modern names like *Sadler's Wells* remind us. For about a century Clerkenwell was a flourishing community. Increasing overpopulation from the end of the 18C onwards led to the development of slums, a development which was furthered by the arrival of manufacturing and industrial settlements in the mid 19C. Most of these industries disappeared in the 20C, but it was perhaps just this and the opening and organization of small craft

Covent Garden Festival

and artistic businesses which led to the redevelopment of a pleasant residential area near to the centre of town.

Covent Garden (WC2): From 1656–1973 this was London's most famous fruit, vegetable and flower market, immortalized in George Bernard Shaw's *'Pygmalion'*. The market moved to a new site in Wandsworth, the *New Covent Garden Market*, between Nine Elms Lane and Wansdworth Road (SW8) in 1974. Covent Garden derives its name from its medieval owner, the convent of *St.Peter* in Westminster (Westminster Abbey). After the dissolution of the monasteries grazing land and gardens passed to the Russell family, Earls of Bedford. Francis Russell, the fourth Earl, bought the privilege of building on some of the land; he chose Inigo Jones, surveyor-general of the royal buildings, as architect. Jones

designed an Italian piazza, which was built between 1627 and 1639, and indeed acquired the Italian name. The square faced *St.Paul's Covent Garden*, and was surrounded by three terraces of spacious houses suitable to the life-style of the nobility (as the Earl of Bedford's commission ran). With the exception of St.Paul's none of these buildings has survived, although Henry Clutton's *Bedford Chambers* (1877–9) are an attractive echo of Inigo Jones' concept. In 1670 the Bedfords were granted permission to hold a market daily except on Sunday and at Christmas. The market hall, which has now been turned into shops, restaurants and offices was designed by Charles Fowler in the 1830s, and its outward appearance has been largely preserved, with the exception of the late 19C iron roofs. Today Covent Garden between *Drury Lane* and *St.Martin's Lane* is an integral part of the West End theatre landscape.

Drury Lane (WC2): In the 16&17C Drury Lane was a distinguished address for persons of rank, but in the 18C it became synonymous with urban vice in contemporary literary and pictorial presentations, dominated by prostitution and gin palaces. When it was cleared in the course of the extension of *Kingsway* and *Aldwych* the street was one of the most dreadful slums in London. *Nos.124–140* are a group of houses financed by George Peabody to accommodate 1,470 poor craftsmen and workers.

Finsbury (EC2): Since the 12C the area of moorland N. of the town, agriculturally a benefice of the canons of *St.Paul's Cathedral*, has been an area of recreation for the citizens of London. The Lord Mayor held hunting parties here. Drainage of the area started in 1511, and *c.* 1600 trees were planted and rubble paths laid to enhance the recreational value of the district. In 1641 the Honourable Artillery Company established a practice area; they were recognized as a guild under Henry VIII, made responsible for the defence of the City, and became a model for the Royal Regiments of Guards. The Great Fire of London drove the inhabitants of the town to this open space, and their emergency accommodation, some of it transformed into permanent residences while the town was being rebuilt, became the starting point for building in the area. Nevertheless open fields remained for a further century. In 1739 John Wesley took over the old cannon foundry and turned it into a Methodist chapel with school and accommodation for the minister. *Wesley's New Chapel* was built in 1778. Finsbury began to develop into a residential suburb when George Dance designed *Finsbury Square*. The plans for *Finsbury Circus* were also the work of George Dance the Younger, realized 1815–17 by William Montague. Only in Finsbury Square have traces of Dance's design survived: all the other buildings are the work of later architects.

Fleet Street (EC4): The ancient connection between the City and the Inns

Covent Garden Festival

f Court, beyond which the road to Westminster then ran. The name is derived from the river *Fleet*, which now lows into the Thames under Farringdon and New Bridge Street. In the Middle Ages bishops and abbots from various parts of the country had their town residences here. Fleet Street was connected with printing from 1500. This was the year in which Wynkyn de Worde and Richard Pynson moved their premises here. The reason for this was probably that their trade was better protected in the area of City jurisdiction, and there were book-binders nearby in Shoe Lane. The first newspaper, Edward Mallett's *'Daily Courant'*, appeared here on 11 March 702, and was shortly afterwards taken over by Samuel Buckley. Other 18C newspapers were *'The Morning Chronicle'* and *'The Diary'*, both projects of William Woodfall's. Fleet Street has become almost synonymous with the British press, encompassing the whole spectrum from journalists' trade union to the international news agency Reuters, and also pubs rich in tradition. Since the industrial disputes of the last few years involving new print-

ing technology, and especially since the editorial office and presses of *The Times* group of newspapers moved to *Wapping* on the Isle of Dogs in 1986, it is, to some extent, difficult to predict how quickly and in what direction the character of London's newspaper quarter will change.

Green Park (SW1): The park W. of *St.James's Palace* between *Piccadilly* and *Constitution Hill* takes its name from the dominant colour of the grass and trees. It is said that no flowers grow here because it was originally the cemetery of St.James's Leper Hospital. In the 18C Green Park was the scene of baroque court feasts and magnificent firework displays, for which court composers like Georg Friedrich Händel provided the music. The present system of pathways leads to the *Queen Victoria Memorial*.

Grosvenor Gardens (SW1): An impressive group of houses in French Renaissance style, arranged around two small gardens.

High Holborn (WC1):This street is now

Strand, view of Law Courts (left), Fleet Street, Ludgate House (right)

dominated by office and government buildings but from the 17C to the 19C it had a flourishing business existence, including specialized firms like confectioners and clockmakers, and above all large coaching inns. The area was originally a possession of the Knights Templar, who built one of their characteristic round churches here. A number of theatres were built here in the late 19C, but they were obviously not popular enough to be worth rebuilding after the Second World War. There are, however, still shops which are worth visiting, such as John Brumfit's old tobacco business at *No.337* or Beatties of London Ltd's model railway shop, one of the most important of its kind in England.

Holborn (EC1): Important even in the Middle Ages as an access road to the City, used by traders in skins, wool, wood, corn and cheese. The road was paved for the first time in 1417, and from the 16C important people such as Sir Thomas More, Sir Francis Bacon and John Milton lived here. The botanist John Gerard had his herb garden here. The 'Daily Mirror' building at No.33 is an interesting example of late 1950s architecture. The district known as Holborn (WC2), now in the Borough of *Camden*, was first mentioned in a document by King Edgar relating to a donation to Westminster Abbey.

Hyde Park (W1, W2, SW7): This site, once part of a large Saxon estate, was given to Westminster Abbey by the Normans after the conquest. When the monasteries were dissolved by Henry VIII, the park fell to the crown. It was opened to the public in the early 17C, but hunting was permitted until the late 18C. Even in the 17C the park was a popular rendezvous for May Day trips and walks, and presented an opportunity for ordinary citizens to be noticed by the monarch. When William III moved into *Kensington*

Whitehall by night

Palace in the late 17C he had *Rotten Row* (originally *route du roi*), the connecting route between *St.James's Palace* and *Kensington* hung with lamps to discourage highwaymen; the measure did not succeed in preventing highway robbery, but it did make Rotten Row the first street in England to be lit at night. Queen Caroline began landscaping the park in 1730. The Serpentine was dammed and two royal yachts sailed upon it. However, the park was so intensively used for public festivals that many contemporary reports complain that there was not a blade of grass to be found anywhere on the site. In 1851 the *Great Exhibition* was opened at *Hyde Park Corner* near the *Albert Gate* (SW1). In 1860 the architect and landscape gardener William Nesfield began to plan the park. The majority of the fountains and water gardens (*Italian Garden*) date from this period. The greenhouses, which

over a huge area, provide seedlings for ll the royal parks.

ermyn Street (SW1): There are many entlemen's outfitters here, and other hops selling items with famous names, uch as a Dunhill pipe to suit your face nd station. This was a residential area for he nobility until Victorian times. Henry ermyn, the Earl of St.Albans, was granted he land by King Charles II and finished uilding the road c. 1680. None of the uildings from that period has survived. relief on *No. 73*, on the corner of Bury treet, commemorates the handing over f the deeds to Jermyn by the King. The dest surviving buildings date from the aid 18C.

ing's Road (SW3, SW6, SW10): This ow world-famous shopping street was ntil 1830 a private road in the possession of the crown E. of the junction with Old Church Street: a special pass was needed to use it. It formed a connection between the palaces in Westminster and Hampton Court and Kew. King's Road is now the heart of fashionable *Chelsea*. Its boutiques set the style for Swinging London in the 1960s, and still have considerable influence on fashion, although the range covered is now too broad to be reduced to a single formula. Some elegant early 18C houses have survived, for example the group opposite Chelsea College W. of the junction of Oakley Street and the King's Road.

Knightsbridge (SW1): The name can be traced back to the 11C, and is associated with a legend that two knights fought to the death on the bridge over the West-bourne, roughly at the point where Albert Gate now leads into Hyde Park. From the

Marble Arch

late Middle Ages to the 18C the settlement was famous for its taverns, but also feared because the company could include highwaymen and bands of robbers from Hyde Park and the fields of Belgravia. *Knightsbridge Green*, the narrow connection between Knightsbridge and Brompton Road to the W. is all that survives as a reminder of the former village green. Architecturally the street is an impressive mélange of late-19C Gothic and large-scale post-war buildings. Knightsbridge, *Sloane Street* and *Brompton Road* form a shopping centre W. of the town centre.

Lincoln's Inn Fields (WC2): This small inner-city park was made up of two areas of pasture, *Purse Field* and *Cup Field*, and took its name from *Lincoln's Inn* to the E. Although the land never belonged to the Inn the name is fitting: it was largely because of barristers' protests that the area was never built up. An important compromise was reached *c.* 1640, namely that the area was to be a square surrounded by smart houses, but that part of the site should never be built on. The *Soane Museum* now stands on the N. side of the square, and on the S. side are the *Royal College of Surgeons* dating from the first half of the 19C and the *Nuffield College of Surgical Sciences*, a modern training establishment. Some impressive 18C houses have survived around the square. The garden has been open to the public since 1894. The buildings of Lincoln's Inn to the E. are examples of urban architecture ranging from the early 16C to the mid 19C.

Lombard Lane (EC4) and **Lombard Street** (EC3): Two of the streets in which Italian merchants and moneylenders

Henry Moore, Locking Piece, near Vauxhall Bridge

mainly from Lombardy, settled to ply their trade from the 12C onwards. Both streets are now dominated by international bankers. The *Institute of Bankers* also has its premises at *No.10 Lombard Street*.

The Mall (SW1): Avenue laid out after the Restoration in 1660, intended to replace *Pall Mall*, N. of St.James's Palace, as a site for the game of pail-mail, a sort of croquet. The game, imported from France, went out of fashion in the 1840s, but The Mall remained popular with strollers, probably because it offered an informal possibility of seeing members of the royal family out for walks. This attraction waned towards the end of the century, and in 1903 the avenue was redesigned to provide an optical connection between *Admiralty Arch* and the *Queen Victoria Memorial*. The street was opened to traffic in 1911.

Marble Arch (W1): This triumphal arch based on the Arch of Constantine in Rome was designed by John Nash as the gateway to the rebuilt *Buckingham Palace*, and this is where it was first placed, but it was moved to its present site in 1851. It has been a traffic island since 1908, and only high-ranking members of the Royal Family and the King's Troop of Horse Artillery are allowed to pass through it. The most-used London gallows stood on this site at the NE corner of *Hyde Park* from 1388–1783. Execution days were public holidays, but many contemporaries doubted whether these shows really had the desired deterrent effect.

Mayfair (W1): Extensive building started in the 1660s along what is now Piccadilly. The area soon became popular with the nobility because of its proximity to St.James's Palace and the declining attraction of Soho and Covent Garden, and by the mid 18C Mayfair covered roughly the same area that it now does within the rectangle bounded by *Hyde Park, Oxford Street, Regent Street* and *Piccadilly*. The May fair, which moved here from Haymarket in the late 1680s and gave its name to the area, was unpopular with the elegant residents, and its licence was withdrawn in 1764. Mayfair is one of the few districts which never ceased to be attractive as a residential area. Country gentry had their town houses here, and they held elegant balls in the season. Many of these houses are still in existence. Mayfair is generally rich in old buildings, although many of the plain brick façades have been covered with stucco and other ornamentation felt necessary by the taste of the times. *Chesterfield Street* probably conveys the best impression of the original Georgian elegance.

Millbank (SW1): This old riverside road from *Westminster* to *Chelsea*, which for a long time was lined only with vegetable gardens for the London market, took its name from the mill of Westminster Abbey, which stood S. of the monastery buildings on the bank of the river. The Grosvenors acquired the area after the dissolution of the monasteries in the 16C, and Robert Grosvenor built himself an impressive house here, which was demolished in 1809. From 1821–1903 a gigantic penitentiary stood on the site of the present *Royal Medical College*. In the 1820s some houses were built on Millbank as part of Thomas Cubitt's Pimlico development. Dominant buildings such as the *Tate Gallery* and *Millbank Tower* were not built until the 20C.

Oxford Street (W1): Although this E.–W. connection existed in Roman times, the street leading from *St.Giles Circus* to *Marble Arch* was not given a permanent name until the 18C. Edward Harley, the second Earl of Oxford, acquired it and the land to the N. in 1713; residential building followed in two waves in the middle and towards the end of the 18C. Theatres and other places of entertainment soon moved here. Oxford Street started to develop as a shopping street towards the end of the 19C, and the

Burlington House, Piccadilly

low of patrons to evening events slowed down, which meant that many of the great houses had to close. Oxford Street became the home of department stores and smaller shops. In 1972 the authorities introduced partial pedestrianization and planted some trees; the street is closed except to buses and taxis during the day.

Palace Gardens (SW1): The Garden of *Buckingham Palace* in the triangle between *Constitution Hill* and *Grosvenor Place* covers an area of about 40 acres. It was landscaped by W.T.Aiton. Large areas of lawn are broken up with numerous flower beds; a lake completes the picture to the W.

Pall Mall (SW1): Laid out for the game of pail-mail under Charles I (see *The Mall*) for the use of the court, this street near *St.James's Palace* soon became a popular residential area for court society. Some specialized shops also established themselves here. The area was considered a calm oasis until the advent of coffee houses in the 18C. Writers and artists sought accommodation here, and debating clubs

and societies formed in the coffee houses, some of which then acquired permanent premises on the S. side of the road. Pall Mall still made an aristocratic impression, however. Since the middle of the present century the residential character of the neighbourhood has been completely changed by the establishment of firms and offices.

Piccadilly (W1): Like Oxford Street an age-old route out of the City to the W., only gradually built up. A rich tailor with house in what is now Piccadilly Circus set the ball rolling. He had made his money by manufacturing and selling 'picadils', a sort of stiff collar fashionable at court. For this reason his house was christened '*Piccadilly Hall*', and despite later attempts to give the street to the W. a proper name the nickname became popular currency. Further building in the street began under Henry Jermyn, Earl of St.Albans, in 1661. In the E. section, around the James's church, numbers of inns and shops were built in the next 20 years. The nobility built some houses on the N. side, W. of *Swallow Street*, including *Burlington*

Regent Street, department store

Regent Street

House. In the last quarter of the 18C more fashionable residences were built in the W. section of Piccadilly, including *Apsley House* at *Hyde Park Corner,* now the *Wellington Museum.* For several generations Piccadilly, and especially the W. section with a view over *Green Park,* was a popular residential area for the gentry. Increasing traffic noise in the late 19C meant that these residences were replaced by clubs and offices. In the meantime most of the clubs have moved away because of high rents in this fine situation, and Piccadilly is now dominated by businesses with a high turnover such as hotels, airline offices and banks. *Piccadilly Circus* was designed by John Nash along with Regent Street, but its symmetry was destroyed in the interests of modern traffic when the ring of façades was pierced to allow access to *Shaftesbury Avenue, c.* 1885.

Pimlico (SW1): The stretch of the river bank between *Chelsea Bridge* and *Vauxhall Bridge* has been known by this name since the 17C. though no-one is clear why. Only a few simple cottages and later a small brewery stood on this damp strip of bank. Thomas Cubitt began to build houses here *c.* 1835, with support from the Grosvenor family, as in Belgravia, but it was agreed from the first that the houses should be aimed at a less wealthy, and therefore less elegant, clientele. Pimlico was thus not favoured by the rich and fashionable, with the advantage that housing designed by a great architect was available at modest prices. As in Belgravia, a number of Cubitt's buildings are still to be seen in Pimlico, and many of the terraces demonstrate that skilful design retains its beauty even amid changing fashions.

Regent Street (W1): Regent Street was

St. James's Park

built to provide a necessary link with land which had fallen to the Crown N. of *St. Marylebone*, but also owes its existence to the desire of the Prince Regent, later King George IV, to transform London into a town with the *joie de vivre* and magnificence of the continental metropolises. He employed John Nash for this purpose, who oversaw the design of the entire street, and also of the area around *Regent's Park*. Nash subsequently laid down the basic structure of Buckingham Palace. In 1813 Parliament passed acts enabling Nash to proceed with his work. He and the Prince Regent agreed that Regent Street was an effective social dividing line between the great residences of the nobility and aristocracy to the W. and the less attractive houses of the craftsmen and merchants who had in the meantime established themselves in Soho and Covent Garden. Access to Regent Street and Port-

land Place was to be subjected to severe restrictions, so that these less elegant people would not spoil the impression made by fashionable ladies and gentleman promenading there. George IV's inclination towards splendour made him unpopular with Londoners, and they would probably have felt his extravagant plans were un-English even without the financial impositions resulting from them. Regent Street was a far cry from the formal style and unity of 18C architecture. The façades were lavishly articulated and structured in different ways; on the one hand they reflected the architects notions of liveliness, on the other hand the particular requirements of the people who lived in them. The heart of the complex was the so-called *Quadrant*, the sweep leading out of Piccadilly Circus in the direction of Oxford Street. Massive colonnades in front of the elegant shops were designed to allow the residents to take their walks in the open air even in wet weather. The terraces above them were intended to allow tenants of the flats above the shops to converse with their friends passing in coaches.

St.Giles in the Fields (WC2): The origins of the district around *St.Giles High Street* go back to the year 1101. At that time the leper hospice founded by Queen Matilda, the consort of Henry I, was dedicated to St.Giles. Condemned men who passed the chapel on their way to execution on the gallows at Tyburn were given their last drink here; this was seen as an act of charity. As the town had in the meantime grown well beyond the walls of the City, St.Giles in the Fields maintained its function as a parish after the hospice had been dissolved in 1539, under Henry VIII. In 1665 the plague which was be the terror of all London broke out here. Parish records show that many important people lived within its bounds in the 17&18C, including the Shelleys and Lord Byron.

St.James's Park (SW1): This is the oldest of the Royal Parks in central London. It covers an area of almost 100 acres between *Buckingham Palace* and the government buildings around *Downing Street* in the E. Henry VIII began to drain the marshes in this area and turned it into a hunting park, along with the adjacent woodland stretching as far as Hampstead and Islington. Queen Elizabeth I still went hunting here. The park was first landscaped under her successor James I, and provided with a herb garden, a small zoo and an aviary. *Birdcage Walk*, to the S. is a reminder of this. The basic layout of the modern park began under Charles II, who is said to have been advised on the matter by Le Nôtre, the designer of the gardens of Versailles. The existing small ponds were combined to form a single lake, which under the humble name of *'canal'* attracted not only the king to walk there,

but also many ordinary Londoners as well. In the first half of the 18C the park deteriorated appreciably, but was restored from 1751 under Lord Pomfret. In subsequent decades it was possible to buy a mug of milk for a penny in the evening, fresh from the cows who grazed in the park. Under George IV the park was further improved by the introduction of gaslight and a final decision about the line of the bank of the lake. The landscape of the park has remained essentially unchanged since this time, but the buildings in it have often been altered or rebuilt. Finally the *Lake House* N. of *Duck Island* was replaced by a tent-like structure containing a mural by Barbara Jones illustrating the history of the park.

Smithfield Market (EC1): The 'Smoothfield', a grassy area just outside the City walls was the home of *Bartholomew Fair* from 1123–1855. In the Middle Ages the horse market, held here every Friday, was particularly important, but sheep, pigs and cattle were also sold here. From 1400 the City coffers received levies from the traders. Before the gallows were built at Tyburn Smithfield was the most important site for public executions, notorious for the stake at which 200 Protestants were burned as heretics under Queen Mary I. As late as 1652 John Evelyn reported the burning of a woman found guilty of poisoning her husband. In 1638 a cattle market was established here by the City of London, and existed until 1855, when trade moved to the Metropolitan Cattle Market in Islington. This happened despite the fact that houses had been built in the surrounding area and the occupants soon began to complain about the noise, mess and smell caused by the market. The **market hall**, designed on the model of Crystal Palace by Henry Jones, was opened as the central London meat market in 1868. It had its own underground station connecting it with th

Smithfield Marke

Smithfield Market

railway termini. The new market hall was built in 1963 at the City's expense. *Smithfield Market* still has its own police and a pub which has the right to sell alcohol from 6.30 am.

Soho (W1): The name of this district is probably explained by the fact that its ecclesiastical owners handed over this medieval pasture W. of St.Giles in the Fields to King Henry VIII in 1536 so that he could create a park and hunting ground for the Palace of Whitehall *(St.James's Park)*; 'so-ho!' is an old hunting cry. The first houses were built here in the early 17C, and some aristocrats built their town houses here in the 1770s and 1780s. The district began to have an international flavour even then, as it started to be settled by Greek Christians and soon above all by French Huguenots fleeing from persecution on the continent. Around the middle of the 18C the native aristocracy had largely left the district (see *Regent Street)* and artists and literary figures started to move into this part of London, which bore the stamp of immigrant trade and crafts. In 1850 Soho was the most densely populated district in the capital, which made it prone to epidemics of infectious diseases, but also formed the basis of its development as a centre of the London theatre and variety scene. Although some of the old-established foreign hotels profited from theatre patrons, it was a different development which was responsible for the rapid spread of restaurants specializing in exotic food: in the early years of the 20C it was the fashion in London society to hold dinners and parties in restaurants rather than in private houses. Soho had a firm place in gastronomic guides in the 20s, and the district has retained a reputation for good food at reasonable prices ever since. The streets have also retained international flair, although the name of Soho is a little suspect today because of the accumulation of sex shops, striptease clubs and similar establishments. Because living accommodation has become more expensive as a result of this, Soho is apparently full of life in the evening and at night, but the actual residential population has sunk below 3,000. The authorities are trying to arrest or even reverse this trend by stricter controls and limited issue of concessions.

Spitalfields (E1): A Roman cemetery was discovered here in the 16C, set on the route out of London, according to Roman custom, in fact on the Colchester Road. Throughout the Middle Ages the agricultural land here belonged to the monastery and hospital of *St.Mary Spital* (hence the name of the district), dissolved in 1538. *Spital Square* (E1) is the only reminder of this institution. Houses began to be built in the area *c.* 1640, and towards the end of the 17C Spitalfields came under suspicion as a possibly dangerous centre

The Strand, Strand Theatre

of nonconformist religion. To counter this Nicholas Hawksmoor was commissioned to design and build *Christ Church* between 1714 and 1729. At that time the population consisted principally of poor workers and craftsmen, and had an international flavour from an early stage, as many refugees found their first, if not permanent, accommodation here. That this is still the case is shown by the building at the corner of *Fournier Street* and *Brick Lane*. It was originally built as a chapel for Huguenots fleeing from France, later it was changed into a synagogue, and today it is a mosque used largely by refugees from Bangladesh. In the 19C attempts to clear the slums in Spitalfields and Mile End were overshadowed by the so-called *'Jack the Ripper'* murders, which brought the area into the public eye. Incidentally slum clearance occurred exclusively as a result of private enterprise;

the Peabody Foundation built a first row of houses in Commercial Street in 1864, intended as dignified accommodation for impoverished craftsmen. *Spitalfields Market*, which has existed since 1682 for trade in imported fruit and vegetables, was a private institution until 1920, when it was acquired by the City of London and redesigned in its present form to fulfil the demands of the times.

Staple Inn (EC4): Sited opposite the junction with *Gray's Inn Road* on the S. side of Holborn, this *Inn of Chancery* gives an impression of the design of these little Inns which were part of the archive of the Lord Chancellor's office. It has survived in its original form because it was bought by an insurance firm in the late 19C with the intention of restoring it.

Strand (WC2): Originally a bridle path

King George IV, Trafalgar Square

along the Thames, thus really on the 'strand', the first houses were built on the N. side of this road linking the City and Westminster as early as the 12C. *Savoy Palace* and *Somerset House* were later to be the most splendid of them, but have not survived in their original form. The names of the side-streets on the Strand are a reminder of the most important bishops' houses and houses of the nobility; most of these urban palaces were replaced in the first half of the 17C by smaller houses belonging to well-to-do citizens, and by shops. Only a few of these half-timbered buildings have survived the development from a residential to a business street which began in the 19C.

Thames: Frequently referred to simply as *'the river'* the Thames was historically one of London's most important thorough-fares. Thames (called *Tamesis* by Julius

Caesar) is the oldest recorded place-name in England after Kent. It leads to just under 200 miles of navigable inland water-way. The Romans established their first settlement at the first point upstream at which it was possible to build a bridge. The stretch between the modern City and Southwark was the only one on which bridgeheads could be built on each bank without reinforcement. This is also emphasized by the fact that, apart from the medieval bridge at Kingston-upon-Thames, other plans for bridging the river had to await the technical capabilities of the 18C. It can also be seen how important these technical developments were for the unhindered growth of the metropolis when one considers that engineers were soon working on plans for a tunnel under the river below London Bridge. Marc Brunel and his son Isambard finally built the first tunnel between Wapping and

Rotherhithe 1823–43, used until 1860 as a pedestrian tunnel, then as a railway tunnel; it is now used by underground trains. In the course of this work the Brunels developed techniques still used for tunnelling under rivers and built-up areas; thus their pioneering work made modern underground railways possible.

Tower Hill and **Trinity Square** (EC3): From 1388–1747 prisoners in the Tower condemned to death for high treason were beheaded at the point where Tower Hill enters Trinity Square, and after that a gallows stood here until 1780. The executions attracted such masses of people that sometimes the number of spectators killed by collapsing stands far exceeded the numbers of those executed. A stone set in a path in the little park today marks the former place of execution. The building designed 1912–22 by Sir Edwin Cooper for the headquarters of the *Port of London Authority* (responsible for the entire tidal area of the Thames from the estuary to Teddington) sets the architectural style of the square. To the right of it is *Trinity House*, a building designed 1792–4 by Samuel Wyatt and accommodating the central authority responsible for lighthouses in England and Wales. The institution and the name go back to medieval guilds in various ports which had the aim of making navigation safer by the use of beacons and other aids.

Trafalgar Square (WC2, SW1): The square was designed by Sir Charles Barry in the first half of the 18C, and is considered the central orientation point for the metropolis: at the corner where *Charing Cross Road* and *Strand* enter the square a plaque marks the spot from which all distances indicated on road signs are calculated. The standard measures for the imperial *inch, foot* and *yard* are set into the N. wall used by Barry to compensate for the sloping site. *Nelson's Column* has been a rendezvous for political meetings and demonstrations since the mid 19C;

Victoria Street, The Albert Tavern

later the square became a destination for protest marches. A Christmas Tree presented by Norway has been a feature here since the end of the Second World War. On New Year's Eve Trafalgar Square becomes a centre of noisy celebration to greet the New Year.

Victoria (SW1):The area is named after Victoria Station, its economic centre. *Victoria Street* was named after the Queen in 1851. This low-lying land on the banks of the Thames was originally a possession of Westminster Abbey. Until the 19C there was no urban development, with the exception of a slum accommodating impoverished petty criminals who had settled here during the Middle Ages under the protection of the nearby Abbey. A settlement began to spring up after the opening of *Vauxhall Bridge* and *Vauxhall Bridge Road* in the early 19C. The opening

Victoria Station

of the *Grosvenor Canal* in 1825 demonstrated the intention of establishing an industrial quarter for Westminster. Victoria Street was finally driven through the slums of Westminster to form a link between Thomas Cubitt's extended Buckingham Palace, which was planned but never built, and the Abbey and Houses of Parliament; administrative buildings and institutions such as the Army and Navy Stores were established along the street. After this the railway was laid in the bed of the Grosvenor Canal. Victoria Station was opened in 1862 as terminus for Dover, the Continent, the West of England and Wales; today services for Brighton and Dover run from here.

Victoria Embankment (SW1, WC2, EC4): After the Great Fire of London, Sir Christopher Wren suggested that an embankment between the City and

Westminster should be included in the plans for rebuilding, but it was not until 1864 that Sir Joseph Bazalgette was commissioned to build both it and the avenue between *Blackfriars* and *Westminster Bridge*. Work was completed in 1870. A number of the buildings date from the 1930s and 1950s, but some of the original Victorian architecture has survived. *Victoria Embankment Gardens* on either side of *Hungerford Bridge*, the railway and footbridge linking Charing Cross and Waterloo Station, are, along with the *York Watergate* the last reminder of the town palaces which stood here before the 17C, and they also give an impression of the original line of the river bank.

Victoria Tower Gardens (SW1): This little park with children's playground stretches along the banks of the Thames from the *Victoria Tower* of the *Houses of*

Parliament to *Lambeth Bridge*. It is one of the few places in Central London where a park is not cut off from the river by a road.

West End: Originally the collective name for the fashionable residential area between the City and Hyde Park, the West End is now known principally for the concentration of theatres, cinemas and restaurants around *Leicester Square* (WC2), offering a wide range of evening entertainment.

Whitechapel (E1): This area had a reputation as bad as that of Spitalfields in the 19C: the press referred to Jack the Ripper's crimes as the *'Whitechapel Murders'*. The living conditions of the dockers and industrial workers who lived here were pitiful; many improvements were brought about by Victorian philanthropists. Whitechapel had once been part of *Stepney*, which dates back to Saxon times, but in the Middle Ages came into the sphere of influence of the City, where the authorities were concerned to site noisy industries, particularly those involving metalwork, outside the town walls. An example of this which is still working is the Whitechapel *Bell Foundry*, founded in 1420 in *Houndsditch* (EC3), which later moved to Whitechapel. The chapel from which the district takes its name was built in the 13C and replaced in the 14C by the parish church of *St.Mary Whitechapel*. *Whitechapel High Street* was principally important to the City as the road to Essex; it was lined with coach stops, and first metalled in the first half of the 16C. The Jewish immigrants who settled here in the early 20C organized trade in old clothes and thus laid the basis of *Petticoat Lane Market* in *Middlesex Street*, which connected the poor immigrant areas of Whitechapel and Spitalfields. The work of 19C philanthropists and the social legislation of this century have made this a densely populated but attractive residential area close to the centre of the town.

British Museum, main entrance

Whitehall (SW1): Almost all government buildings are concentrated in and around this street connecting *Trafalgar Square* and *Parliament Square*, and its side streets (such as *Downing Street*). The name comes from King Henry VIII's *Palace of Whitehall*, and was at first associated only with the N. part of the street, in which the Palace was actually sited; it may be that it was a contemporary designation for any hall or palace used particularly on festive occasions. The S. section, then known as *The Street*, and *King Street*, contained market stalls and street traders until well into the 17C; they were often prosecuted for obstructing the traffic. In the mid 18C *King Street Gate* and *Holbein Gate* and some of the surrounding buildings were pulled down so that the street could be duly widened, but it was not until the late 19C that the stretch S. of Downing Street was extended to its present width by the removal of obstructive buildings, creating *Parliament Street* as a link with *Parliament Square*. The *Banqueting House* was built by Inigo Jones S. of the Tudor palace in 1625, and was the only building in the palace complex to survive a fire in 1698 which destroyed the buildings opposite the *Horse Guards*.

Museums

Anna Pavlova Museum (North End Road, NW11): The great Russian ballerina *Anna Pavlova* (1881–1931), who so fascinated the world with the expressive grace and lightness of her performances, lived in this house for a few years, and memorabilia of her life and career are displayed here.

Baden-Powell Museum (Queen's Gate, SW7): General *Robert Stephenson Smith, Baron Baden-Powell* (1857–1941) founded the Boy Scouts in 1907&8. This house belongs to the organization, and memorabilia of the founder are on show.

Bear Gardens Museum (Bear Gardens,

British Museum, Rosetta stone

SE1): Little museum of Elizabethan and Jacobean theatre, and the period in general.

Bethnal Green Museum (Cambridge Heath Road, E2): This museum was established in 1872 in an interesting brick, iron and glass building. Exhibits include toys, dolls, costume and other craft objects, and will appeal to both adults and children.

Blindania Museum (Great Portland Street, W1): This little museum presents an interesting survey of the history and development of aids for the blind.

British Dental Association Museum (Wimpole Street, W1): If one is not actually compelled to sit in the notorious chair, a glimpse of the history of dentistry and its technical aids can be most interesting.

British Museum (Great Russell Street, WC1): The history of this museum goes back to 1753, when Sir Hans Sloane (1650–1753) bequeathed his art collection and library to the state. Subsequent additions have included the family treasures and scientific collection of Robert and Edward Harley and Sir Robert Cotton, consisting mainly of manuscripts and books, a valuable royal library and unique exhibits from ancient high cultures in Africa, Asia and Europe. In 1832 Robert Smirke was commissioned to design a building worthy to accommodate all these treasures, which task he completed by 1857, with the help of his brother Sidney, and Sir Robert Westmacott. Early this century the present building, neoclassical with three wings, was completed. The main entrance is in Great Russell Street. It is surrounded by a façade gallery supported on Ionic columns and topped by a triangular pediment with frieze.

There is not sufficent space in the present work either to list or describe all the exhibits which make this one of the finest and most interesting museums in the world. It is probably also quite impossible to find and do justice to all the treasures of the museum in a single visit. The ground plans and text are thus intended simply to help the visitor to find his or her way around and to make it possible to establish priorities according to personal interests and the time available.

In the section of the ground floor to the right of the *main entrance* (1) is the *British Library*; its collection of European and Asian books and manuscripts is among the most valuable and distinguished in the world. Religious manuscripts are displayed in the *Grenville Library* (3), named after Thomas Grenville (1755–1846). In the *Manuscript Room* (4) is the original of Magna Carta, and also manuscripts by most great British poets and writers and other literary and historical documents from Britain and abroad. The *Crawford Room* (5) is used for temporary exhibitions. The *King's Library* (6) is built around the library of King George III, presented to the museum by George IV. Particularly fine among the European and other manuscripts are the

Gutenberg Bible and the First Folio of Shakespeare. The *Map Room* (7) leads to the *King Edward VII Gallery* (9). The *Chinese Collection*, showing art treasures from many centuries, has a world-wide reputation for the quality of its exhibits. There are also exhibits from India and the Islamic countries. This exotic area is completed by a room of *Japanese treasures* (10).

The section of the ground floor to the left of the main entrance is devoted to ancient high cultures. The *Egyptian Collection* (12) brings alive the old civilization of the Nile with its display of reliefs, statues, works of art and ritual objects. Probably the most valuable item is the *Rosetta Stone*, found in 1799. In 1822 the French Egyptologist Jean-François Champillon solved the riddle of its hieroglyphics, which enabled him to read written material from the empire of the Pharoahs. From Egypt we move to nearby *Palestine* (13) and a survey of its history in documents, equipment and cult objects. The *Greek Collection* (14) gives a comprehensive picture of life and art in the first high culture on the continent of Europe. Particularly striking

British Museum, Bassae temple

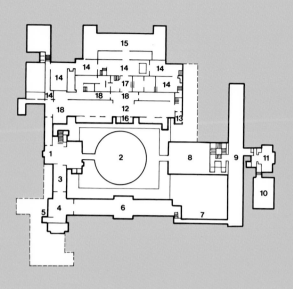

British Museum, ground floor 1 Main entrance (Russell Street) **2** Large reading room **3** Grenville Library **4** Manuscript room **5** Crawford Room **6** King's Library **7** Map room **8** N. library room **9** King Edward VII Gallery (Oriental collection) **10** Art of Japan **11** N. entrance (Montague Place) **12** Egyptian collection **13** Finds from ancient Palestine **14** Greek collection, beginning in the Bronze Age **15** Elgin Marbles **16** Etruscan room **17** Roman collection **18** Assyrian collection

among the countless architectural fragments, statues, sculptures, reliefs, amphoras, vases, utensils and cult objects, arranged in chronological order, are the original caryatids from the Erectheion on the Acropolis in Athens (*c.* 405 BC), the frieze from the Temple of Apollo at Bassae (*c.* 400BC), the façade of the Temple of the Nereids at Xanthos (*c.* 400BC), the sculptures from the Mausoleum in Halicarnassus in Asia Minor (*c.* 355BC), and of course the celebrated *Elgin Marbles* (15). These masterpieces of Greek sculpture, created 447–32BC, still impress

and amaze the visitor. They once adorned the Parthenon and other buildings on the Acropolis in Athens. Thomas Bruce, Earl of Elgin and Kincardine, Ambassador of the British Crown to the Porte in Constantinople, assembled this collection from 1803–12, and sold it to the British Government in 1816. The sculptures are beyond price. The gem of the *Roman Collection* (17) is the hand-blown blue and white *Portland Vase*, dating from around the birth of Christ and brought here by the Dukes of Portland. The Assyrian Empire flourished *c.* 9000BC in modern Iraq, and the *Assyrian Collection* (18) documents its late period, the last few centuries BC. The First Floor houses a collection on *Prehistory* (19). Via the *Romano-British Room* (20) we reach the *Medieval Room* (21), with its display of largely religious art. The *Gallery of Clocks and Watches* (22) is very fine. *Renaissance*

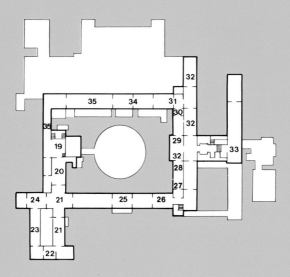

and Later Arts (23) is a collection of pictures, religious vessels, porcelain, seals and other gems. The *European Glass and Porcelain* department contains fine pieces from all the important manufacturing houses. The *Department of Coins and Medals* is of specialized interest. Further collections (26–31) open up the magic world of Asia, and the parts of the *Egyptian Collection* accommodated here are concerned with the cult of Isis and Osiris, and everyday life under the Pharoahs. This is probably the main attraction on this floor, although the somewhat grisly mummies may cause the visitor to wonder what can have possessed human beings to put their fellows, formerly persons of rank and status, on show in this way. A fine collection of *ancient vases* (34) and other finds from *Greece and Rome* (35) show how much these two ancient cultures had in common.

British Museum, upper floor 19 Early history of man **20** Roman Britain **21** Medieval art **22** Clock collection **23** Art since the Renaissance **24** Glass and porcelain from Europe **25** Coins of the British Isles **26** Art of Anatolia and the Hittites **27** Prehistoric finds from W. Asia **28** Ancient inscriptions **29** Finds from Syria, Phoenicia and Carthage **30** Nimrod Ivories **31** Finds from S. Arabia **32** Egyptian collection II **33** Rooms for special exhibitions **34** Ancient vases **35** Finds from Greece and Rome

British Museum of Natural History (Cromwell Road SW1): Alfred Waterhouse completed this unusual building in 1880; it is Byzantine in style, with battlements, turrets and lavish decorative detail on the outside walls. The ceilings and walls of the galleries are also richly decorated with designs on the theme of 'Nature'. This museum too is based on an original collection by Sir Hans Sloane, originally in the British Museum, and moved here in 1883. The present museum illustrates the history and development of animals, plants and minerals from

*British Museum, details of the frieze which formerly adorned the Parthenon on
the Acropolis in Athens (above and below)*

British Museum, Greek sculpture c. 400 BC (above)

British Museum, the Elgin Marbles, details from the Parthenon (above and below)

prehistoric times to the present day, arranged under the headings *zoology, botany, mineralogy, palaeontology and ethology*. The mineral and fossil collections and the ornithological gallery are of particular interest.

Broadcasting Gallery (Brompton Road SW3): Comprehensive permanent exhibition covering the history, development and future prospects of audio and visual communications.

Broomfield Museum (Broomfield Park, N13): This charming 17C house with garden has a fine entrance hall and staircase, a permanent exhibition of pictures by the 18C artist Gerrard Lanscroon and items on the natural history of the area.

Cabinet War Rooms (Whitehall, SW1): These nineteen underground rooms were used as the base for British strategic conferences and operations. The visitor still has the impression that Churchill and his war cabinet could return at any moment. The table in the conference room is laid with name cards and writing materials, and jackets, protective helmets and gas masks hang in the hall. Churchill's study, in which he could also sleep, still seems to be waiting for the Prime Minister.

Clock Museum (Guildhall, EC2): This little museum contains more than 700 clocks and other devices for measuring time from the 15–20C and gives a comprehensive view of the history of mechanical time measurement.

Commonwealth Institute (Kensington High Street, W8): Frequent temporary exhibitions in this museum convey an impression of the history, culture and daily life of Commonwealth countries; further information is provided by the library and films.

Courtauld Institute Galleries (Woburn Square, WC1): Viscount Lee of Fareham and Samuel Courtauld founded the *Courtauld Institute of Arts* by handing over their private collections to the University of London in 1932. As there is not room to show the whole collection at the same

British Museum, detail of tombstone frieze of Xanthos (470 BC)

ime in the galleries, the works are divided into six separate collections. The two collections mentioned above are a particular treat for art lovers. The *Courtauld Collection* includes paintings by French Impressionists and their pupils and successors, including in particular Cézanne, Gauguin, Manet, Renoir, Toulouse-Lautrec and van Gogh, represented by his 'Self-portrait' (1889). Almost all the great names of European painting are featured in the *Prince's Gate Collection*, which includes an excellent library. Lord Lee of Fareham's *Lee Collection* is distinguished by old masters such as Bellini, Botticelli, Goya, van Dyck, Rubens, Tintoretto and Gainsborough. Mark Gambier-Perry contributed 13–17C Italian paintings and sculptures. The *Witt Collection* includes paintings by British, Italian, Flemish and Dutch masters. The *Fry Collection*, a gift of the painter and art critic Roger Fry (1866–1934) includes pictures by his friends in the Bloomsbury Group and African and Australasian sculpture, as well as his own work.

Cuming Museum (Walworth Road,

SE17): This museum in the upper storey of the local library is again based on a private collection: it gives an impression of the social history of the area.

Faraday Museum (Albemarle Street, W1): A Corinthian columned portico leads into this building owned by the *Royal Institution of Great Britain*. This was founded *c.* 1800 to promote the natural sciences. The museum accommodated here is devoted to the physicist and chemist *Michael Faraday* (1791–1867), director of the society from 1825. Experts and laymen can visit the laboratory in which the Faraday's laws were established, benzole discovered in 1825 and other important discoveries made.

Flaxman Gallery (Gower Street, WC1): This domed building with Corinthian columned portico houses original models and designs by the neoclassical artist and sculptor *John Flaxman* (1755–1826), famous above all for tombs in *St. Pauls's Cathedral* and *Westminster Abbey* and illustrations for the works of Homer, Dante and Milton.

British Museum, relief of Harpven tomb (480 BC)

Courtauld Institute Galleries: 'A Bar at the Folies Bergère' by Manet (above)

Foundling Hospital Museum (Brunswick Square, WC1): In 1729 Thomas Coram established a home for foundlings and orphans, the *Thomas Coram Foundation for Children*, to which the (modern) building still belongs. Coram managed to acquire support for his Institution from such famous names as William Hogarth and Georg Friedrich Händel. Hogarth painted the portrait of Coram (1740) which is displayed here, and the Händel donated the organ, on which he gave many concerts to raise money for the foundation. The museum contains some of the original furnishings from the old hospital, such as the fine staircase and the Court Room, decorated by Hogarth, which was transferred to the new building. There are also Händel memorabilia, including a manuscript of 'Messiah'. Valuable painting were also presented to the Foundation, outstanding among which are more works by Hogarth and a picture by Thomas Gainsborough.

Geffrye Museum (Kingsland Road, E2) Thomas Geffrye was a 17C leader of the Ironmongers' Guild. In 1714 he built fourteen single-storeyed almshouses for the poor and needy on his land. The present museum shows the development of the English domestic interior from the 17C to the present day, using individual rooms furnished and decorated in the style of their period.

Geological Museum (Exhibition Road SW7): The museum has a fine collection of precious stones, and shows how they are cut for use in jewellery. The geology of England, Scotland and Wales is illustrated by a collection of fossils, minerals, other finds, and documents. It also covers Earth's natural resources, and

'Cain slaying Abel' by Rubens (left), 'Doubting Thomas' by Caravaggio (right)

the ways in which they are mined and exploited. Another excellent feature is an exhibition on the origin and evolution of the Earth, in which visitors can experience simulated earthquakes and volcanic eruptions.

Goldsmiths' Hall (Foster Lane, EC3): This museum can be visited only by arrangement; it has a collection of antique silver cutlery and modern English jewellery.

Guildhall Art Gallery (Guildhall, EC2): Part of the *Guildhall* is used for series of exhibitions by groups of London artists, changing at irregular intervals. Today it is amalgamated with the Barbican Gallery.

Hayward Gallery (Belvedere Road, SE1): The *Arts Council of Great Britain*

mounts art exhibitions in this striking modern building.

Heinz Gallery (Portman Square, W1): This fine late-18C building is used for exhibitions on themes relating to architecture and architects.

Historic Ship Collection of the Maritime Trust (St.Katharine Docks, E1): The old dock has been well restored and contains English ships used in recent times for exploration, now open to the public. The best known is probably the 'Discovery', on which Sir Robert Falcon Scott (1868–1912) made his first expedition to the South Pole.

HMS Belfast (Symons Wharf, Vine Lane, Tooley Street, SE1): This old cruiser has probably found her final anchoring place here by Tower Bridge,

Hayward Gallery

where she has been since 1971. The ship was built in Belfast and launched by Mrs Neville Chamberlain in 1938. One of her most important Second World War missions was on D-Day, 6 June 1944, as part of the Allied invasion of Normandy. Later she served in the Korean War under the auspices of the United Nations, and was stationed in the Far East. Visitors are admitted to the decks and various sections of the ship.

Horniman Museum (London Road, SE23): This art nouveau building by Charles Harrison Townsend (1901) has a large façade mosaic showing the cycle of human life and houses an interesting museum with ethnological exhibits from various parts of the world, mainly relating to religious rites and cults of the dead. The collections also include applied art, musical instruments and an extensive natural history section showing fossils and stuffed animals from all over the world. *Frederick Horniman* was a rich, well-travelled tea merchant, and this trade and its products are also illustrated in the museum.

Imperial Collection (Central Hall, Westminster, SW1): This unique collection shows *c.* 180 faithful reproductions of crowns and regalia from all over the world. It includes the crown of the Holy Roman Empire, the Hapsburg crown, the St. Stephen's crown from Hungary, the papal tiara, the Romanoff crown jewels including Catherine the Great's magnificent crown, Marie-Antoinette's celebrated necklace and the royal regalia which disappeared during the French Revolution, and the crowns of Frederick the Great, Ludwig II of Bavaria, Napoleon and the Shah of Persia.

HMS Belfast

Imperial War Museum (Lambeth Road, SE1): This domed building dating from 1813 houses an interesting collection exhibited on two floors and devoted to 20C warfare. The museum was founded in 1917 and accorded offical status by Parliament in 1920. The two world wars and other armed conflicts in which Great Britain and the Commonwealth have been involved in this century are documented with weapons, equipment, ammunition, vehicles, the spoils of war, uniforms, orders, decorations, pictures, documents and posters.

Institute of Contemporary Art (The Mall, SW1): This neoclassical building concerns itself with modern art of all kinds. The complex includes a gallery, a theatre, a cinema and a bookshop, and also arranges temporary exhibitions, discussions and lectures.

Jewish Museum (Tavistock Square, WC1): This little museum is devoted to the history of Judaism in England, illustrated by pictures, portraits, documents, religious and ritual exhibits and everyday objects.

Jewel Tower (Old Palace Yard, WC1): This 14C tower is one of the few surviving sections of the old *Palace of Westminster*, and contains finds from the palace.

Linley Sambourne House (Stafford Terrace, W8): *Edward Linley Sambourne*, the great political caricaturist of 'Punch', founded in 1841, lived in this building, reminiscent of an Italian terraced house, from 1874 onwards. The interior decoration and furnishings give a good impression of upper-middle-class life in the late Victorian and early Edwardian periods.

London Dungeon (Tooley Street, SE1): This 'chamber of horrors' illustrates, in pictures and tableaux, some quite violent and realistic, methods of torture and execution used in England from the Middle Ages to the 17C. The visitor is also shown how various dastardly deeds and historical plots were actually carried out.

London Transport Museum (Covent Garden WC2): This museum housed in a fine Victorian building has a interesting collection of old horse trams, buses, locomotives and other vehicles and also shows films on the theme of transport. Some of London Transport posters from the early years of the present century, also on show, were the work of distinguished artists.

London Toy and Model Museum (Craven Hill, W2): Small private museum which appeals not only to children; exhibits include an old model railway, other toy vehicles and playthings of almost every kind used by boys and girls before the age of computer games.

Jewel Tower

Madame Tussaud's (Marylebone Road, NW1): *Marie Tussaud* (1761–1850), a portraitist in wax at the court of King Louis XVI of France, was thrown into prison during the French Revolution and fled to London in 1802. Here she founded what is probably the world's best-known waxworks, which no visitor to London will want to miss. The *Grand Hall* shows figures from world history, including Madame Tussaud in the form of of model she made of herself in 1850. Great care is taken that the collection acknowledges changes of government and other great events by removing old and creating new figures. *'The Tableaux'* is a sequence of historic scenes partially prepared from pictures; they include the murder of the Little Princes in the Tower in 1483, the execution of the unhappy Mary Stuart and 'The Sleeping Beauty', who is in fact Madame Dubarry, the mistress of Louis XV of France; close examination shows that the figure is breathing deeply and peacefully. *Heroes Live* shows famous personalities from various spheres, such as the first two men on the moon, Rudolf Nureyev, Elizabeth Taylor and Richard Burton, and the Beatles. The *Hall of Kings* presents English monarchs from the time of William the Conqueror. The famous Battle of Trafalgar, in which the English fleet defeated the French on 21 October 1805, can be experienced complete with thundering cannon and the tumult of battle from a copy of the gun deck of the flagship 'Victory'. The visitor also sees the death of Lord Nelson, the great victor, whose life history is depicted around the walls of the room. The *'Chamber of Horrors'* is not for the fainthearted. These gloomy, subterranean rooms show particularly horrific criminals and their victims. There are also a model of a cell from the Bastille in Paris, remains of the death cell of Newgate prison, the death masks of Louis XVI and Marie Antoinette, made by Madame Tussaud herself, a model of the Parisian revolutionary guillotine and the original blade of this gruesome device.

'The Arcade' is rather more cheerful, a kind of amusement arcade with shops, hall of mirrors and fruit machines. It also contains a collection commemorating the legendary 'Battle of Britain' in 1940. Anyone who has still not seen enough can move on to the Planetarium for a show on the universe and its stars.

Mall Galleries (The Mall, SW1): Temporary art exhibitions.

Maugham Collection of Theatrical Paintings (South Bank, SE1): This exhibition of pictures of famous theatrical scenes is based on the writer *Somerset Maugham's* (1874–1965) collection.

Museum of Leathercraft (Basinghall Street, EC2): All kinds of leatherwork from Roman times to the present day.

Museum of London (London Wall, EC2): This modern building houses a museum which is a must for every visitor interested in the history and development of London from its beginnings to the present day, opening with prehistoric finds

and exhibits from the Roman and Anglo-Saxon periods, continuing to a major section on the Tudors and Stuarts, and concluding with exhibits from the 18,19&20C. The collection is built principally around archaeological finds, costume, furniture and domestic utensils.

Museum of Mankind (Burlington Gardens, W1): This building dating from the middle years of the last century now houses the ethnological section of the *British Museum*. Exhibitions of art from primitive tribal cultures mainly in Africa, Australasia and the Americas are changed regularly.

Museum of the Chartered Insurance Institute (Aldermanbury, EC2): Museum devoted to the history of insurance, and also to past and present methods of firefighting.

Museum of the Order of St.John (St.John's Lane, EC1): Former gatehouse of the monastery of the Order of St.John founded *c.* 1130, and rebuilt after a fire in the early 16C. It is now the head-

Henry Moore, Knife Edge 2

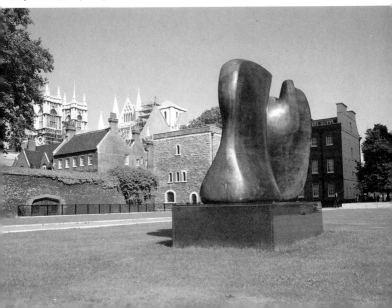

Madame Tussaud's and Planetarium

quarters of the St.John's Ambulance Brigade, and houses a small museum on the history of the monastery, which was dissolved by Henry VIII.

National Army Museum (Royal Hospital Road, SW3): This museum founded in 1971 illustrates the history of the British Army from the late 15C to the present day, in an interesting and often quite unusual manner. A collection of hand guns on the ground floor shows the development of these weapons. The 'History of the Army' collection has various exhibits. Particularly interesting is the gallery covering uniforms, decorations and orders, with adjacent art gallery showing pictures of famous war heroes, including several paintings by Gainsborough.

National Gallery (Trafalgar Square, WC2): The long, massive, balustraded façade of the *National Gallery* is on the N. side of Trafalgar Square. This building (1834–8) by William Wilkens is dominated by a central dome with lantern and two small side domes. The façade, articulated with Corinthian pilasters, has a broad central portico with Corinthian columns and triangular pediment and several narrower Corinthian porticoes with cornices. Edward M.Barry was principally responsible for the interior design. The mosaics in the vestibule, allegories of famous people from various walks of life, are particularly unusual.

The history of the gallery began in 1824, when the government purchased for exhibition 38 paintings from John Julius Angerstein's collection. Subsequent purchases were made regularly all over the world when famous paintings were on sale. Thus the National Gallery is one of

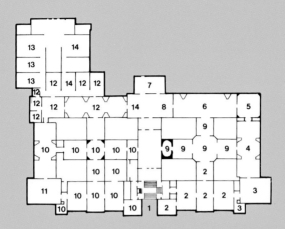

the most comprehensive and valuable collections of paintings in the world, containing works by the best and most famous artists from all European schools up to the 20C. It is therefore also not surprising that the gallery is a mecca for art lovers and connoisseurs, who often come to study a single movement. In fact it is simply impossible to absorb and pay due attention to all the works of art exhibited here. Similarly if we were to attempt to name artists and works it would rapidly degenerate into a wearisome list of names, dates and titles which would be of no help to anybody. Thus the ground plan showing the various galleries and the individual schools and periods covered should enable the visitor to settle his or her own priorities. Individual artists and works are not discussed here, as excellent detailed catalogues are available at the gallery.

National Gallery 1 Main entrance 2 French painters (19C, Impressionists and their successors) 3 Spanish painters 4 Italian painters (18C) 5 French painters (18C) 6 French painters (17C) 7 Italian painters (16C) 8 Italian painters (17C) 9 English painters (13-15C) 10 Italian painters (16C) 11 Italian painters (16C) 12 Dutch painters 13 Flemish painters (17C) 14 Austrian, German and Swiss painters

National Museum of Labour History (Mile End Road, E1): This museum offers a lucid survey of the history of the labour movement and the trade unions which are of particular significance in Britain, the cradle of the Industrial Revolution.

National Portrait Gallery (St. Martin's Place): This building in Italian Renaissance style opened its doors at the end of the last century to a collection which now has more than 10,000 items devoted to all the men and women who have attained distinction in Britain in some way. It includes sculpture and photographs as well

King James II outside the National Gallery

as paintings, and is arranged in chronological order on two floors, starting with the Tudor period. Each gallery is furnished and decorated in the style of the period covered. The collection includes a number of valuable works of art, including pictures by Holbein, van Dyck, Hogarth, Gainsborough, Rysbrack and Roubillac, and it also offers an interesting cross-section of British history.

National Postal Museum (King Edward Street, EC1): Interesting collection of stamps and everything associated with them, accommodated on the first floor of the main Post Office, and not exclusively of interest to philatelists. Temporary exhibitions also show the history of the British postal system.

Old Operating Theatre (St.Thomas Street, SE1): The only surviving operating theatre of the period, formerly in *St.Thomas's Hospital,* in the tower of the chapter house of *Southwark Cathedral,* shows how and under what conditions surgical operations were performed in the 19C. The former herb store contains 18&19C surgical instruments and medical apparatus, and also memorabilia of *Florence Nightingale* (1820–1910).

Passmore Edwards Museum (Rumford Road, E15): Small museum housed in an unusual 19C building and devoted to the history, archaeology, geology and natural history of the county of Essex; exhibits include archaeological finds, weapons, ceramics, porcelain, clothes and stuffed animals.

Percival David Foundation of Chinese Art (Gordon Square, WC1): *Sir Percival David,* China expert and lover, donated his valuable collection of Chinese porcelain and ceramics in 1951. It has subsequently been enlarged, and makes this little museum, which shows fine 9–19C pieces, a gem for lovers of Chinese art.

Petrie Museum of Egyptian Archaeology (Gower Street, W1): *Sir W illiam Matthew Flanders Petrie* (1853–1942) conducted excavations in Egypt and Palestine from 1884. He made important finds in the sphere of Egyptian prehistory, for which he established a chronology. He presented these finds and some purchased pieces to the University of London, which exhibits them in this little museum, of interest to all lovers of the Egyptian high culture.

Pharmaceutical Society's Museum (Bloomsbury Square, WC1): This little museum can be visited only by arrangement and illustrates the history of pharmacy in England since the 17C.

Photographers' Gallery (Great

Newport Street, WC2): Temporary exhibitions by British and international photographers.

Pollock's Toy Museum (Scale Street, W1): This charming museum featuring dolls, dolls' houses, teddy bears and other toys from Europe, China and Japan will appeal particularly to children.

Public Record Office Museum (Chancery Lane, WC2): This neo-Gothic building by Sir J.Pennethorne built 1851–71 and extended late in the last century on the Chancery Lane side houses part of the British *state archive*, and is not open to the general public. The building houses a public museum, however, showing letters, seals, documents, decrees etc. connected with the history of London and Britain, including *Shakespeare's will*, Lord Nelson's *'Victory' logbook* and, perhaps its greatest treasure, the original *'Domesday Book'*, William the Conqueror's survey of property in his kingdom, prepared against the Day of Judgement.

Queen's Gallery (Buckingham Palace, SW1): Temporary exhibitions of fine works of art (paintings, drawings, sculpture, silver, cutlery etc.) from the Queen's private collection.

Royal Academy of Arts (Piccadilly W1): The Royal Academy was founded in 1768 to promote the visual arts, with Sir Joshua Reynolds as its first president. It is now administered by Royal Academicians, including architects, sculptors, graphic artists and painters, and also extraordinary members drawn from these professions, It is based in *Burlington House*, a three-storey building with neo-Renaissance façade. The elegant galleries are used not only for the annual summer exhibition of work by contemporary British artists, at which works are on sale, but also other exhibitions on particular themes, which have an outstanding reputation.

George Washington outside the National Gallery

Royal College of Music Collections (Prince Consort Road, SW7): This museum shows portraits, engravings, photographs and sculptures of world-famous musicians as well as an interesting and valuable collection of all kinds of musical instruments.

Royal College of Surgeons (Lincoln's Inn Fields, WC2): This museum may be visited only by arrangement and illustrates experiments by the surgeon *John Hunter* (1728&9).

Royal Fusiliers' Museum see *Tower*.

Royal Geographical Society (Kensington Gore, SW1): There is a fine collection of maps and an interesting library in this house belonging to the *Geographical Society*, founded in 1830.

Royal Mews (Buckingham Palace Road, SW1): This Nash building with clock tower is the home of the royal horses, but they are not always on show to the public. The royal coaches and other ceremonial vehicles are exhibited, however, provided they are not in use, along with harness, uniforms and other accessories, a collection considered to be one of the finest and most valuable in the world. The most impressive of the vehicles is undoubtedly the *Golden State Coach*, in fact gilded, with paintings by the Florentine Cypriani, four winged titans, lions' heads, palm fronds and crown borne by putti; for centuries it has been used by monarchs riding to their coronation in Westminster Abbey. The *Irish State Coach* of 1851 is used annually for the State Opening of Parliament, while the *Glass Coach* dating from 1910 conveys royal bridal couples, and the contemporary *State Landau* visiting heads of state.

St.Bride's Crypt Museum see *St.Bride*.

Salvation Army Museum (King's Cross, WC1): In 1865 the Methodist preacher *William Booth* (1825–1912) founded a tented mission in E. London which he renamed *'Salvation Army'* in 1878. Over two million 'soldiers' of this peaceful army fight vice throughout the modern world, above all alcohol and drug abuse, and concern themselves with the homeless and unemployed. This little museum is devoted to the Army, and includes documents and other exhibits concerning the history of the organization, as well as memorabilia of Booth.

Science Museum (Exhibition Road, SW7): This museum is devoted to the history and development of technology and the natural sciences and their influence on industry and everyday life; it extends over five floors, and is of equal interest to adults and children, experts and laymen. Exhibits include apparatus, machines and models with which visitors

can experiment, and also memorabilia of great scientists and inventors, from Galileo's telescope to Stephenson's legendary 'Rocket', historic Daimler, Ford and Rolls Royce cars and Apollo 10, a capsule from the US space exploration programme.

The same building also houses the **Wellcome Museum of the History of Medicine**, concerned with the subject throughout the centuries.

Serpentine Gallery (Kensington Gardens, W2): Temporary exhibitions of 20C art.

Soane Museum (Lincoln's Inn Fields, WC2): The house, simple and unassuming at first sight, built in 1812 by the neoclassical architect *Sir John Soane* (1753–1837) and occupied by him from 1813 is on the N. side of *Lincoln's Inn Fields*. The unusually-organized interior is a surprise to the visitor, with its central dome and rooms giving the impression that one is in a mysterious ancient palace, because of the architectural and decorative effect of galleries, arches, niches and mirrors. The house is literally crammed with works of art of all shapes and sizes from the most varied periods, consisting of drawings, pictures, sculptures and antiques collected by the former occupier in the course of his life. The most impressive items are the sarcophagus of the Egyptian Pharoah Seti I, Hogarth's 'Rake's Progress' cycle, and sculptures by Flaxman. Experts differ over the point at which art and aesthetics stop and kitsch begins in this highly individual museum, but nevertheless no lover of art and antiques should fail to visit it.

South London Art Gallery (Peckham Road, SE5): This little gallery presents

Tate Gallery, 'Carnival' by M.Beckman

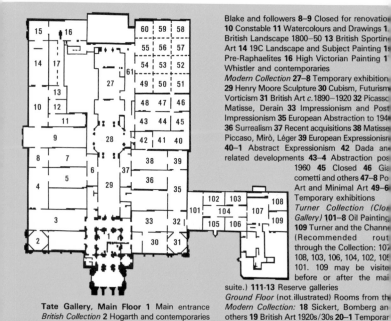

Blake and followers **8–9** Closed for renovation
10 Constable **11** Watercolours and Drawings 1.
British Landscape 1800–50 **13** British Sporting
Art **14** 19C Landscape and Subject Painting 1!
Pre-Raphaelites **16** High Victorian Painting 1
Whistler and contemporaries
Modern Collection **27–8** Temporary exhibition.
29 Henry Moore Sculpture **30** Cubism, Futurism
Vorticism **31** British Art *c.*1890–1920 **32** Picasso
Matisse, Derain **33** Impressionism and Post
Impressionism **35** European Abstraction to 194(
36 Surrealism **37** Recent acquisitions **38** Matisse
Piccaso, Mirò, Léger **39** European Expressionisn
40–1 Abstract Expressionism **42** Dada and
related developments **43–4** Abstraction pos
1960 **45** Closed **46** Gia
cometti and others **47–8** Po
Art and Minimal Art **49–6**
Temporary exhibitions
Turner Collection (Clo
Gallery) **101–8** Oil Painting
109 Turner and the Channe
(Recommended rout
through the Collection: 10?
108, 103, 106, 104, 102, 10£
101. 109 may be visite(
before or after the mai
suite.) **111-13** Reserve galleries
Ground Floor (not illustrated) Rooms from th\
Modern Collection: **18** Sickert, Bomberg an\
others **19** British Art 1920–40 **23** Britis\
Abstraction 1945–60 **62** Temporary exhibition

Tate Gallery, Main Floor 1 Main entrance
British Collection **2** Hogarth and contemporaries
3 Early British School 16-18C **4–5** Late 18C painting **6** Painters of the Exotic and the Sublime **7**

temporary exhibitions from its fine
collection of Victorian and 20C works.

Tate Gallery (Millbank SW1): This
neoclassical building on the bank of the
Thames with Corinthian portico topped
with triangular perdiment and statues and
similar 'side temples' with balustrades was
built by Sidney Smith in the late 19C, and
later extended. In 1897 the gallery based
on *Sir Henry Tate's* collection of mainly
Victorian pictures was opened. This core
has been built upon until today and makes
the Tate Gallery, along with the National
Gallery, a must for art lovers visiting
London. The *British Collection* is probably
the most comprehensive anywhere of
British painting from the 16–20C, and the

Modern Collection consists of pictures an\
sculptures by British and internationa\
artists from the Impressionists to th\
present day. The items exhibited ofte\
change, as there are not sufficient gallerie\
to show all the pictures owned by or o\
loan to the gallery at the same time. Fo\
this reason it is impossible to lis\
individual works and their positions here\
It would also, as in the case of the *Nationc*\
Gallery, simply become a list of names\
dates and titles which would bore rathe\
than inform the art lover. Thus the groun\
plan is intended as a guide to the build\
ing which will help the visitor to identif\
his or her priorities. Catalogues and othe\
detailed information are available in th\
main entrance. The high spots of the *Bri*

Tate Gallery, painting by Picasso (left), 'Two Women' by K.Schmidt-Rottluff (right)

sh Collection are works by Blake, Constable, Gainsborough, Reynolds and the Pre-Raphaelites. The *Clore Gallery* collection of paintings, drawings and sketches by J.M.W.Turner (1775–1871), best known for his atmospheric landscapes, is the most comprehensive, beautiful and valuable homage to this artist anywhere in the world. The *Modern Collection* includes excellent and well-known works by artists of the following schools: the French Impressionists and their successors; the Fauves (especially Matisse); Cubism, Futurism, abstract artists; European and American Expressionism; Dada and Surrealism; American Pop-Art and its successors; 20C British artists.

Theatre Museum (Covent Garden WC2): The *Victoria and Albert Museum's* collection on the history and development of world theatre and rock and pop music is soon to be transferred to the old *Flower Market*.

Tower Bridge Museum (EC3): Museum housed in the towers of *Tower Bridge* devoted to the building history and function of the famous bridge and other London bridges over the Thames.

Treasury of the Diocese of London see *St.Paul's Cathedral*.

Victoria and Albert Museum (Cromwell Road, SW7): This museum was founded in the middle of the last century on the initiative of the Albert, the Prince Consort (1819–61), married to Queen Victoria from 1840. Like Elizabeth I, Victoria made such a mark on the history of her country that her reign has gone down in the history of Britain as the

Tate Gallery, 'Woman' by Henry Moore (left), 'Pietà' by M.Ernst (right)

Victorian Age. Prince Albert was also closely concerned with the organization of the Great Exhibition in 1851. The museum named after the royal couple is now accommodated in Aston Webb's complex, capricious and overdecorated neo-Gothic building. It offers a comprehensive view of fine and applied art from the Middle Ages to the 19C in Europe and the Near and Far East. There are exhibitions of pictures, sculptures, costume, textiles, jewellery, tableware and porcelain, prints, musical instruments— in fact everything which could be classed as art and gives information about a period by dint of characteristic qualities, design, pattern etc. Here again, as the sheer number of exhibits precludes a complete description and would degenerate into a mere list, a ground plan has been provided to assist the visitor in finding his way around. Detailed plans and surveys of the museum, which is again often rearranged, are obtainable in the vestibule. Several visits will be needed to form an impression of the collection and gain a comprehensive view of individual periods or types of art, as each section includes so many valuable and characteristic individual pieces that a mention of an individual exhibit would seem like a value judgement better left to the visitor. Travel guides and experts alike assess the Victoria and Albert Museum as 'particularly worth seeing'.

Wallace Collection (Manchester Square, W1): The third and fourth Marquesses of Hertford asembled this valuable private collection in France in the 17&18C. It later passed to a descendant, *Sir Richard Wallace*, who brought it back to England. His widow presented it to the nation, making the Wallace collection the most valuable private collection in the world.

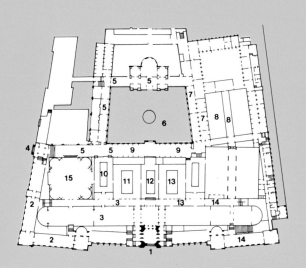

Victoria and Albert Museum, lower storeys **1** Main entrance **2** Furniture and crafts from England (mainly 17/18C) **3** European art in the 17/18C **4** Entrance from Exhibition Road **5** Italian Renaissance art **6** Garden **7** Renaissance art in Europe **8** Tapestries and wall hangings from various centuries **9** Gothic art works (mainly sculptures) **10** Indian art **11** Islamic art **12** Early medieval art **13** Asian art **14** Sculptures from the British Isles and the Continent **15** Clothes museum

ever to have been donated in this way. It is now accommodated in *Hertford House*, an elegant late-18C town house. The beautifully furnished rooms enjoy magnificent furniture, porcelain, mainly Italian ceramics, tableware, 16–18C gold and bronze work and European and oriental weapons, armour and uniforms. Art lovers will be attracted above all by the paintings, which include works by Hals, Rembrandt, Rubens, van Dyck, Watteau, Boucher, Fragonard, Velàsquez, Titian, Murillo, Gainsborough, Romney and Reynolds.

Waterloo Place Gallery (Waterloo Place, SW1): Temporary exhibitions of works by British artists and extensive transparency archive.

Wellcome Institute for the History of Medicine (Euston Road, NW3): This little museum, with extensive library of oriental and occidental medicine attached, has a collection of documents, drawings and pictures on the history of medicine. The rest of the collection is now in the *Science Museum*.

Wellington Museum (Apsley House, Hyde Park Corner, W1): *Arthur Wellesley, Duke of Wellington* (1769–1852), who with Field Marshall Blücher finally defeated Napoleon at the Battle of Waterloo and thus removed him from the imperial

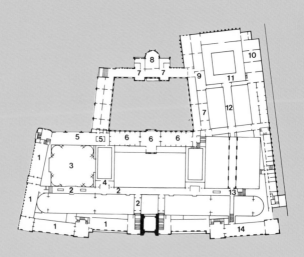

Victoria and Albert Museum, upper storeys 1 English art from the 18/19C **2** Plates, porcelain, faience etc. from England and the Continent **3** Collection of musical instruments **4** Wrought-iron works **5** Prints and printing **6** Library **7** Jewellery, gold, gems **8** Lecture room **9** Metal processing and metal working **10** Textile manufacture and processing **11** Works by John Constable (1776-1837) **12** Glass-blowing workshop and glass works **13** Far Eastern art **14** Tableware

throne of France, bought this late-18C red-brick house in 1817 and in the years immediately following had Benjamin Wyatt extend it by adding the Corinthian columned portico, the dining room and the Waterloo Gallery; Wyatt also restored the exterior. The beautifully furnished rooms are to a large extent still as the Duke left them.

The furnishings consist largely of valuable silver, tableware and booty accumulated by Wellington from the French. The *Waterloo Gallery* houses the Duke's valuable collection of pictures, some of which were formerly the property of the Spanish crown and presented to Wellington after victories over the French, as well as his own tastefully and expertly assembled collection of Dutch masters. Names such as Velàsquez, Goya, Murillo, Rubens and van Dyck speak for themselves. Finally there is a collection of portraits of famous contemporaries and military opponents of Wellington.

Whitechapel Art Gallery (Whitechapel High Street, E1): This gallery has made a name for itself with temporary exhibitions of modern art.

Whitechapel Bell Foundry (Whitechapel Road, E1): The foundry made bells for numerous churches in London and elsewhere in England. A small museum illustrates its history and work.

Victoria and Albert Museum, sculpture (left), Hercules and Hebe (right)

William Morris Gallery (Forrest Road, E17): This picturesquely sited Georgian house was the home of the writer, artist-craftsman and early socialist *William Morris* (1834–96). Together with Rossetti, E.Burne-Jones and other artists he founded small applied art businesses intended to compete with large industrial operations based on commercial principles of mass production and to maintain humanity within the world of work. The museum displays furniture, textiles, tableware and other work by Morris, and from his workshops.

Events

The British have a way which is unique in Europe of celebrating festivals, holidays and great events with a mixture of splendour, pomp and tradition which casts a spell over even the most sceptical spectator. The most recent example was probably the 1986 'wedding of the year' of Prince Andrew and Sarah Ferguson, which not only brought thousands of people on to the streets of London, but also enchanted millions of television viewers all over the world. The following is a chronological list of the most important regular events.

Daily events

Changing the Guard: The changing of the guard at *Buckingham Palace* takes place daily in the late afternoon; the Foot Guards are unmistakable in their red uniform jackets and tall dark bearskins. A band accompanies the new guard from their quarters to the Palace, and returns with the old guard after the relief ceremony.

Mounting the Guard: The mounted

Life Guards, recognized by their red coat and white plumes, and the Blues and Royals, with blue coat and red plumes, are relieved at the Horse Guards in *Whitehall* at about the same time as the changing of the guard at Buckingham Palace.

Ceremony of the Keys: The *Tower* is locked each evening shortly before ten o'clock; the ceremony may only be attended with prior notice. The highest in rank of the Yeoman Warders, conspicuous in their magnificent 16C uniforms, locks the gates of the Tower in a fixed sequence, and hands over the keys in a traditional ceremony to the Resident Governor, who lives in the Queen's House. The Yeoman Warders in their red and gold coats and flat black top hats with floral bands are better known by their nickname 'Beefeaters', a corruption of the French phrase 'Buffetier du Roi'; they were established by Henry VII in 1485.

Annual events
Charles I Commemoration Ceremony: The execution of Charles I is commemorated on 30 January by a processsion ending at the *Banqueting House*.

Oranges and Lemons Service: A service is held in *St.Clement Danes* around 28 March in memory of the hanging of the bells featured in the famous nursery rhyme. Each child present is given an orange and a lemon.

Maundy Thursday: The Queen distributes the specially minted Maundy money to old people and children in a different church each year. The ceremony is a continuation of the old custom that the monarch made gifts to the old and needy on the day on which Christ washed his disciples' feet, and thus made himself their servant.

Hot-Cross Buns Service: This ceremony held annually after the Good Friday service in *St.Bartholomew the Great* is also a reminder of alms-giving in former days. The children of the parish are given hot-cross buns.

Easter Parade: London too has an Easter Parade of the kind for which American towns in particular are famous. It used to be the custom for society ladies to parade their new spring clothes in *Battersea Park*. Today the parade consists of musicians, decorated floats and people dressed up in carnival costume.

Harness Horse Parade: Horse lovers meet in *Regent's Park* on Easter Monday for a colourful parade of carriages drawn by horses of all breeds.

Spital Sermon Procession: The Lord Mayor and other City dignitaries process to a service in *St.Lawrence Jewry* on the second Wednesday after Easter.

Queen's Birthday: Queen Elizabeth II's 'real' birthday on 21 April is celebrated with gun salutes in *Hyde Park* and on Tower Wharf, and with a small military parade at midday.

Ceremony of the Lilies and Roses King Henry VI was murdered on the orders of his rival Edward in the *Wakefield Tower* on 21 May 1471, during the Wars of the Roses. Henry was the founder of *King's College*, Cambridge and *Eton College*, and representatives of these two educational institutions lay roses and lilies at the scene of the murder in memory of the unfortunate king.

Chelsea Flower Show: Magnificent show held each year in late May in the grounds of Chelsea *Royal Hospital*.

Oak Apple Day: A memorial parade of the pensioners is held, again in the *Royal*

Victoria and Albert Museum, God of
Thunde

Hospital, in memory of their founder Charles II on 29 May. As the King is held to have hidden successfully from Cromwell's executioners after the defeat at Worcester (1651) in an oak, his statue is crowned with leaves of the tree which saved him.

Trooping the Colour: In the hope that the weather god who blesses London with the proverbial grey skies, mist and rain at certain times of the year will be in a better mood than in the at best temperamental month of April, the Queen celebrates her birthday a second time on the second Sunday in June, officially and somewhat exhaustingly: together with Prince Philip, the latter half hidden under one of the famous bearskins, she takes the salute at the impressive parade of her red and black foot guards, an occasion which lasts for several hours.

Royal Ascot: It is no distance at all from the capital to nearby *Ascot* in Berkshire, where this famous race meeting is held in the third week in June. Society ladies traditionally steal the horses' thunder with their expensive clothes and, in particular, their hats.

Garter Ceremony The knights of the *Order of the Garter* meet on the third Monday in June at *Windsor Castle* to pay their respects to the Queen.

Election of the Sheriffs: The new Sheriffs of the City are elected in a majestic ceremony in the *Guildhall* around 22 June.

Wimbledon All England Tennis Championships: Famous for many years, the English open championships take place in late June/early July, attracting competitors from all over the world.

Henley Royal Regatta: Regatta famous in both social and sporting circles, again taking place in late June/early July.

Royal Tournament: This 'Olympic Games' of Her Majesty's forces begins in July with a great parade in the *Mall*.

Swan Upping: Only the Vintners' and Dyers' companies and, of course, the monarch, have the right to own swans on the Thames. In the third week in July, when the brood has reached a decent size, representatives of the parties concerned make an inventory and ring the young birds.

Admission of Sheriffs: On 28 September the sheriffs elected in June are led in a splendid procession from the *Mansion House* to the *Guildhall*, where they are installed.

Election of the Lord Mayor: On 29 September the new Lord Mayor is elected in the **Guildhall** and escorted by a magnificent procession to the *Mansion House*; all the bells of the City churches are rung.

Judges Service: On 1 October the new legal year begins throughout Britain. The judges in their gowns and wigs celebrate this event with a service in *Westminster Abbey*, from which they process to the Houses of Parliament; there are also festivities in the *Royal Courts of Justice*.

Pearly Harvest Festival: Not only the rich and the great 'glitter' on festive occasions in London. On the first Sunday in October Cockneys celebrate around St.Martin in the Fields. The 'Pearly Kings and Queens' wear costumes decorated with shiny buttons and pearls.

Harvest of the Sea Thanksgiving: On the second Sunday in October the fishmongers and City dignitaries give thanks in *St.Mary at Hill*.

Tate Gallery, 'The Child' by E.Munch

Quit Rents Ceremony: On 26 October in the *Royal Courts of Justice* a representative of the City hands a royal official an axe, a domestic knife and two bundles of twigs as the token rent for lands in Shropshire, and also six horseshoes and 61 nails for a long since defunct smithy.

Trafalgar Day: On 21 October, the day on which Lord Nelson paid for his victory over the French with his life, London remembers the admiral and all others who died for their country at sea with a service in *St.Paul's Cathedral* and a parade ending in *Trafalgar Square*.

Opening of Parliament: In late October/early November the Queen and members of her family process to the *Houses of Parliament*, where she opens the new session from the House of Lords.

Veteran Car Run: On the first Sunday in November veteran cars assemble at *Hyde Park Corner* for the start of the London to Brighton race.

Guy Fawkes Night: On the 5 November London and the rest of Britain celebrate with bonfires and fireworks the discovery of the 'Gunpowder Plot' of 1605, when the Houses of Parliament were to have been blown up.

Lord Mayor's Show: On the second Sunday in November, on which his period of office officially begins, the new Lord Mayor of London processes to the *Royal Courts of Law* in medieval pomp and splendour.

Greater London environs

Map pp. 190/191
Index 313

London is a city embracing many districts whose different characters and attractions make it a source of fascination for the visitor, as well as for the capital's seven million inhabitants. Much of this variety reflects the history of those areas outside the City of London proper which were for a long time independent. A uniform administration for the more immediate environs of the city was not set up until 1855, when it was called the *Metropolitan Board of Works*. However, the City of London still preserves its privilege of self government. The *County of London* was created in 1888, when it was legally separated from the surrounding counties of *Essex, Kent, Middlesex* and *Surrey,* and its inhabitants directly elected their local government, *London County Council. County Hall,* on the south bank of the Thames opposite the Houses of Parliament, became the administrative centre. In 1961, over three million people lived in this area which comprises over 100 sq.miles.

The *Greater London Council* was created in 1965 by another administrative reform. This was once again a directly elected regional parliament, and the area it administered covered 600 sq.miles. The number of inhabitants in this area exceeds even million. County Hall continued to be the central administrative office. The region was subdivided into the *City of London* and 32 *boroughs*. The GLC was

dissolved in March 1986, some of its function reverting to the boroughs, while genuinely central services are now performed by corporations appointed by the Borough Councillors. The express intention of this reform is to strengthen the local responsibilities of the 32 boroughs on the one hand and, on the other hand, to increase the influence of central government and parliament. In this new system, central government and parliament can decide the allocation of tax revenue. However, there has been much discussion to date as to the viability and efficiency of this administrative re-organization of the Greater London area. In the present section of the volume, only boroughs have a separate alphabetical entry where the Greater London area is concerned. It is true that the organization of these boroughs in 1965 was determined solely by administrative criteria. However, this method of alphabetical arrangement appears worthwhile because it opens up quite clearly delimited areas which enable the traveller to find his bearings. In 1965 the boundaries were laid down in such a way that the boroughs each had an average population of 250,000. For this reason borders sometimes ran through the middle of old, expanded neighbourhoods, which in the present book are dealt with under the borough where their old core lies.

A selection of some towns around London which have a special relationship with the

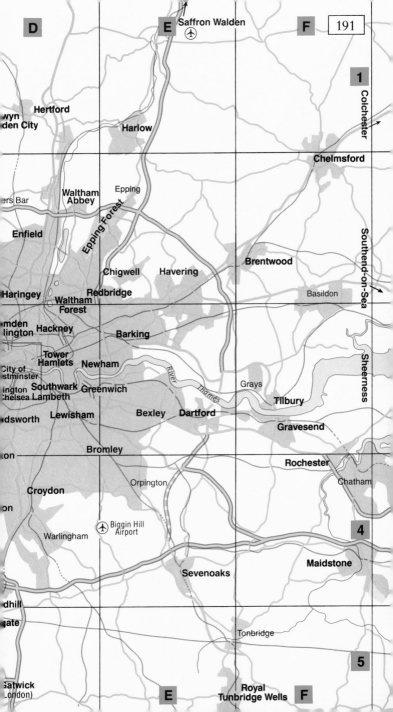

1

Colchester

Hertford

wyn
den City

Harlow

Chelmsford

Southend-on-Sea

**Waltham
Abbey**

Epping

ers Bar

Epping Forest

Enfield

Brentwood

Basildon

Chigwell

Havering

Haringey

Redbridge

**Waltham
Forest**

Sheerness

mden
lington

Hackney

Barking

**Tower
Hamlets**

Newham

River Thames

Grays

City of
stminster

ington
helsea

Southwark

Greenwich

Tilbury

Lambeth

dsworth

Lewisham

Bexley

Dartford

Gravesend

Bromley

on

Rochester

Croydon

Orpington

Chatham

on

4

✈ Biggin Hill
Airport

Warlingham

Maidstone

dhill

Sevenoaks

gate

Tonbridge

5

Gatwick
London)

E

Royal
Tunbridge Wells

F

capital is included too. Examples are *Windsor,* the Queen's summer residence, and day-trippers' destinations in Essex. However, towns are also described which, because they are residential towns alleviating the pressure on London, have long been regarded as a part of London's cultural and economic life. The decline in the population of most boroughs of Greater London should not be taken to mean that the city has diminished in importance with regard to people's everyday lives. Rather, it indicates a modern continuation of the centuries-old endeavour to live in quieter and comparatively rural surroundings.

Barking (Borough of Greater London)

Essex p.190☐B 3   (IG11, RM8, RM9, RM10)

This borough has existed since 1965 and was created from the two former urban districts of *Barking* and *Dagenham.*

BARKING (IG11): *Berecingum* on the E. bank of the *River Roding* was one of the oldest Saxon settlements in Essex. *Barking Abbey* was built in *c.* 666. An important town developed around the abbey and exerted its influence from the Thames up to Ilford and Chadwell in the N. Barking was the centre of a significant fishery industry and had a large fishing fleet from the 15C to the 19C. When the railway was opened in 1854, agriculture and horticulture became important. At the same time, the area began to develop into a suburban residential area for London, or for the new industrial enterprises which were establishing themselves in the region. The new industries were set up to the S. of the old core of the settlement, along *Barking Creek,* the mouth of the Roding.

Barking Abbey: The Benedictine Abbey of *St.Erkenswald's* was a religious and economic centre from the 7C until it was dissolved in the 16C; it was pulled down

in 1541. Excavations in 1910 uncovered most of the building, and today these provide a good impression of the convent setup. The discovered remnants derive from 12C (the church) and 13C buildings. Only the E. gatehouse tower *(Fire Bell Gate),* with a chapel above the gate proper, still survives in its entirety.

St.Margaret: The parish church, wider N. aisle; W. tower. Apse from the early 13C, when the church seems to have been redesigned with a transept. Older components are integrated into the E. chapel of the N. part of the nave, and into the N. chapel of the apse. Other very old features, such as Norman stonework, were included again when the other parts of the church were restored in the 15&16C, so that the architectural result may certainly be confusing to the onlooker. A number of picturesque tombs from the 14C to 18C are also worth looking at.

St.Patrick (Blake Avenue): A somewhat irritating attempt at modern religious architecture, the work of A.E. Wiseman (1940). The round E. tower has the bells and also encloses the church's choir.

Eastbury Manor House (Eastbury Square): Today a community centre occupies this splendid medium-sized Elizabethan manor house. An H-shaped building, it was completed in 1572 and much of the the original structure has survived. However, the strict symmetry of the original was impaired by the addition of a porch at the front of the W. wing, and by tearing down one of the spiral staircases in the courtyard by the wings. The original interior decorations unfortunately do not survive, apart fom mural paintings in the *Great Chamber* on the 1st floor of the W. wing and in a room in the E. wing.

DAGENHAM (RM9, RM10): *'Daecca's home'* was a another old Saxon settlement, similar to Barking. Both were part of the possessions of Barking Manor, and surrounded an area extending as far as some 8 miles N. of the Thames. When the urban community was incorporated into the borough of Barking, the N. section, *Hainault Forest,* was added to *Redbridge.* The area retained its exclusively rural character until the first few decades of the 20C. Only in the 1920s did the urbanization around *Chadwell Heath* and *Beccontree* (RM8) begin in the N. of *Dagenham Village.* The District Line of the London railway system was opened, and this certainly assisted the region in the tremendous impetus which it achieved between 1920 and 1950 in the erection of both council and private houses. These houses quickly caused the whole area to conglomerate into a large suburb.

St.Peter and St.Paul (RM10): The old village church (13C) stands in an unexpected site facing the Thames between the council housing estate (see *Beccontree*) in the NW on the one side and the Ford works on the other. The oldest section is the choir, which has Gothic windows. The chapel, incorporated into the choir's N. side, was completed in the late 15C. Nave and W. tower were built by William Mason in 1800. Here, the use of old materials indicates that this work was primarily conceived as an act of restoration; the result was a laymanlike Gothic style, which chiefly arouses mild surprise from today's onlooker.

Cross Keys Inn: This inn to the N. of the church is the oldest surviving secular building in Dagenham. A half-timbered hall structure, it was probably completed shortly before 1500 and is a very impressive example of that style.

Vicarage: The vicar's house to the E. of the church was built in the early 17C and enlarged in the second half of that century. Its architectural substance survives, but later alterations unfortunately caused it to lose more and more of its character.

Environs: Becontree Housing Estate (RM8, RM9): This enormous council house estate built in the 1920s was owned by the London County Council and has about 100,000 people. It attempted to retain a rural style of domestic architecture, somewhat out of place on this scale. On the other hand, public planning had the advantage that such parks as *Parsloes Park* were laid out in addition to private gardens. Some of the churches built in the 1930s in imitation of traditional styles are certainly worth visiting (e.g. *St.Elizabeth* in Wood Lane or *St.John-the-Divine* and *St.Martin* in Goresbrook Road).

Heath Park Estate (RM10): Another housing estate from the late 1950s and early 1960s. In this estate, the problems of size were taken into account and there is more of a mix of architecture (cottages, houses and blocks), which better suits the area's urban character.

Valence House (Becontree Avenue, Becontree, RM8): An L-shaped 17C manor house with an irregular gable, timber framing and plastering. It was built on the site of a medieval manor which, in 1309, came into the hands of Aymer de Valence, Earl of Pembroke (hence the name). Some remains of the medieval castle moat are still discernible. The house is now owned by the borough. Today it houses a small collection of documents on regional history.

Barnet (Borough of Greater London)
Hertfordshire, Middlesex p.190□C 2(NW2, NW4, NW7, NW9, NW11, N2, N3, N11, N12, N20, EN5, HA8)

Since 1965 this borough has consisted of the former districts of *Chipping Barnet, East Barnet, Finchley, Friern Barnet* and *Hendon.*

BARNET (Hertfordshire, EN5): This place name is Saxon in origin and refers to the clearing of a section of woodland by burning it down. The landed property was probably founded by the monks of *St.Albans* to whom, in 1199, King John granted the privilege of holding a market; hence *Chipping* (=market) *Barnet*, and more recently also *High Barnet*. Over the following centuries, the market and its location on the main road leading N. out of London caused the town to experience a continuing impetus which, in the 15C, was concentrated in *High Street* and *Wood Street*. This town became the first important stopping point to the N. of London and its coach houses and inns became central to the region's economy. Some of the buildings in Wood Street still bear witness to this former heyday. Chipping Barnet became a fashionable climatic health resort and spa for Londoners in the 17C. The coach houses lost their importance when the town was joined to the railway in the 19C; later it became part of the Northern Line of the London underground railway system. High Barnet quickly established itself as a residential area for people who, using the new means of transport, commuted to and from their place of work in the city centre. Since then, High, New, East and Friern Barnet have developed into a largely compact residential area.

St.John-the-Baptist (Wood Street): The church lost much of its original character when it was restored by William Butterfield in 1875. Some 17C tomb monuments have survived.

Tudor Hall (Wood Street): This complex of buildings opposite St.John-the-Baptist was built in *c.* 1577 to accommodate *The Free Grammar School of Queen Elizabeth*, which received its foundation charter from Elizabeth I in 1573. Funds for this were provided by the schools' 24 curators, and by collections in London churches. In 1932, the school moved to a modern building in Queen's Road, but the borough bought Tudor Hall and completely restored it.

Environs: East Barnet (Hertfordshire EN4): Originally the centre of the landed property of *St.Albans* abbey in this area, in the 13C it lost in importance to the market in Barnet. Its exclusively rural character was maintained until the mid 19C. In the 16C, and especially in the 17C, some large country houses were built along the little river *Pymmes*, of which the street names are the only reminder today. The area developed rapidly after the New Barnet railway station started operating and an abrupt structural transformation resulted. The population of East Barnet increased tenfold between 1840 and 1880. The church of *St.Mary the Virgin* (Church Hill Road) was enlarged to meet the new requirements in the 19C, as was the village itself. But this church is still worth seeing for some parts of it which are very old. Part of the Norman N. wall of the nave survives from the 11C. The apse is 15C. The gallery was added in the mid 17C. The major 19C alterations are the addition of the S. aisle and the second tower and the installation of the organ in the choir.

Friern Barnet (Middlesex, N11): Known as *South Barnet* in the 12C, and thereafter as *Little* Barnet. Today's name *'Friern'* came into use when the Bishop of London let the Order of St.John of Jerusalem have the area in the 13C. Their title as members of a lay order was 'frere' in Franco-Norman colloquial tongue. The town was at that time on the N. exit route (today known as *Friern Barnet Lane*) which also made Barnet what it is. From the late 14C onwards, the manor also included *Whetstone* (q.v.) in the NW and *Colney Hatch*, now called *New Southgate*, in the SE. After the Dissolution of the monasteries, the *Manor House* fell in ruin and was replaced by *Friary House* in 1551. Elizabeth I presented Sir Walter Raleigh with the house, and it then remained in the possession of the Bacon family until the 19C. At that time, the village only consisted of the church of *St.James*, the manor and two farms. As with the other towns in this area, urbanization did not begin until the mid 19C. All that survives from earlier times, apart from some street-names, are the *poorhouses* along *Friern Barnet Lane*. These were donated by Lawrence Campe in 1612. The history of the parish church of *St. James* (Friern Barnet Lane/Friary Road) dates back to the 12C; however, the structure was so thoroughly rebuilt and enlarged in 1853 that none of the original design survives except the Norman frame of the S. entrance. *Friern Hospital* (between Colney Hatch Lane, Friern Barnet Road and Station Road) was built as *Colney Hatch Asylum* in 1849, and was at the time Europe's largest and most expensive institution for the mentally ill. The building, whose foundation stone was laid by Prince Albert, was built with the purpose of making possible the complete self-sufficiency of 1,250 patients, who were employed in agriculture, as well as in various trades and service industries. The number of patients rose to 2,000 in the late 19C. After World War 1, the district, and later also the mental institution, were re-named, because the old designations were regarded as discriminatory towards the surrounding residential area.

Whetsone (Middlesex, N20): From the 15C on, this hamlet stretching along the *Great Northern Road* profited from the need for coach-houses and inns along this route. In the late 19C, it then also became interesting as a residential area, and housing estates such as *Oakleigh Park* to the E. of the main road enjoyed a very good reputation.

HENDON (Middlesex, NW4): In the 14C, the landed property of Hendon was owned by Westminster Abbey, and fell to the Crown in the Dissolution of the Monasteries. Lent to William Herbert, Earl of Pembroke, in the 1550s, it remained in the family's possession for 200 years. Industrial settlements developed rapidly along the *Edgware Road* between the two World Wars, and this of course also influenced the increasing density of the surrounding residential areas.

St.Mary (Church End, NW4): This parish church, originally mainly 13–15C, was given a new aisle in *c.* 1914.

Friern Barnet (Barnet), Peace Memorial

Church Farm House (Church End): Today this 17C house accommodates a regional museum. Fine fireplaces.

Hendon Hall Hotel (Ashley Lane, NW4): David Garrick, the great Shakespearean actor, bought himself this lordly house in 1756. It was built in the 17C on the site of the old manor. Although it did not attain its present form until the mid-19C, it continues to be worth seeing as an example of an early and successful combination which has been adapted to contemporary requirements but which has preserved the original structural components.

Newspaper Library (Colindale Avenue, NW9): Built around the turn of the century as a store for the *British Museum's* newspaper collection. Enlarged in the 1930s, it is now part of the *British Library* with reading rooms for the users of the collection. Newspapers published in the United Kingdom since 1840 are extant almost in their entirety, but the works preserved date back to the 17C and also include many foreign publications.

Hendon (Barnet), St.Mary

Royal Air Force Museum (Grahame Park Way, NW9): Founded in 1963 and opened by H.M. The Queen in 1972, the museum has an extensive assortment of exhibits on the history of aviation, with the focus on *British Military Aviation.* The hangars of the former *Hendon Aerodromes* are an integral part of the complex. The *Battle of Britain Museum,* a separate exhibition building on the same grounds, was opened by the Queen Mother in 1978. Here there is a unique collection of aeroplanes used by the British, Germans and Italians in the air battles over England in 1940.

Watling Estate (HA8): An attempt (1926) by the architect C.Topham Forrest to adapt the concept of a middle-class garden town to the financial restrictions applicable to the construction of workers' housing estates.

Environs: Edgware (Middlesex HA8): Inhabited in the pre-Roman period, it was later used by the Romans as a stopping post along *Watling Street* (today *High Street*). During the Middle Ages, it changed hands again and again between ecclesiastical and secular owners. Before it was joined to the underground railway system in 1924, the area developed in relatively organic fashion, and this is probably one reason why houses in rustic style survive along the High Street. On its W. side there are 15C–17C houses, and the poorhouses built by Samuel Atkinson (1680) and Charles Day (1828) are in the transitional zone leading to *Stonegrove* in the N. The parish church of *St.Margaret* (High Street/Station Road) was converted and enlarged in several sections, but its tower is 14C. *St.Lawrence* (Whitchurch Lane) was built in the 16C, but has unusual decorations, for contemporary artists such as Louis Laguerre painted it in Italian baroque throughout in the 18C. This church represents one of the few attempts to introduce the style to England. The church goes back to James Brydges,

Duke of Chandos, who appointed Georg Friedrich Händel as a music teacher in his house in 1718. Apart from the church and the family vault, only the remains of *Canons Park* still remind the visitor of the Chandos family's splendid manorial seat.

Finchley (Middlesex, N2, N3, N12): From earliest times this area was part of the church's possession called *Fulham*, the park of the Bishop of London stretching here from Hornsey. The first housing estates, *Church End* (N3) and *East Finchley* (N2), were both built along the borders of the park. East Finchley, formerly called *East End*, attained some importance because of its position on the *Great North Road*, but the entire area, and especially Church End, remained a rural idyll until the late 19C, from which time the population increased spasmodically until today the Finchleys present themselves as a uniform urban settlement extending as far as Whetstone and South Barnet in the N. The parish church of *St.Mary* (Hendon Lane, N3) is 15C, but a surviving Norman font and documentary evidence suggest that a church had been built here in the 12C. An interesting collection of tomb-stones is to be found on the church walls. The best is that to *Thomas Sanny* (d. 1509), which has an extract from his will upon it. Some of the old buildings survive along *East End Road*, the road linking it to East Finchley.

Golders Green (Middlesex, NW11): This wooded area to the SE of Hendon was made arable in the mid 18C and divided into several large farms. The final station on the Northern Line of the underground railway system was opened here in the open country in 1905, and speculators then invested successfully in building residential houses around this centre of communications. These investments were worthwhile, as the fact that the *Hippodrome*, a concert hall with 2,300 seats, which was opened here in 1913, suggests. (Today used by the BBC as a studio).

Hampstead Garden Suburb (Middlesex, NW11): After *Letchworth Garden City*, this is the second experiment with the garden city idea conceived by the architects Raymond Unwin and Barry Parker. The present experiment derives from the endeavours of Dame Henrietta

Hendon (Barnet), Church Farm House

Barnett, whose particular philanthropic concern was to bring different strata of the population into contact with one another. She hoped to be able to achieve this best by starting at the very beginning and paid particular attention to the architecture of the new residential area. The experiment clearly failed where its social intention was concerned, because today Hampstead Garden Suburb is a solidly middle-class residential area. However, the harmonious town planning around *Central Square* is not merely a good example of Sir Edwin Lutyens' architecture, but also a continuing memorial to the lady philanthropist's social involvement. *St.Jude-on-the-Hill*, the *Free Church* opposite, and the *Institute* of adult education, form the centre of the suburb. These buildings, along with the variously designed surrounding houses, were designed by Lutyens between 1908 and 1910.

Mill Hill (Middlesex, NW7): In the 17&18C, this village was a popular rural haven frequented by important Londoners, including Lord Mayors. It has remained largely spared of the demolitions resulting from the spasmodic urbanization of the last hundred years. In the 19C, before Catholics and non-conformists became socially emancipated, they set up seminaries for priests and also ordinary schools here. *Mill Hill School* was founded by a private group in 1807, to enable the sons of Protestant non-conformists to have an education on a par with that available in the Public Schools, which were closed to them. Today this boarding school is attended by some 550 pupils. The school buildings can almost all be found along *The Ridgeway* and the side roads leading off it.

Berkhamsted

Herefordshire p.190□B 1/2   HP4

This town grew up along the old Roman road (today *Akeman Street*). The Norman *castle* was one of the town's landmarks until the 16C, but today the earthworks on the N. edge of the town are the only discernible surviving remnants of the castle. Buildings on the N. side of the *High*

Aldbury (Berkhamsted), St.John-the-Baptist

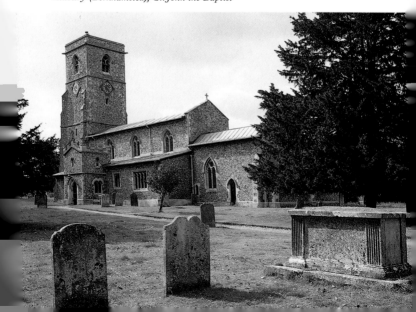

Street give a historical backdrop of the town's development. The urban character is emphasized by the visually unified front created by the church with the houses, which are 16C and later.

St.Peter (High Street): Norman church with a transept. Additional building in the architectural styles of the following centuries can be seen in the structure. The architect William Butterfield completely restored it in 1871. Some of the leaded windows are 14C.

Environs: Aldbury (3 miles NW): The 13/14C church of *St.John-the-Baptist* was altered inside in the 15C, when the *Pendley Chapel,* which includes a monument with recumbent sculptures on the sarcophagus, was added. One rarity is the priests' dormitory above the entrance gate. **Ashridge** (2.5 miles N.): The country house was built in Gothic style in 1808 by James Wyatt for the seventh Earl of Bridgewater. In the 20C it was used as a college and most recently as a training centre for managers. The *chapel* has a tower which rises above an open arcade. The original 13C *monastery* was altered after the Dissolution of the Monasteries under Henry VIII, when it became a residence for his children. The monastery crypt, and a 16C barn, still survive. The park designed by Humphry Repton, and the landed property, are today administered by the National Trust and are open to the public.

Tring (4.5 miles W.): It was in this little town that Lord Rothschild built a *zoological museum* for his private collection. The museum was opened to the public in 1892. Exhibits include prepared mammals and birds, and also interesting examples of reptiles and fishes. The building and its collection were handed over to the British Museum at first, although since 1938 they have been a permanent external department of the *National History Museum.*

Bexley (Borough of Greater London)

Kent p.190☐E 3   (DA5, DA6, DA7, DA8, DA14, DA15, DA16, DA17, DA18)

This borough has existed since 1965 and

Aldbury (Berkhamsted), Pendley Chapel, monument

Ashridge (Berkhamsted), country seat

consists of the former districts of *Bexley, Erith, Crayford* and *Sidcup.*

BEXLEY (DA5) and **BEXLEYHEATH** (DA6, DA7): Until the 20C, *Bexley Village* was a flourishing agricultural area, and rich Londoners built their country houses here. Today the parks of some of these houses break the monotony of an essentially urban landscape. Bexley Village was owned by the Archbishop of Canterbury from 814 until the time of Henry VIII. Bexleyheath, which grew up in the early 19C as a workers' suburb in the untouched heath near *Crayford*, is today the region's residential and administrative centre.

St.Mary (Bexley Village): The 13C church was much altered in the late 19C, but the unconventional tower with its pyramidal base and octagonal super-structure still retains its original form. *High Street House*, very close to St.Mary, was built in 1761 and still gives a vivid impression of the town's period of middle-class prosperity in the 18C.

Danson Park (Bexleyheath, DA6, DA16): John Boyd, an ambitious London councillor, purchased this landed property in 1751. It was first mentioned by the name of *'Dansington'* in 1284 in a document belonging to the Archbishop of Canterbury and listing the possessions in the area of his manor in Bexley. Boyd ordered Sir Robert Taylor to build him a Palladian-style villa here. The landscaped park, with a lake now used for sailing, was designed by 'Capability Brown' in 1761; it has been open to the public since 1924.

Hall Place (Bourne Road, DA5): Built

Hall Place (Bexley)

for Sir John Champneys in 1537 in the style of a lordly medieval house. A brick annexe, which took no account of the original stone construction, was added in 1649 after the house had been purchased by Robert Austin, a rich London citizen. However, both parts of Hall Place bear faithful witness, each in their own way, to the architecture of their time. The building's architectural charm is accentuated by the small surrounding park. The barn to the SE of the house is contemporary with the house. Usually open to the public.

Red House (Red House Lane, DA6): In 1859, William Morris commissioned Philip Webb to build this house. Morris was influenced by the architectural harmony of the medieval cathedrals along the Seine, which he had visited on a journey with his friend Dante Gabriel Rossetti. The owner's idea was that it should be a medieval house, however, Webb built a house which, despite employing clear and plain Gothic stylistic elements, is by no means an imitation of the Gothic style. Despite the building's asymmetrical, towering lines, the result is essentially a harmonious piece of architecture. Today Red House is still inhabited.

Environs: Crayford (DA1): The history of settlement in this area dates back to the Iron Age. It is said to have been here in AD 457, where the Roman road from London to Dover crossed the River Cray, that the Jutes gained their military victory against the Britons which was so decisive in their conquest of the country. Since the late 16C, Crayford has been an industrial town whose architecture and economy are today characterized by the Vickers factories. Vickers, which originally specialized in weapon manufacture, today creates a wide range of industrial products. In the early 20C, *Barns Cray* in the E., and *Slade Green* in the N., were designed on the drawing board as workers' suburbs. The only notable building to date from earlier than 1930 is the church of *St.Paulinus,* which is Norman in origin. It was probably in the early 15C that it was enlarged in an unconventional, if not unique, manner, when the nave was simply doubled in size. The arched buttresses remained in the middle, and these now form an open arcade which divides the nave and reaches as far as the apse. The N. half of the nave mostly consists of the Norman section of the church, apart from the roof (c. 1630). The enlargements, and also the W. tower and the new choir for the double nave, are all in the Perpendicular style, although some components from the original Norman S. wall survive here. The *monument to Elizabeth Shovel* is at the same time a testimony to her husband's extraordinary career in the late 17C. She was the widow of Sir Cloudsley Shovel, who moved up the Royal Navy from the rank of cabin boy to that of admiral.

Erith (DA8): This area on the bank of the Thames was also a prehistoric settlement. The place name, which means 'muddy harbour', was first mentioned in a Anglo Saxon document dating from 695. After the Norman invasion, the manor was part of the English possessions of Bishop Odos of Bayeux. It was here, in the reign of Henry II, that Richard de Luci founded *Lesnes Abbey* in reparation for the share he had in the murder of Thomas Becket. Thomas Wolsey secularized the abbey in 1525. Henry VIII ordered the building of a wharf and his warships were equipped here and at the docks in Woolwich. After 1849, the year in which the *North Kent Railway* was opened, the town rapidly developed into an industrial centre, which was soon followed by the residential areas of *Belvedere* (DA17), *Northumberland*

Heath (DA8) and, most recently, *Thamesmead* (DA18). The Vickers company was established here in the late 19C and because of its connections with the armaments industry, the area suffered severe damage in bombing raids in World War 2. The ruins of *Lesnes Abbey* in Lesnes Abbey Wood are today a part of the charming public park (DA17, SE2). The parish church of *St.John-the-Baptist* lost much of its former character and magic when it was restored and enlarged in c. 1877. The Norman origins of this religious building are still discernible in the choir, although much of the building was early Gothic (before c. 1300). The church also has a rich collection of 15C tombstones and some good individual monuments. *Christ Church* (Victoria Road), built in brick by J.P. St.Aubyn (1874), is a good example of Victorian Gothic (Early English style). The nave and choir were decorated throughout with wall paintings in the early 20C. An 'Adoration of the Magi', in 15C Italian Renaissance style, was painted by A.O. Hemming on the altar superstructure in 1904. The stained-glass windows on the E. side are 13C in style, and complete the impression of a medieval church interior. The *Ои Works* (Church Manorway) in the marsh land on the shore of the Thames are a pioneering work by the Danish firm Christiani & Nielsen. 1913–17 this company, working to plans by S.Rowland Pierce, built 24 silos of reinforced concrete, a new building material at that time. Even today, these silos are more conspicuous than the other factory buildings and some elements of their style anticipates work by Le Corbusier. Building on the modern *Thamesmead* housing estate has been in progress since 1967. From the very outset, the rather unfavourable soil conditions were made an advantage and the design included the digging of canals and lakes to dry the marshland, which in turn made for a more interesting site for the housing development. This architectural experiment,

Hall Place (Bexley)

consisting of a heterogenously designed but nevertheless united row of houses more than half a mile long, forms the backbone of the estate which, after its most recent phase of expansion, is intended to be a suburb for 60,000 inhabitants.

Sidcup (DA14): Originally a hamlet in the *Foots Cray* community, it became a suburb in the 18C. However, the real impetus to the area's development did not come until the railway was electrified (1926). Today the area is heavily built up and almost all the signs of earlier habitation, including the modest detached houses from the 1920's and 1930's, has been masked. Some fine houses still survive: *Frognal House* (Frognal Avenue), today part of Queen Mary's Hospital; *Lamorbey Park* (Burnt Oak Lane; DA15); *Manor House* (The Green); and, to the S. of it, *Sidcup Place.* The latter two houses are today used as offices by the council. All these four build-

ings date from the 18C, but were subsequently altered in varying degrees. The least-altered building is Manor House. To the NW (DA15), it is only the names of the modern districts of *Halfway Street, Blendon* and *Blackfen* that still preserve the memory of 13C manor houses which were formerly at the centre of the villages. *Foots Cray* and *North Cray* were absorbed by Sidcup in the E., and the former rustic charm of these communities is still largely discernible in North Cray. Their former significnce may still be guessed from their parish churches. *All Saints* in Foots Cray was built in wood in *c.* 900, and replaced by a stone structure in the 1st half of the 14C. Elements of this latter building were included in Henry Hakewill's enlargement of the church (*c.* 1862). *St. James* in North Cray was rebuilt in its present form by Edwin Nash in 1851. The origins of this church date back to Saxon times and the little town was evidently a flourishing agricultural community from that period onwards. In the 17C, wealthy London citizens built their country houses here (as they did in Bexley), and some of the parks of those houses still survive.

Brent (Borough of Greater London)

Middlesex p.190☐C 3   (NW2, NW6, NW9, NW10, HA0, HA9)

Since 1965 this borough has included the former districts of *Wembley* and *Willesden*.

WEMBLEY (HA0, HSA9): A settlement by the name of *Wemba Lea* existed here in the 9C. The former settlements developed around *The Green* (HA1) and *Wembley Hill* (HA9). Only after the station on the London-Birmingham railway line was opened in 1837 did the modern town centre (*Wembley Central,* HA0) develop around the station. In 1889, *Wembley Park* was bought by the Metropolitan Line company so that a leisure centre for NW London could be set up along the underground railway line. The park had its origin in a private park designed by Humphry Repton in 1793. The *British Empire Exhibition* was held here in 1924/5 and the occasion was used to provide the surrounding area with the transport facilities to accommodate the expected stream of visitors. It was only then that Wembley began to develop into a residential suburb.

Brent Town Hall (Forty Lane, HA9): Built in the late 1930s as a town hall and administrative centre for the district of Wembley, this building is now used as a council office for the whole borough. It is a lucidly designed functional building in which the public library, the large assembly hall, and the offices are merged into a clearly arranged whole. The design,

Wembley (Brent), Wembley Stadium

by Clifford Strange, was the winning entry in a competition organized in 1934.

Wembley Stadium (HA9): Built for the *British Empire Exhibition* in 1922 and 1923, this complex was opened in 1923 when the F.A. Cup Final between Bolton and West Ham was held here. Most of the exhibition buildings were designed by Sir John Simpson and Maxwell Ayrton and constructed of reinforced concrete. The open air stadium was designed to hold 120,000 spectators. *Wembley Arena,* built by Sir Owen Williams, was added to the original complex in 1933/4. This arena is now used for sporting events and entertainment. The facilities were fully stretched when the Olympics were held here in 1948. Today the stadium is used for international football and hockey matches, greyhound racing and speedway events.

Environs: Kingsbury (NW9): In the 14C, after the Great Plague, the centre moved from the medieval core around *Old Church Lane* N. to around *Kingsbury Road*, where the unimpressive *Holy Innocents* church stands. The best buildings are the two parish churches between Old Church Lane and Church Lane. *Old St.Andrew's* was recently secularized, and is used by the Wembley History Society as a museum and studio. The church was probably not built until the Norman period, but has discernible Saxon stylistic elements which made many think the building may be earlier. However, the re-use of some building materials suggests that settlement in Kingsbury dates as far back as the Roman period. One of its three rare bells was cast by Peter de Weston in c. 1340. The new *St.Andrew's church*, which is today within the same graveyard, was originally built in Wells Street (E. of Oxford Circus, W1) in 1847. It is the earliest example of a liberal and deliberately Victorian neo-Gothic style. Its interior decorations reflect the religious understanding of the Anglo-Catholic movement in the 2nd half of the 19C. The church was pulled down in 1933 and rebuilt in Kingsbury, a suburb which it now dominates. *Blackbird Farm*, which is probably 17C like the barn attached to it, survives to the SW of these two churches. **Sudbury** and **Alperton** (HA0): It was here that Charles Holden built the Piccadilly Line stations *Alperton, Sudbury Town* and *Sudbury Hill* in 1932/3. These buildings prove that careful modification of details can transform standardized structural elements into functional buildings showing an individual style. **Willesden** (NW10): Willesden is today directly interwoven with the central region of London. Along with the surrounding hamlets of *Neasden* and *Harlesden,* it was a rural idyll to the SE of Wembley up until the 19C. From 938 onwards it was a possession of the Dean and Chapter of St.Paul's Cathedral. During the 19C, wealthy Londoners built themselves impressive houses in the area of *Craven Park Road* and *Nicoll Road.* These houses have largely survived but exude little character of their own. Almost all the historical architectural buildings were pulled down when the area was later built up with houses for those on lower incomes. The parish church of *St.Mary,* together with its sacristy and Church Cottage, forms the only surviving medieval ensemble. This mainly 13&14C building consists of a choir, nave and S. aisle, with a tower to the SW of the nave. The homely character of a village church survives in the modest interior architecture. *All Souls,* an octagonal structure in Harlesden High Street, has a good wooden roof but the original architectural concept by E.J. Tarver (1879) was much impaired by the later addition of a nave. *St.Andrew* (Willesden Green High Road) was designed in the late 1880's and differs from the old parish church mainly in its ambitious dimensions, which are accentuated by their imitation of the Early English style. Some of the secular buildings are worth seeing: *Dollis Hill House* (Dollis Hill Lane, NW2) is an unadorned but impressive building by Joseph Finch (1923) which is today used for receptions. Its hilly location in the NE of Neasden and Willesden gives a panoramic view of Harrow and Ealing. A part of the park was opened to the public and given the name *Gladstone Park.* William Gladstone the politician, and also Mark Twain, were often the guests of the owner, Lord Aberdeen. *The Grange* (Neasden, NW10) results from the conversion of a group of old stable buildings into an L-shaped house in 1810. This building in the Gothic style has a good hip roof with two ridge lines, similar to an upside down 'W'. Today the building houses a *museum*

of the borough's regional history. Oxgate Farmhouse (Coles Green Road, NW2), the oldest residential building in the Willesden area, is still a private house, and is also all that remains of the *Manor of Oxgate,* first mentioned in 1246. The N. wing of the house is 16C; the S. wing was added in the 17C. The original timber framing was covered by external plastering, but elements of the original design have been preserved inside.

Brentwood
Essex p.190☐F 2   CM14

Industrial development in the SW of Essex has obliterated almost all traces of the historic significance of *Brentwood.* The town's present suburban character arose mainly in the 2nd third of the 19C. In previous centuries, Brentwood's economy was associated with its location on the road from London to Colchester and inn and coach houses did well in the town.

Cathedral (Ingrave Road): This Roman Catholic cathedral (1861) surprises the onlooker with its slender, polygonal, high-rising tower. The Munich artist Mayer was commissioned to carry out the stained-glass work on the E. window.

St.Thomas: All that survive of the 14C *St.Thomas's Chapel* in the High Street are ivy-covered remnants of the walls of nave and tower. The new St.Thomas town church was built by E.C. Lee in 1882–90. In its new dimensions, it reflects the town's size in modern times. The interior design is Early English in style; the exterior is more interesting.

Brentwood   School   (Shenfield Road/Ingrave Road): This group of buildings reflects the styles employed in the various phases of construction. The outer wall and a gate still survive from the original Tudor brick building (1568) in

Ingrave Road; the dormitory above dates from 1856. The main building dates from 1910, but is outshone in its appearance by the Georgian houses on the school premises: *School House, Barnards House* and *Roden House*, which are all 18C. *Mitre House* (c. 1600) was for a while also part of the school. Some good Georgian town houses are still to be found in *Shenfield Road*, opposite the school.

White Hart Hotel (High Street): This hotel still has its old coach yard. The overhanging first storey, with timbering, was formerly part of a long gallery probably dating back to the late 15C.

Environs: Great Warley (6 km. S.): The ruined tower of *Christ Church* is not, as one might suppose, a medieval relic, but the tower of an early Art Nouveau church from 1855. The same style, more successfully realised, is seen in the new parish church of *St.Mary-the-Virgin*, in which the architect Charles Harrison Townsend collaborated successfully with William Reynolds-Stevens, the latter being mainly responsible for the interior decorations. Some old houses, notably the 15C and late-16C *Wallets*, survive on the green to the N. of the church.

Laindon and **Basildon** (16 km. SE): The town of Basildon was built to a drawing board design in the post war years, with the aim of relieving the pressure on London. When finally developed it was intended to have some 100,000 inhabitants. Today it comprises the old villages of *Basildon* and *Laindon*. *St.Nicholas* in Laindon is the best of the old village churches integrated into the modern housing estates. Nave and choir are 14C, the roof and S. entrance hall 15C. The conspicuous bell tower is a free standing wooden structure inside the church walls. The *Priest's House* is a two-storeyed 17C annexe on the W. side. *Holy Cross,* the small parish church of Basildon Village, is also 14C. *St.Mary-the-Virgin and All Saints* in *Langdon Hills* (S. of

Laindon) is a small early-16C brick church, which was partly redecorated in the 2nd half of the 17C.

Thorndon Hall (4 km. SE): This country seat built from 1764 onwards by James Paine for Lord Petre stands in a park designed by 'Capability' Brown (1766–72). The house, a large rectangular block connected by colonnades to side pavilions, is in the Italian style, with classical façade decorations. The portico facing the garden is particularly good. The house burned down in the 19C, and the only room which has survived in its original form is the *chapel* in the E. wing. The domestic buildings on the hill are also by Paine. The *mausoleum* and *Chantry Chapel* for the Petres were built in the park by A.W.N. Pugin. Remains of the old 15&16C hall were uncovered in the 1960s.

**Bromley
(Borough of Greater London)**

Kent p.190☐D/E 3   (BR1, BR2, BR3, BR4,
                       BR5, BR6, BR7, TN16)

BROMLEY and **BROMLEY COMMON** (BR1, BR2): The manor and common were in the possession of the Bishops of Rochester from Saxon times onwards. The landed property was first mentioned in a document in 862, and remained within the Bishops' domain until 1845. The first documentary confirmation that *Bromley* was a market dates from 1205 and Bromley's central function in the region was thereby secured. *Bromley Common* was largely a fallow heath where, until the late 18C, coaches en route from London to Tunbridge Wells had to reckon with the possibility of encountering highwaymen. In the 1st half of the 19C, the common began to develop into a residential area for the rapidly growing town of Bromley.

Holy Trinity (Bromley Common, BR2): Built by Thomas Hopper in 1839, with a tower also dating from 1839, the church was intended to be the centre of the new residential area. However, the building displays no great expressive power. It is chiefly of interest because of C.Pemberton's endeavours (1884) to improve its architectural decoration by the use of Gothic motifs.

St.Luke (Bromley Common/Southlands Road, BR2): A church (1886–90) by Arthur Cawston, in Early English Style, built in brick partly faced with stone and yellow brick. The exterior has a conventional appearance, and the visitor may be pleasantly surprised by the spacious interior, which is uninterrupted throughout its length and constitutes a contemporary religious structure of interesting design.

St.Peter and St.Paul (Church Road, BR2): The only part of the 13C church to survive the bombing of World War 2 was the tower, and J.Harold Gibbons adapted his modern design (1948–57) to the tower's style and dimensions.

Bromley College (London Road, BR1): A poorhouse dating back to an institution founded by Bishop John Warner for 'twenty poor widows of loyal, orthodox clergymen'. The original late-17C block of houses, grouped around a courtyard with a colonnaded passage, was enlarged in the first few years of the 18C by the addition of a second block on the same design. Further houses were added in 1840 as dwellings for the widows' daughters, who were able to live here only while their mothers too were alive. Bromley College is the oldest surviving building of this kind in England, and it is still used exclusively for the purpose specified by the foundation.

Bromley Palace (Rochester Avenue, BR1): The *manor* of the Bishops of Rochester stood here in the Norman period. The building soon developed into a palace and became one of the Bishops' most important residences. The old palace was pulled down and replaced by the present building in 1775; only the red brick section of the building still remains of the palace. The annexes date partly from the Victorian period after the Bishops had relinquished the palace in 1845, and partly from the 1930's, when the building housed a teachers' training college. Today it is borough council offices.

Sundridge Park (BR1): Originally also in the possession of the Bishops of Rochester, *Sundridge Manor* has been in secular hands since *c.* 1301, the year when John le Blunt (or Blound), a London clothier, was named as its owner. Claude Scott, a banker and member of parliament, took over as owner in 1801 and he had the present mansion built and the park landscaped. John Nash, Humphry Repton and Samuel Wyatt were jointly responsible for the design of house and park. Repton later described the manner in which the proportions of house and landscape were allowed to interact, for example, the gradient of the slope was altered so as to give the house, designed by Nash in 1799, an appropriate site with the corresponding panoramic view. Nash and Repton seem to have been primarily responsible for the harmonization of 'nature' and architecture, while the decorations are evidently largely Wyatt's work. Unfortunately, not all of the park survives, because parts of it were given up in the 19C for building land for Bromley; in 1901 another section was converted into a golf course, although this has not had too dire an effect on the design of the former park. After Scott's family gave up the house, it was for a time run as a hotel. Today it is a managerial training college.

Environs: Beckenham (BR3): The Saxon and Norman *manor* also contained the *Shortlands* district in the E., and bordered on *West Wickham*, a landed property in the S.. Beckenham remained a small village until the 19C, but little of this traditional character remained preserved in the subsequent rapid urban development. Two interesting inns which have survived in the High Street are the *Three Tuns*, and the *George Inn*, which was important in the 17C as a coach house. *St. George's* parish church at the N. end of the High Street originated in the 12C, but today's church was not built until the turn of the present century. A fine collection of monuments were taken from the old 14C church and integrated into the modern building. *Coper's Cope House* (Southend Road) is the only surviving 18C town house. The urbanization of Beckenham began in *Southend Road* in the 19C, with large town houses in Italian style being the first to be built. The houses at the W. and S. edges of *Beckenham Place Park* are also mid-19C. *Beckenham Place* itself, built by John Cator in 1773, is one of the few surviving lordly mansions. Apart from the latter, all that has survived to remind us of such mansions takes the form of isolated buildings and small parks such as *Kelsey* and *Langley Park*, and *Eden Park*. The best impression of the development and style of domestic architecture over the last two centuries can probably be seen in *Wickham Road*. In the S., *West Wickham* (BR4) stands at the beginning of a predominantly modern residential area. *Wickham Court*, with the old church of *St. John the Baptist*, is to be found about a mile SE of the modern High Street, and stands on a slope above the 20C houses. The church and house were enlarged for Sir Henry Haydon in *c.* 1500, and met with much approval from his contemporaries. Sir Henry had acquired the property in 1469, and subsequently arranged for it to be restored and enlarged. Rather restrained in its proportions, its appearance nevertheless, resembles a fortified castle; elements of early Tudor style can also be discerned. However, the fact that there are neither castle moat nor gatehouse makes it clear that it was never intended to serve as a fortified building.

Chislehurst (BR7): It is here that the character of an old town has best been preserved within the borough. The spacious impression which the place creates is mostly due to the *common* in the middle of town. The town has a rich diversity of old houses, most of which are 19C. *St. Nicholas* (between Church Row and Church Lane) has largely preserved its 15C architectural style, despite being rebuilt and enlarged in the 19C. The church is also worth seeing for its splendid monuments. The best of the surviving lordly houses is *Camden Place* inside Camden Park, where Napoleon III spent his period of exile at the invitation of Nathaniel Strode, the owner at the time, who is also reponsible for the interior decorations in French style. The name of the house is a tribute to *William Camden*, the historian. The oldest parts of Camden Place are early 18C, but the original simple articulation is today overshadowed by 19C ornaments and annexes. The building is now used by the Chislehurst Golf Club as a clubhouse. The streets around *Camden Park* have a number of interesting houses designed around the turn of the century by Ernest Newton for William Willett junior, who wanted to house the upper middle classes (1890). The best-preserved 18C house is probably *Chesil House* (St. Paul's Cray Road); not particularly large, it displays fashionably Venetian features in the façade. The two old villages of St. Mary Cray and St. Paul's Cray stand invitingly at the E. edge of town. *St. Mary Cray*, with its 13C church, sits almost hidden under the large railway bridge, but somehow it is not entirely devoid of its former delightful character. In *St. Paul's Cray*, a modern suburb comes into direct contact with the quiet of the countryside: in the W. there is a large housing estate from the 1950s, while to the E., there is much open countryside. When *St. Barnabas* was being built in the 1960s, it was discovered that the area was already inhabited in the Bronze Age. The old parish church of *St. Paulinus*, built in a loop of the river, combines Saxon and Gothic elements; most of it was completed in c. 1200, but restoration work of c. 1860 has spoilt much of its original character.

Downe (BR6): This is still a country town. Its documentary record dates back to c. 1100. The centre of Downe is a village in character. *Orange Court* in the N., and *Downe Court* in the S. (1690), two medium-sized landed properties, stand at the edge of the village. *Down House* in Luxted Road is the house in which Charles Darwin pursued his studies. *Biggin Hill* (TN16) in the SW is dominated by the airfield at its N. edge. Today, low-density settlements are indiscriminately spread across it. To the W. is the charming *Norheads Farm,* made more attractive by the farmhouse dating from 1715.

Hayes (BR2): This village, which probably dates back to Roman times, evidently became a parish of its own in the 12C. The village's Norman origins are still discernible in the church of *St.Mary-the-Virgin,* although Sir J.J. Scott (c. 1860), and later J.Oldrid Scott, did convert and enlarge the church. People of renown, including Elizabeth Montagu and her literary circle known as 'The Blue Stockings', began to settle in Hayes in the mid-18C. *Hayes Grove* (Prestons Road) from the 1730s, and *Oast House* designed by Philip Webb (1873/4), have both survived from the period before Hayes finally developed into a suburban housing estate. Here Webb continued to develop his ideas which, in the case of Red House (Bexleyheath; see *Bexley*), built for William Morris, largely consisted merely in imitating medieval models. The history of human settlement in *Keston* in the SE can be traced back to the 3rd millennium BC. The oldest large landed property in the area is *Holwood House*, first mentioned in 1484 as a possession of the manor of West Wickham. The present house was built by Decimus Burton in 1827. Remains of an old early-18C windmill can still be seen in the *common*. Traces of

prehistoric *hillforts* remain on the common and in *Holwood Park*.

Orpington (BR6): This area has been in continuous use as a human settlement ever since the Stone Age. Since at least Norman times, the church has been of central importance to the entire area to the E. and S. of the modern borough, probably because the benefice was held alternately by Christ Church Canterbury and the Archbishop of Canterbury until the Dissolution of the Monasteries in the 16C. *All Saints* was greatly enlarged by Geddes Hyslop in 1957/8, so that the medieval church, whose Saxon elements are the result of restoration work in c. 1200, is now merely the portico of the new town church. *The Priory,* begun in c. 1393, has preserved its medieval character, although renovation work performed in subsequent centuries did not pay very much attention to the manner in which the building was originally divided up.

Camden
(Borough of Greater London)

London County p.190☐D 3   (NW1,
                                    NW3, NW5, NW6)

Since 1965, this borough has comprised the former councils of *Hampstead, Holborn* and *St.Pancras.* The S. section (Holborn) is dealt with under inner city London.

CAMDEN TOWN (NW1): The area belonged to *Cantelowes Manor,* and was in the possession of St.Paul's Chapter from at least as early as the 11C. The possession later fell into secular hands. In 1749, it came through marriage, into the possession of Sir Charles Pratt, who acquired the title of Earl of Camden for his family. At this time it was still cattle pasture, but in the late 18C the Earl of Camden drew up leases permitting 1,400 houses to be built. The development of

Hampstead (Camden), Kenwood House

Hampstead (Camden), Kenwood House

Camden Town as a residential area began rather hesitantly, but from the 1820s onwards it was given a strong economic impetus by being connected first to Regent's Canal and then to the railway. However, it subsequently became mainly a business district rather than a residential district although the present trend shows Camden Town once again serving increasingly as a residential area.

All Saints (Camden Street, NW1): Today this is a Greek Orthodox church intended mainly for the Greek Cypriot immigrants resident here. The interior decoration with an iconostasis was installed after the church had been consecrated anew for this purpose. The church was built by William Inwood and his son Henry William in 1824 in the style of a Greek temple.

Royal College Street School (Royal College Street, NW1): This school (1910–13) by the architect W.E. Riley was at the time thought to be the finest school building in the entire County of London. The stone façade decorations give the building a handsome appearance.

Royal Veterinary College (Royal College Street, NW1): This building (1937) designed by H.P.G. Maule stands on the site where this institution was founded in 1791 along the model of Continental veterinary colleges (especially that in Lyons, France). The training school was integrated into the medical faculty of the *University of London* in 1949.

Working Men's College (Crowndale Road, NW1): The appearance of this college built by W.D. Caroe in 1905 is that of a public building intended to impress

Kenwood House, Dining Room

rather than an institution for the further education of underprivileged sectors of the population. The college is one of a number of adult education establishments set up around the turn of the century by socialist groups who were involved with education.

Circular Factory (Oval Road, NW1): An interesting functional building from the Victorian period, stating clearly that the Victorian style cannot simply be equated with the neo-Gothic. Built for a piano manufacturer in *c.* 1860.

Environs: Kentish Town (NW5): *Kentystone* and *St.Pancras* seem initially to have been two names for one and the same area. What is today the centre of this area was formerly a village in the Fleet valley. This village flourished from about the mid-15C onwards. In the late 18C it became a fashionable urban suburb for the

middle classes, and lost its rural character. The parish church of *St.John-the-Baptist*, a work by James Wyatt, dates from this period. The entrance hall and dome are in Tuscan style, but older components from a previous church seem to have been incorporated with them. When the railways expanded, Kentish Town became a workers' suburb, supplemented by small and medium-sized industrial enterprises. The church of *St.Martin* (Vicars Road) was built by E.R.Lamb at this time and this Victorian building makes a startling impression today. An architectural style imitative of the Tudor period, combines with 19C ideas and makes for a somewhat unhappy interior decoration.

Somers Town (NW1): Until 1784, the area between today's *Euston* and *Kings Cross Stations* was owned by the family of Baron Somers, and was largely devoted to agriculture. In 1784 *Brill Farm* was leased to Jacob Leroux for building, but by the time the building boom had slackened off, only patches of the projected high-class suburb had been constructed. Some buildings then had to be sold off at less than their value and consequently Somers Town became a suburb for workers. These were joined in the following decades by refugees fleeing from the French Revolution and from Spain. By the mid-19C the area was a slum, although matters were improved to some extent by the construction of further railway lines. A slum area was razed to the ground in order to build St.Pancras *Station*. *St.Pancras Station and Hotel* (today an office building), gives an impression of how far technical progress was at that time (1868) also regarded as a blessing. This enormous Gothic structure distinctly suggests a religious building. When the medieval parish church of *St.Pancras* (Pancras Road) was restored in 1848, it was given a Norman style despite its 13C Gothic origin, which unfortunately quite spoilt the building. *St.Aloysius* (Phoenix Street) was built by French immigrants between 1808 and 1816 as a Roman Catholic church. It displays Southern European stylistic elements, and is also of interest because it is one of the few Roman Catholic churches to have been completed in its present form before the Catholics became emancipated.

HAMPSTEAD and **HAMPSTEAD HEATH** (NW3): Tribes settled on the hills here in prehistoric times. Hampstead is mentioned as a manor in a 10C document and King Ethelred presented it to Westminster Abbey. Originally a part of Hendon (Brent), the village became a parish of its own in *c.* 1598. Many of the trees in the area were cut down in the late 17C in order to rebuild London after the Great Fire. Hampstead became popular as a spa in the early 18C (*Well Walk* still reminds the onlooker of this). Daniel Defoe noted in 1725 that Hampstead had changed from a village into a town. Since then it has continued to be a sought-after residential area.

St.John (Church Row, NW3):

Hampstead (Camden), Kenwood House Library (left), portrait in Breakfast Room (right)

Hampstead parish church (1744–7) by John Sanderson stands on the site of the old 14C village church. Alterations to the interior continued until the present century, with side chapels and other decorations being added.

High Street (NW3): The High Street still presents a handsome collection of 18C town houses, although the ground floors have been altered by shop fronts.

Hampstead Heath (NW3): In 1871, these grounds were declared to be public property in perpetuity. In the following decades they were enlarged by the incorporation of adjoining districts such as *Parliament Hill* and *Kenwood Avenue*. During the Great Plague of 1665, court hearings were held in *Judge's Walk* and *King's Bench Avenue.*

Fenton House (Hampstead Grove, NW3): This plain red brick house (1693) is a fine example of the Dutch style so typical of William III's period of rule (1650–1702). Housed here are a collection of instruments and a large collection of

fine porcelain from Europe and China; rooms have splendid English furniture.

Freud Museum (20 Maresfield Gardens, NW3): The house was opened as a memorial to the founder of psychoanalysis in mid-1986 at the request of Anna Freud, daughter of Sigmund Freud. His study survives in its original state. His library numbers some 3,000 volumes, and there are over 1,000 sculptures on display from his collection which comprised some 2,500 items in all. Researchers can have access to part of his correspondence, although most of the letters are in the *Sigmund Freud Archives* in New York.

Keats' House (Keats Grove, NW3): *John Keats* (1795–1821), the romantic poet and writer of some of the English language's best-loved odes, lived in one of the two Regency houses here and *Fanny Brawne,* his great love, lived in the other. (Today they have been knocked into one house.) Keats' 'Ode to a Nightingale' was written in the splendid garden of the house. The young poet left here for Italy where he hoped that his tuberculosis would be

Hampstead (Camden), Keats' House

Hampstead (Camden), Freud Museum, Study

cured, but he died shortly after his arrival. Letters, manuscripts and other Keats memorabilia are on display in the house.

Kenwood House (Hampstead Lane, NW3): The original house was built in *c.* 1616, but a later owner pulled much of it down in the late 17C and rebuilt it with the rooms newly divided. This second building is substantially the house which stands today, although the façade and annexes date mainly from the second half of the 18C. Robert Adam was responsible for parts of it; his masterly work is mainly seen in the design of the library. Today this house contains the *Iveagh Bequest*, a rich collection of mostly English and Dutch paintings belonging to Edward Cecil Guinness, first Earl of Iveagh.

Environs: Highgate (N6, N19): This region is now divided administratively between the boroughs of Camden, Haringey and Islington, but much of its historical core is in Camden. Here, at the entrance to the former park of the Bishop of London, there was probably a small village in very early times. The hamlet achieved its first expansion no later than the 13C, and by the 14C it was probably concentrated around a toll-gate which the Bishop of London had set up on a hilltop on the *Great North Road* which ran through his possession. The burden of traffic was reduced in the early 19C by the construction of *Archway Road*, and Highgate was able to retain its elegant village structure in the expanded central area. The village character is accentuated by a rich diversity of old houses and pubs. The relatively new parish church of *St.Michael* was built in 1831/2 to designs by Lewis Vulliamy, after the citizens had been forbidden to continue using the

Hampstead (Camden), Freud Museum, Library

chapel of Highgate School because the Court of Chancery considered that this imposed an unreasonable strain on the school. The church's architecture is Gothic. *Highgate Cemetery* (Swain's Lane) was consecrated in May 1939 and from the outset it was a successful project of the London Cemetery Company. David Ramsay, the landscape gardener, contributed to its design and it soon developed into a popular spot for an outing, because of its hilly location with a view across London. The E. part is today administered by the Camden Borough Council; the *tomb* and *monument* of *Karl Marx* are to be found here. The W. section is still privately owned. The Friends of Highgate Cemetery, a private association, organizes the maintenance of the cemetery and the restoration of the monuments. It has been doing this work since the 1960s, when the cemetery was in danger of fall-

ing into ruin and being closed down. Hence today's restricted opening hours. Cromwell House and Lauderdale House are the best of the stately homes. *Cromwell House* (104 Highgate Hill) was built in *c*. 1637. Its original character has been preserved to a certain exent, but alterations include an extension of the roof (*c*. 1860). The name was selected arbitrarily in *c*. 1833, and there is no historical background to it. *Lauderdale House* (Waterlow Park) was converted into its present form by the second Earl of Lauderdale in *c*. 1645, after he had come into the possession of this originally Elizabethan house by marriage. Sir Sidney Waterlow, the last private owner, presented the house and park to the London County Council in 1889. The house suffered severe fire damage, but was completely restored in the 1970's. Today, exhibitions and concerts are held here. The building also

Highgate Cemetery, monument to Marx

houses a permanent exhibition devoted to the region's history, and a restaurant.

Chelmsford
Essex p.190☐F 2   (CM1)

This town is the administrative centre of Essex, and today has a very modern face. However, some of its historical dignity survives around *St.Mary* in the town centre.

St.Mary: This parish church was elevated to the status of a cathedral in 1914. Its appearance testifies to the town's flourishing medieval past and the church's dimensions are still generous despite radical 19C restoration. The 15C tower and the library above the S. portal (17C) survive in their original form.

Shire Hall (Tindal Square): A very solid and dignified government building by John Johnson (1789–91). Its effect derives chiefly from perfect craftsmanship and the absence of artistic originality.

Corn Exchange (Tindal Square): Built by F.Chancellor in Renaissance style in 1857 in yellow brick. Outside the building there is a *statue of Chief Justice Tindal*, who gave this central square of Chelmsford its name.

Environs: Ingatestone (6 miles SW): A large village with rows of good 16C houses. The church of *St.Edmund and St.Mary* is Norman in origin, but was later altered. The tower is 15C. The Petre family lived in Ingatestone Hall from 1539 onwards, and some members of the family are commemorated in 16&17C monuments and in a side chapel. *Ingatestone Hall* was previously a manor belonging to the convent of Barking. The Petre family's impressive house was grouped around two courtyards, and most of the inner courtyard still survives. Building work was completed in 1548. Many of the 16C interior decorations survive in the original.
Margaretting (3 miles SW): The 15C church of *St.Margaret* has a three-part window in the E. with a Tree of Jesse originally 15C but much restored. The church tower has an unusual beam structure. The moated house called *Killigrews* is built of Tudor material, but the E. façade was rebuilt in the 18C and the W. wing was added later.

Chesham
Buckinghamshire p.190☐B 2   (HP5

The town centre still reflects its citizens' wealth in former centuries. Stylishly designed houses are to be found in *Church Street, Fuller's Hill, Germain Street* and *Market Square*.

St.Mary: The exterior of this parish church has been neo-Gothic since it was restored by Sir George Gilbert Scott in 1869. However, the original Perpendicular and Decorated styles have survived in the details.

The Bury (take a turning off Church Street for the approach road): This, the only large country house in Chesham, was built for William Lowndes in *c.* 1712. There are two porters' lodges in Church Street. The façades of the house were redesigned in the early 19C. Later the W. part of the building was also extensively enlarged.

Blackwell Grange Farm (SE edge of town): Originally a 15C half-timbered building. The panels between the timbering were later filled with bricks. The form of the windows also dates back to 16C alterations.

Great Hundridge Manor (W. edge of town): The manor house was built in 1696 for a member of the London apothecaries' guild and is a splendid example of late-17C style. The 13C manor *chapel* survives behind the house.

Environs: Amersham (2 miles S.): The imposing town church of *St.Mary* has had an entirely Victorian appearance ever since 19C restorations. However, it dates back to the mid 12C. In the late 1960s, serious endeavours restored the medieval character of the building and this was especially successful with the interior decoration. One of the richest collections of tombstones and monuments in all Buckinghamshire is to be found here. The core of the town, around *High Street* and *Whielden Street,* has preserved the character of a traditional country town with stylishly designed but not excessively large houses built at different periods.
Chenies (6 km. SE): This town was among the possessions of the Bedford family, who left their cultural impression

Highgate (Camden), sculpture in cemetery

on it. *St.Michael* was built in the 15C on the site of a former church. The church has good interior decorations, but acquired its real importance when *Bedford Chapel* was added in 1556. The chapel has tomb monuments to the Bedfords dating from the 15C to the late 19C, but is not generally open to the public. The chapel and church were later restored and altered. The architectural history of the *Manor House,* which stands very near the church, is not sufficiently well known. The Tudor architecture of the older sections is unmistakable, but the exact year of its construction is unknown. Some parts of the buildings were redesigned and enlarged in the first two-thirds of the 19C. *Woodside House* in the N. was built for Adelina Duchess of Bedford in 1897 above the little river Chess. Building was supervised by C.E. Kempe, the glass-stainer and

IN EVER LOVING MEMORY
OF

t reflects the new residential architecture
of the late 19C. The garden was designed
by Sir Edwin Lutyens. *The Village* is a
housing estate which the administrators
of the Bedford landed properties ordered
to be built in *c.* 1850; houses are solidly
designed in the style of that period.

Chigwell
Essex p.190□E 2   (IG7)

Until the late 1960s, this town retained
its rural character to a greater extent than
would be expected for a town on the very
borders of Greater London. Today it is
linked to the London underground railway system by the Central Line.

St.Mary: Although extensively enlarged
in the 1880's, this is still unmistakably a
village church. The original style of
architecture was Norman; N. arcade, roof
and belfry are all 15C.

Grammar School (to the E. of the
church): This school was founded in 1629
by Samuel Harsnett, Archbishop of York,
who is commemorated by a monument,
with an almost life-sized sculpture, in the
village church. The school room, a large
hall, and much of the adjoining *Head
Master's House,* survive in their original
form.

Convent of the Sacred Heart (on the
southbound road, near Woodford Bridge):
The façade of this old Georgian mansion
was unfortunately later adapted to the taste
of the times.

Environs: Chigwell Row (2 miles E.):
The town church was built in the 2nd half
of the 19C in 13C style. *Hainault Hall,*
a solid brick structure, stands opposite *All
Saints,* also on the green.

Highgate (Camden), cemetery, angel

Colchester
Essex p.190□F 1   (CO1)

COLCHESTER: One of the most important historical towns in England. It was
here that King Cunobelin, the Cymbeline
of Shakespeare's play, had his seat of
government before the Romans took possession of the town in about the mid-1C.
It was here too that Queen Boudicca's
revolt was temporarily successful in *c.*
AD 60. Hardly any traces survive from
the Anglo-Saxon period, although the
town was evidently important enough for
the Danes to raid it repeatedly. The Normans built a major fortification and the
town subsequently became a monastic
centre. Cloth manufacture and cloth trading were the most important feature of the
town's economy until the 18C. The old
section of town, on a hill, is surrounded
by a wall.

Holy Trinity (Trinity Street): The only
part surviving in its original form is the
Anglo-Saxon W. tower. The rest of the
church was built in 1886, incorporating
parts of the 14&15C church. Today the
church has a collection of artistic han-
dicrafts and an exhibition of the history
of transport and shipping.

St.Botolph's Priory: The ruins of a
11&12C complex—the first establishment
of the Augustinian hermits in England—
can be seen here. The only surviving sections are parts of the large church: nave,
W. façade, two towers, and the N. foundation wall of the cloister. *St.Botolph's
church* was built in Norman style by
William Mason to the S. of the ruins in
1836.

St.James-the-Great (East Hill): The
choir and its adjoining chapels are fine
examples of the Perpendicular Style.
Norman masonry is still discernible to the
NW of the nave. Some other details date
from the 13&14C. However, the overall

Colchester Castle, seen from the E.

design of the church was altered in restoration work in the late 17C and 19C.

St.John's Abbey (St.John's Green): All that survives of this Benedictine abbey is the *gatehouse*, which was restored in the 19C. The previous structure was pulled down, and in 1591 its stones were used to build *Bourne Mill* (Bourne Road), a building charmingly displaying the ornateness of Elizabethan architecture.

St.Martin (West Stockwell Street): This church in Perpendicular and Decorated styles has preserved its original structure particularly well. The N. aisle and the tower are Norman, while the main section of the church is 14C.

Castle: This, the largest surviving fortified castle, dates from the 11C, like the White Tower in London (see *Tower*),

although it is considerably larger. The original castle was probably two storeys taller but these upper sections were pulled down in 1683. The present top of the roof dates from the mid 18C, when the castle stood in the park of *The Hollytrees* and was regarded as a kind of historical adornment to the garden. The entire castle was built above the roof vaults of the Roman temple of Claudius. Today it is the appropriate setting for an exhibition of the region's cultural history from the Stone Age until the 17C, an exhibition which is part of the *Colchester and Essex Museum.*

The Hollytrees (High Street): This house was built in 1716 and its W. wing was added in 1748. The best example of architecture of this date in Colchester, it today houses the *Colchester and Essex Museum's* department of ancient furniture, household objects and clothing.

Colchester, County Hall, detail

High Street and **East Hill:** Both these streets, along with their side roads, are rich in 18C and early-19C buildings, some of which, such as *The Minories* (1776), have collections open to the public.

Environs: Dedham: (8 miles NE): The cloth industry made this an important and prosperous little town from the 14C to the 17C and some charming buldings survive from that period. The cloth trade suffered great losses from about the mid-17C onwards, due to Dutch competition. One testimony to the town's heyday is the parish church of *St.Mary the Virgin,* which is the finest Perpendicular church in Essex. Completed between 1492 and 1520, it appears to be based on a unified design which was not altered in the course of construction. Of the secular buildings, the *Marlborough Head Inn,* one of the town's finest houses, was completed in *c.*

1500. At about the same time, a rich clothier built himself the house (S. edge of town) called *Southfields,* which has a round courtyard. In this building, store-house, office and house are all combined. A timber-framed structure, it is plastered in parts and has a visible beam construction in others. The *former poorhouse* is on the E. side. The *Sun Inn* with its delight-ful yard also dates back to the early 16C. The *Grammar School* (Mill Lane) and *Sherman's* (opposite the church in the High Street) were erected by the same architects in *c.* 1730.

Great Bromley (7 miles E.): The church of *St.George* is a fine example of 15C architecture. The S. arcade appears to date back to the 14C.

Great Coggeshall (9 miles W.): This town is of interest for its unconventional layout. The town lies on the important traffic route from Colchester to Braintree,

Colchester, Castle, pub sign

but the church and market place are located away from the main road, as if in a medieval desire to reduce the traffic volume. *St. Peter-ad-Vincula* is a large 15C church built to a uniform design. It was restored after being damaged in World War 2. *Paycocke's House* (West Street), built in a mixture of the solid construction system and the half-timber style, is a charming building from *c.* 1500. Built for William Paycocke, a well-to-do clothier, the interior decorations of the house are largely original. Apart from this, the late-15C *Woolpack Inn* near the church is also of interest. About a mile S., near *Little Coggeshall* or *Coggeshall Hamlet,* are the *ruins of the Cistercian abbey,* which dates back to a foundation by King Stephen in the 1140's. Only a few fragments from the 12&13C have been discovered. A house was built among the ruins in 1581 and some materials and

ornaments from the monastery buildings were used in its construction. The only part of the monastery to have survived in its original form is the gatehouse chapel of *St. Nicholas* (1225).

Layer Marney (10 miles SW): This was owned by the Marney family from the 12C onwards, but they did not become public figures until the last two generations of their existence. Henry Lord Marney, and later also John Lord Marney, became members of the Tudors' Privy Council. From *c.* 1505–25 they applied themselves to the task of enlarging the church and manor house in Layer Marney. *St. Mary-the-Virgin* to the W. of the gatehouse was the first to be rebuilt. Its brick walls have blue geometric patterns. A priest's chamber is installed at the W. end of the N. aisle, and this has a fireplace which it is somewhat surprising to see incorporated into a religious build-

Colchester, Bay Hall, room

ing. The monuments to Sir William Marney, Henry Lord Marney and John Lord Marney inside the church reflect the transition from traditional English sculpture to the Italian Renaissance models. This transition also characterizes the completed sections of the new mansion. The *Layer Marney Towers*, eight storeys high, form the tallest gatehouse ever to have been completed in England. They give an impression of the dimensions planned for the manor house itself. After the family died out in 1525, the main house was not built. The gate between the two pairs of towers has above it two spacious halls between the towers. This gate was intended to open into a courtyard which was to have had low wings at the sides. A section of the W. wing adjoining the gatehouse survives in its original form. The E. wing with the adjoining buldings was later converted.

Croydon
(Borough of Greater London)
Surrey p.190☐D 4   (SE19, SE25, CR0, CR2)

CROYDON: Until around the mid 19C Croydon was a small market town, which attracted people from a large area, its sphere of influence becoming almost as large as the present borough. From the 11C onwards Croydon was in the possession of the Archbishops of Canterbury, who had a summer residence here. The *Surrey Street Market* has been in existence since the 13C, when the Archbishop granted the town the right to hold a market. Today the market is increasingly threatened by competition from the large department stores. After a railway connection to the City of London was opened in the mid 19C (today the journey takes 18 minutes), middle-class

Londoners began to build themselves houses in and round about. Croydon Airport was set up during World War 1, and in 1920 it was enlarged into London's main civilian airport. It was, however, replaced by *Gatwick Airport* in 1958. As a result of these developments, the main focus of the town shifted to the E., where a whole new town may be said to have grown up after the war. As the old part of town was mostly destroyed, new buildings predominate over the buildings of historical interest in the old sector too.

St.John the Baptist (Church Street; CR0): This medieval parish church was built by order of the Archbishops and was therefore the largest in all Surrey. The original structure was completely burned down in 1867 after being struck by lightning. Shortly thereafter it was rebuilt by Sir G.G. Scott in accordance with the original.

St.Mary Magdalene (Canning Road; CR0): This church by E.Buckton Lamb clearly shows that the Victorian preference for medieval stylistic elements was not an imitative cult, but rather provided the framework for the individual architects' particular preferences. This is particularly noticeable in the interior, where all the traditional structural elements seem only to serve the purpose of supporting Lamb's unconventional roof design. The church was completed in 1868–70, the tower in 1928–30.

Archbishop's Palace (Old Palace Yard; CR0): An archbishop's manor was first mentioned in 1215, but some of the structure points back to the 12C. The building is mainly 14&15C, but the palace was later converted. The archbishops sold it in 1780. The palace consists of mainly two storey, irregularly grouped around two small courtyards. Only the *Great Hall* is on the ground floor, all the other main rooms being on the upper storey. The *chapel* in the N. of the complex was probably built under Archbishop Bourchier in *c.* 1460–80, and enlarged under Archbishop Morton in the early 16C.

St.Bernards (Park Hill Road, CR0): Built by *Atelier 5*, the Swiss group of architects who were influenced by Le Corbusier, the resulting estate of 21 terraced houses is one of the most architecturally harmonious in England.

Whitgift's Hospital (North End/George Street, CR0): This hospital (1596–9) founded by John Whitgift was built of red brick around a courtyard. The façade facing the street was designed strictly symmetrically.

Wrencote (High Street, S. of the flyover, CR0): This early-18C town house was built in the style of the preceding century and is one of the best from its period to have survived in Croydon. A few similar houses are to be seen in *South End*.

Ruskin House (formerly *Coombe Hill House,* Coombe Road, CR0): Another Queen Anne House built of red and yellow brick, it makes a pleasant impression.

Environs: Addington (CR0): The church of *St.Mary* is mostly in the Norman and early Gothic styles. Despite later additions, it still gives the impression of adhering to the original styles. *Addington Palace* (Gravel Hill) by Robert Mylne (1773–9) is built of Portland stone ashlars with no superfluous ornament; later additions preserve this quietness of style. The palace later came into the possession of the Archbishops of Canterbury, and today houses the *Royal School of Church Music.* **Coulsdon** (CR3): The only parts of the church of *St.John-the-Evangelist* dating from later than the late 13C are the tower, which is a 15C addition and its even younger spire. Beside the church is a 16C *barn.*

Colchester Castle, Roman ceramics

Taunton Farmhouse (Taunton Lane) has a 15C roof surviving in its original form; the upper storey just beneath the roof was added in the 17C. Traces of former human settlement, as well as some burial mounds, have been discovered along the *Ridgeway* (Farthing Down in the S.). Excavated ceramics and weapons point to the Roman and Saxon periods.

Sanderstead (CR2): The 13C nave of *All Saints* was considerably altered in the 14C when the tower was incorporated. A chancel was added at about the same time, but its effect was impaired by renovation work performed in 1832. The late-17C *Sanderstead Court* was destroyed by bombing in 1944 and it has since been almost entirely replaced by a housing estate, although large parts of the surrounding garden have survived, as has a N. section of the N. wing, now used as a clubhouse.

Dartford

Kent p.190□E 3   (DA1, DA2, DA9)

DARTFORD (Kent, DA1): The traces of man's presence in this area date back to the second interglacial period, although there were evidently no permanent settlements here at that time. The area along the River Darent seems to have been of some importance from at least as early as the Roman period onwards. Today Dartford is one of the region's large industrial towns.

Holy Trinity: The present exterior is the result of restoration and reconstruction work by A.W. Blomfield (1862/3). All that survives of the originally Norman structure is the tower in the N. Inside the building, certain parts of the 13C church were included in the two 14C conversions and the overall style is a mixture of Decorated and Perpendicular.

Priory (entrance above Hythe Road, DA1): The ruins of this 14C foundation are today in the middle of an ironworks. This, the only Dominican nuns' priory in England, was founded under Edward III. Until its dissolution it was among the most important educational establishments for daughters of the distinguished aristocracy.

Darenth (Dartford), Roman villa

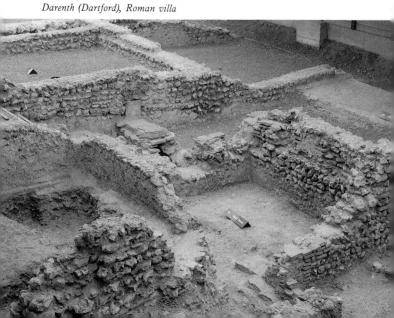

It was discovered by Sir Alfred Clapham in archaeological work in 1913. Henry VIII built himself a house in the monastery grounds in *c.* 1542, and stayed there at times. Its SW corner survives.

Royal Victoria and Bull Hotel (High Street, DA1): A coach station from 1703. The *Bull Head Yard* survives in good condition.

Environs: Darenth (2 miles E., DA2): The church of *St.Margaret* has an interesting architectural history. A large number of Roman flagstones have been used in the nave which dates from Saxon times (*c.* late 10C). The choir and sanctuary are Norman in origin, the sanctuary being the older structure. A detached sanctuary of this kind is very unusual. Here it consists of two storeys, a chamber above a lower room which is the sanctuary proper. A *Roman villa* was uncovered in the 19C on the E. bank of the Darent some 450 ft. S. of the church and it covers an area of some 14,500 sq.yds.

Eynsford (6 miles S., DA4): From the 13C church of *St.Martin,* which shows traces of the previous Norman structure (mid-12C), a route leads across a 17C stone bridge over the Darent to the *Plough Inn* with its half-timbered façade. A few hundred yards to the NE is the early-Norman *castle,* the best-preserved example of a castle to have been built without the addition of a fortified tower. Excavation work has shown that a wooden watchtower stood on the castle hill *(motte).*

Farningham (4 miles S., DA4): In the 18C this little town was a resting-place on the route to Dover. Today's arterial road (the A20) passes around the town, so that the old period of prosperity is still visible in many buildings, especially in *High Street* and *Sparepenny Lane: Farningham House, Lion Hotel, White House, Mill, Mount Pleasant* and *The Mount. St.Peter and St.Paul* (High Street) has a fine 13C interior, whose effect was scarcely impaired by the two 19C renovations to the exterior.

Horton Kirby (4 miles SE., DA4): This town is of importance for the splendid Elizabethan house called *Franks,* which is one of the best-preserved of its kind in

Darenth (Dartford), Roman villa

Darenth (Dartford), Roman villa, mosaic

Kent. On the SW outskirts of the town, it was built around a small courtyard which now contains a roofed Victorian stairwell. The interior and the division of the rooms are still largely in their original state, but the exterior and some of the windows were redesigned by R.M. Roumieu in *c.* 1860. The broad, light-coloured stairwell in the courtyard is also by the latter. The mortar ceilings in the dining room and in the bedroom above it display the date 1591 when they were built. *Reynolds Place* on the S. outskirts of town dates from the same period but was torn down in 1703. Only its E. wall is integrated into the present building.

Lullingstone (6 miles S., DA4): Church, mansion and gatehouse are here charmingly grouped together around a meadow with a lake in the S. *St.Botolph* is 14C, but was redesigned and decorated

in the 1st half of the 18C; imposing tomb monuments. *Lullingstone Castle* is in its present form an aristocratic seat from the early 18C, with a gatehouse from the 16C. The former buildings are quite like a castle, and were surrounded by a defensive moat. Traces of an *Iron Age settlement* have been discovered on the hill above the house. A *Roman villa,* inhabited at various times between *c.* AD 80 and the 5C AD, is to be seen in the valley between here and Eynsford Station. This is one of the few strictly scientific excavations carried out in Kent, and suggests that Roman-Celtic heathen cults were here replaced by Christian cults.

Stone (2 miles E., DA9): The church of *St.Mary-the Virgin* has an impressive-looking site on a limestone prominence above the Thames. The building's outward appearance is rather plain, however, its interior has surprisingly rich and

Darenth (Dartford), Roman villa, tools

valuable decorations. The church was under the patronage of the Bishops of Rochester and therefore very probably had funds at its disposal. Westminster Abbey builders were used for the stone carvings, and probably also for the building work as a whole, which fact dates the church as *c.* 1260. G.E. Street preserved the particular character of this church in exemplary fashion in his careful restoration work performed in *c.* 1860. *Stone Castle*, some 900 yards S. of the church, is a 19C Tudor building; the fortified tower (*c.* late 12C) in the SE corner has been incorporated into its structure. An *Iron Age settlement* with huts arranged in a circle was uncovered in the quarry beside the castle in the 1960's. Further to the E., beyond Greenhithe, is *Ingress Abbey* (1832/3), a large complex by Charles Moreing.

Sutton-at-Hone (2 miles SE, DA4): The church of *St.John-the-Baptist* stands a little to one side. *Poorhouses* date from 1597. *St.John's Jerusalem* stands by the Darent on the SE outskirts of town. From the late-12C onwards it was a manor of the order of St.John of Jerusalem, which set up headquarters here. The chapel, which still survives, was completed in *c.* 1234. The house itself was altered and enlarged several times between the 16C and 18C, but parts of the original walls can still be found in the W. wing.

Ealing (Borough of Greater London)

Middlesex p.190◻C 3   (W3, W5, W7, W13, UB1, UB2, UB5, UB6)

The present borough comprises the former districts of *Acton, Ealing* and *Southall-Norwood.*

EALING (W5, W13): Ealing existed as a Saxon settlement. Belonging to the Fulham possessions of the Bishops of London, it was a long time before the town was able to develop as an independent community between the Rivers Brent and Thames. In the 18C, Ealing's rural character made it a prime site for the building of country houses. At that time the area around Brentford was also part of the municipal area. The further development of Ealing into a residential suburb did not have such a radical effect on the old village as elsewhere, because the important E.-W. routes such as the Uxbridge Road by-passed the outskirts of the historical settlement around *St.Mary's Road* and *Ealing Common,* and hence some of the village charm survives to the present day.

St.Mary (St.Mary's Road, W5): There was a church here from the early 12C. However, the present parish church by S.S. Teulon was not completed until *c.* 1873, when it replaced a more modest structure from the 1st third of the 18C. Its monumental character makes it an almost stifling impression.

Ealing Studios (Ealing Green, W5): The production studios used for the famous British comedy films from the 1940s and 1950s date back to the beginning of the history of film. Between 1907 and 1912, William George Barker *(Barker Motion Photography Ltd.)* built the largest film studios in England on an area of 25,000 sq.yds. The studios have been owned by the BBC since 1955, and are still used for its television productions.

Factories (W5): Two factory buildings from the 1930s exemplify the spirit of those times. The palatial white *Hoover Factory* (Western Avenue) was built by the architects Wallis Gilbert & Partners in 1932–5. In 1936, Sir Banister Fletcher, an early-20C authority on architectural history, built the *Gillette Factory* in Syon Lane, the entrance gate of which, with its tall clock tower, is reminiscent of religious architecture.

Pitshanger Place (Ealing Green, W5): John Soane built himself this mansion on the grounds of the former manor. In 1801, there was a house belonging to his teacher George Dance the younger, but Soane incorporated only the S. wing of this into his own building. The house has recently been opened as a museum. The garden, known as *Walpole Park* (open to the public) is named after the politician *Spencer Walpole,* the last private owner of the estate.

Environs: Acton (W3): Practically the entire history of this district, from the old Saxon village to the large 18C houses, was swept away when the area was industrialized. However, this independent industrial area is not entirely devoid of architectural achievements of its own; these are to be found around the *High Street* and *Acton Park,* and include some of the more modern churches e.g. *St.Aidan's,* the Roman Catholic church built in 1961 to a contemporary design by John Newton. *Bedford Park,* the first London garden suburb, lies on the S. outskirts of the district. The central group of buildings, around *St.Michael and All Angels* and the *Tabard Inn* (Bath Road, W4), by Norman Shaw, is not without its charm.

Greenford (UB6): In the 1930s, the historical structure of the village which goes back to the 9C was completely masked by industrial and housing estates. It is only in Oldfield Lane that the former *Greenford Hall* (community centre), *Betham School* and the two *Holy Cross churches* form an attractive group beside some good modern industrial buildings.

Hanwell (W7): The core structure of the village (facing the W. end of *Church Road*) is a surprising feature here amidst the suburban and industrial buildings. In the S. the large *viaduct of the Great Western Railway* spans the River Brent.

Northolt (UB5): The old village centre, with the small church of *St.Mary-the-Virgin*, is now under a preservation order. The village is of interest for its overall character.

Southall (UB1): The present centre is a rather colourless suburb which passes over into Greenford. The former area of *Norwood* is in the S. and, in spite of the Grand Union and Paddington Canal, some good buildings have survived here. The best is *Southall Manor House* (South Road, UB1, now an office building) which dates from 1587, except for the NW wing,which was added in the 18C. This building still has its ornate original façade facing the street. *St.Mary-the-Virgin* (Norwood Green, UB2) was built in the 12C and enlarged in the 13C; 15C roof. The design of the exterior façade and tower is the result of 19C restoration. The *Free School* (Tenderlow Lane) to the N. of the church is a fine example of a late-18C village school.

Enfield, Gentlemen's Row

Enfield (Borough of Greater London)

Middlesex p.190□D 2   (N9, N13, N14, N18, N21, EN1, EN2, EN3, EN4)

This borough was created in 1956 by combining the districts of *Edmonton*, *Enfield* and *Southgate*.

ENFIELD (EN1, EN2): The area around Enfield is one of the few parts of London developed and cultivated by the Saxons. Enfield was a flourishing independent town until the 18C but in the late 19C, industry settled along *Cambridge Road* (EN1). Today, this town seems to be less dependent upon inner London than are other boroughs of Greater London.

St.Andrew (Market Place, EN2): This church with its nave and two aisles still has the character of a town church and various phases of construction from the 13C to the 16C can be discerned in it. The

severe rectangular form, with the exception of the tower in the W., was respected in later restoration. Today there are some good monuments in cemetery and church.

Grammar School (Market Place, EN2; W. of the church): A two-storeyed brick building from the mid 16C. The dormer windows in the E. façade, and the large schoolroom on the ground floor, both survive in their original form.

Gentlemen's Row (EN2): A group of fine 18&19C houses stands in the N. half of this street. The modern villa at the S. end has an annexe in which the villa's owner has preserved some parts of Enfield Palace. '*Enfield Palace*', the former manor house which stood opposite St.Andrew's on the S. side of *The Town*, was pulled down in 1927.

Forty Hall (Forty Hall, EN2): Elegant houses stand in the two streets called *Forty Hill* and *Bull's Cross*. Since 1951, the *Borough Museum* has been in Forty Hall, the best of these houses. It stands back from the street and is surrounded by a large garden.

Environs: Edmonton: After the railway line opened in the 19C, a workers' suburb was built out of the two villages of *Upper Edmonton* (N18) and *Edmonton* (N9) on the N. exit road to Hertford and Cambridge. A few old cottages survive around *All Saints* (Church Street, N9) and there are some Georgian and Victorian terraced houses here and there along the chief streets. *Salisbury House* (Bury Street West, N9), the only remaining large house, is a public centre for arts and crafts today. The original 16C panelling has been preserved in some of the rooms.

Southgate (N14): Until at least the 16C, the municipal area of Edmonton contained densely wooded countryside with some scattered hamlets from which the names of today's districts are derived. The area also had some large country houses. Of these, *Arnos Grove*, (Cannon Hill, N14), *Broomfield House* (Broomfield Park, N13) and *Grovelands* (The Bourne, N14) still survive. The best of these is probably Grovelands (today *Grovelands Hospital*), designed by John Nash in the late 18C and set in a spacious park laid out by Humphry Repton. The *Friends' Meeting House* (Winchmore Church Hill, N21) from 1790 is an early example of a Quakers' assembly hall.

Trent Park (EN4): Part of *Enfield Chase*, the former royal hunting forest, it was presented by George III to Sir Richard Jebb, his personal physician, as a reward for Jebb's having cured the Duke of Gloucester, the King's brother, in Trient. This explains the name of this park designed by Humphry Repton. The buildings in the ground are more recent. Today it is a teachers' training college.

Epping
Essex p.190☐E 2   (CM16, IG10)

EPPING (CM16): Epping Forest, much

Enfield, Forty Hall

reduced in size over the centuries, has survived London's eastward and northward expansion. The town of Epping has continued to be rather small, its several inns serving as a reminder of its past importance as a resting place for travellers. There were never any especially fine houses here, but *Winchelsea House* and *Epping Place* (both 18C) at the S. end of the High Street are of interest, as are some early-19C cottages in St.John's Road.

St.John the Baptist: The town's parish church was not built until 1889, and the free-standing tower was only completed in 1909. Built in the style of 14C eastern English churches, this structure is surprising in lacking the fashionable excesses of Victorian architects.

Environs: Copped Hall (1 miles SW): The ruins of this large house built in 1753 to the designs of John Sanderson can be seen from the S. end of the town. C.E. Kempe added a N. wing in the same style in the late 19C.

Epping Forest (in the SW of the town, extends far into the borough of *Waltham*

Forest): Primeval forest extended over practically the whole of Essex, from the Thames to the coast. Queen Boudicca is said to have fought her final battle against the Romans here, and to have killed herself and her daughters with poisonous berries when defeat was in sight. The forest was a royal hunting preserve from the Middle Ages on, and from 1226 the citizens of London had the right to hunt here on Easter Mondays. The monarchs' interest in hunting decreased from the 17C, and more and more of the forest was fenced off and incorporated into the surrounding manors, which reduced the area of the forest. In 1882 the forest was declared a permanent recreational area, and was thus in some degree protected from further devastation. It was at about this period that the Easter hunt was held for the last time. Today Epping Forest is the most extensive beech wood in England with large herds of red deer living here in an unenclosed game park. Earthworks of two large Iron Age fortifications survive in the N. section. *Loughton Camp* has an oval defensive rampart, as well as the remains of a defensive ditch some 45 ft.

Enfield, Forty Hall, room (left), chest (right)

wide. Better preserved is *Ambersbury Banks,* a rectangular hill fort with a rampart still over 6 ft. high in places, and a ditch only about half as wide but with a depth of 10 ft. (see *Waltham Forest* and *Waltham Abbey*).

Greensted-juxta-Ongar (15 miles E., near Chipping Ongar): This town is famous for the church of *St.Andrew,* whose nave still has pre-Norman wooden beams some of which were felled in the mid 9C although used in a section probably built in the early 11C. More recent excavations suggest that there were some earlier parts of the choir which were built of wood. The present choir is 16C, although the brick foundations and surroundings date from restoration by Thomas Henry Wyatt in 1848. The roof was rebuilt in the late 19C, but some of the windows in the roof survive in their 16C Tudor frame. *Greensted Hall,* outwardly 19C, has Elizabethan panelling and a stairwell of the same date.

Epsom

Surrey p.190□C 4   (KT17, KT18, KT19)

Epsom's great heyday was in the 17&18C. It first became important as a spa after salt springs were discovered in 1618, with the result that many citizens moved their summer residences into the town and round about. The second attraction was *Epsom Derby,* the great horse race organized by the twelfth Earl of Derby in 1780. The area is very rich in buildings from the late 17C to the early 19C. The town's churches, all built in the 19&20C, are unimpressive. However, an interesting walk may be taken through some streets which have good secular buildings. Epsom's influence extended far into today's borough of *Sutton.*

Church Street (KT17): After the Fire Station, comes *The Cedars,* an impressive house from the 1st half of the 18C. Some

good house fronts from the Queen Anne period are to be found between here and *Ebbisham House,* which is of the same date.

South Street (KT18): The best houses in this street are *The Shrubbery* (early 18C) and *Woodcote Hall* (late 18C). The latter is a mansion with pavilions around a small forecourt.

Woodcote Road (KT18): The first striking feature here is *Woodcote End House,* built partly in *c.* 1700 and partly in the mid 18C; interior completed in *c.* 1770. The late-17C *Woodcote Grove,* now tastefully restored, is today an office building. *Green House* in Woodcote Green Road is also late 17C. Behind it, clearly set back from the road, is the early-19C *Woodcote House.* At the end of Woodcote Road, where it passes into Wilmerhatch Lane, is the drive up to *Woodcote Park,* the finest house in Epsom until a fire in 1934. This building is still quite impressive despite the damage; parts of the original stone façade have been rebuilt in brick. The large stables in the N. also give an impression of the life-style of the house's inhabitants in the mid 18C. A dovecote and a 17C barn stand beside the drive.

Environs: Ewell (1 miles NE, KT17): All that survives of the medieval church is the tower to the S. of the new church of *St.Mary,* built by Henry Clutton in 1848. The large secular buildings are more modest than those in Epsom, but are impressive when seen as a group because they stand close together in a small area. The best are *Ewell Castle, Watch House* and *Well House* in Church Street. *Bourne Hall* in the High Street is a modern building (completed 1970) which comprises exhibition hall, library and museum. The old building (*c.* 1775) was unfortunately pulled down in 1962, but parts of the original garden have been preserved, including the entrance gate, guarded by a lion, to the little park. About half a mile

NE, on the border with the borough of Sutton, is *Nonsuch Park*. This park marks the place where Henry VIII, in the 16C, ordered Cuddington to tear down the village and church in order to build an incomparable, that is to say 'nonsuch', palace here. A splendid Renaissance palace was indeed erected, mostly with the aid of Italian foremen. Henry VIII used it from 1538 onwards as a hunting lodge and guest house for important foreign envoys. Elizabeth I also liked to live in this palace, although the twelfth Earl of Arundel owned it at the time. The fluctuating fortunes of the lands caused the palace to be torn down in the late 17C. Its ruins provided building materials for some of the large houses in the area around Epsom. Excavation work performed in 1960 showed where the palace was located and how its rooms were divided up; the finds were handed over to the Museum of London. The excavation site in the SW corner of today's park was once again filled with earth, and today it is overgrown. *Nonsuch House* which stands here today is not related to the palace, but is a 17C farm which, in *c.* 1804, was converted by Sir Jeffrey Wyatville into an aristocratic house in the style of the times.

Leatherhead (4 miles SW, KT22): This town, originally very small, was overrun by modern developments, and adapted to the requirements of the times with little regard for its cultural heritage. The interior (restored in 1965) of the *St.Mary and St.Nicholas* parish church still exudes the original early-13C charm. In Bridge Street, the inn called *The Running Horse* has outlasted the alterations of the centuries and parts of its timber-framed structure date back to the 15C, when it was designed by John Skelton, the poet.

enlarged from 1952 onwards in order to replace *London Airport Croydon* (see Croydon) as London's airport. The last phase of reconstruction and enlargement, making it the fourth largest airport in the world, was completed in 1978. *London Airport Gatwick* is now a functional modern building, clearly arranged. It is of importance not merely for regularly scheduled inland and international flights, but also for European charter flights and it has thus become the gateway to London for many visitors.

Environs: Horley (1 mile N.): Horley developed most when the railway line to Brighton was built. The early-14C church, *St.Bartholomew*, has survived but even in its original state it was a building of unorthodox design; A.W. Blomfield's restorations of 1881 made little improvement.

Lowfield Heath (1 mile SW): This hamlet stands roughly at the end of the newly lengthened runway, and suffers a good deal from modern traffic conditions. The church of *St.Michael*, although Victorian, is interesting. Built by William Burges in 1867, it radiates the unponderous, lightness of design of the original early-Gothic style, something rarely achieved by other 19C architects.

Smallfield Place (2 miles E.): The manor was built in *c.* 1600, converted in the 2nd half of the same century, partly pulled down in the 18C, and is one of the few big houses in this area to have been built of ashlars. The façade has hardly any decorations although the house is so large. Some of the interior decorations survive in the original, but the house's internal divisions have been altered, as has the use to which the rooms are put.

Gatwick

Surrey p.190☐D 5   (RH6)

The airport dates from the 1930s and was

Gerrards Cross

Buckinghamshire p.190☐B2/3   (SL9)

The church and some isolated early-19C

houses are grouped around the common. In *Bulstrode Park* to the SW of the common, remains of an *Iron Age hill fort* can be discerned. This has a double defensive ring, and is the largest fort of its kind in the county.

St.James: The daughters of Major-General Reid founded this church in his memory. It was built by Sir William Tite in 1859, and designed as a domed church with a campanile, probably in imitation of those adaptations of the Byzantine style which are frequently met with in the Veneto. On the other hand, the capitals of the columns are decorated with English early-Gothic motifs.

Camp Keep (Camp Road): One of the conspicuously individual-looking houses in this typically wealthy residential area. Building in the area was begun in the 1940s on the outskirts of an 18C land-scaped garden. Camp Keep was erected in 1937 using old building materials; the gargoyles are from a church in Scotland.

Environs: Chalfont St.Giles (3 miles N.): The church of *St.Giles* has 13C choir and font, 14C S. aisle and parts of the pews which are probably from the turn of the 16C. A few old half-timbered and brick cottages are grouped around the *green*, which is the centre of the village, including *Milton's Cottage* (17C), where the poet *John Milton* lived during the Great Plague of London and worked on his great epics 'Paradise Lost' and 'Paradise Regained'. The *Rectory* to the SW of the church is also 17C.

Denham (3 miles E.): A very attractive and inviting village on the outskirts of London with some good houses and cottages, especially along the street leading from the church to the small Village Green in the W. *St.Mary* may be Norman in origin (tower), although the building materials, except for the restorations, are mostly 15C. *Denham Place* stands on the other side of the little River Misbourne. This stately home was built for Sir Roger Hill in 1688–1701, with alterations dating from the 1770's. Later a chapel was also installed. The splendid ceilings are the most striking feature of the interior decorations. Garden by Capability Brown.

Denham (Gerrards Cross), Denham Place

Jordans (2 NW): A village designed by Fred Rowntree before World War 1. However, the fame of the town comes primarily from the *Friends' Meeting House,* the Quakers' foremost meeting place. Built in 1688, it comprises the meeting hall and the caretaker's two-storeyed lodging. *Old Jordans Farm* to the N. is a hostel for Quakers today. Meetings were held here from at least as early as 1669 onwards, until the new house was completed. The large barn is said to have been built from the wood of the 'Mayflower'.

Gravesend

Kent p.190☐F 3   (DA11, DA12)

The old harbour of *Gravesend,* the first important berth on the Thames downriver from London, was entirely burned down in 1727. A century later, work began on the town's planned expansion, in the course of which it coalesced with the village of *Milton.* The town is of no importance today as a berth, but its piers still stand.

Denham, Denham Place, coat-of-arms

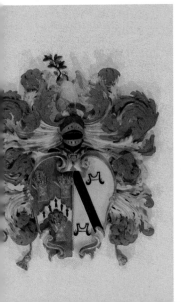

St.George: Charles Sloane, a joiner from Milton, completed the present church in 1733 on the site of the medieval parish church which had burned down. The resulting building was not especially inspiring and later alterations did not particularly improve the building's appearance. A Red Indian princess, Pocahontas, is buried here and there is a life-sized statue in memory of her.

St.Peter and St.Paul (Milton Road): Milton's 15C parish church was given a new roof by Thomas Hall from Dartford in 1790–2. The single-aisled church appears rather small beneath this roof.

Environs: Cobham and **Cobham Park** (4 miles SE): *St.Mary Magdalene,* the village's most eye-catching feature, was built in three phases of construction in the 13C. The choir is very fine, and was probably built in a single phase. The choir also contains the famous collection of tombstones commemorating the Cobham and Brooke families. Sir John de Cobham founded a *college* for a teacher and four priests in 1362 and shortly after, he obtained permission to erect suitable buildings for the college to the S. of the church. During the Reformation the buildings were converted into poorhouses, which they still are today. *Cobham Hall,* the stately home in Cobham Park, is very spaciously laid out. The present structure dates from the Elizabethan period; S. and N. wings were added to an older central structure at that time and in design they probably blended in it. For political reasons, the Cobhams lost their title and their possessions in 1603, so that building stopped. The sixth Duke of Lennox and Richmond became the building's new owner and he ordered a suitable new section to be incorporated between the two wings in 1662–72. In the early 19C, the house was given a new internal arrangement, along with other alterations, which related to the landscaping work performed by Humphry and J.A. Repton. For exam-

Greenwich, pedestrian tunnel to the Isle of Dogs

ple, the entrance was moved from the W. to the N. side, which was fitted with more windows to make it look more plausible as the new main façade.

Luddesdown (6 miles S.): *Luddesdown Court* lies just to the W. of the church of *St.Peter and St.Paul,* which dates from the 13&14C, but was practically rebuilt by R.P. Pope in 1866. A manor house built of flint, it is thought to be the oldest permanently inhabited house in England. L-shaped, there is a brick-built addition in the E. It may date back to the 11C, although the interior arrangement would rather suggest the 13C. In the *hall* on the first floor there is an open fireplace which, to judge by its mode of construction, may be 11C. The entrance to the hall was formerly in the wall next to this, with an external staircase on the outside of the building leading up to it. Additional brick buildings were added in the 16C.

**Greenwich
(Borough of Greater London)**

London County p.190☐D/E 3   (SE2, SE3, SE7,
SE9, SE10, SE18, SE28)

Today's borough unites the former districts of *Greenwich* and *Woolwich.*

GREENWICH (SE10): This town, like the entire borough, seems to have been inhabited in parts in the Roman period. It was later part of the Saxon manor of *Lewisham.* Before the beginning of the present millennium, this area was owned by the monastery of St.Peter in Ghent, and handed over to the Carthusian monastery in Sheen (see *Richmond-upon-Thames)* in 1414. Church property in England was secularized and nationalized under Henry VIII, and possession passed to the crown. In the 15C, Humphrey Duke of

St.Alfege

Gloucester enlarged the manor house and thus created the basis for the royal palaces etc. This residence near London was popular with the Tudor and Stuart monarchs, a fact which contributed considerably to the significance of Greenwich as a town in its own right. Greenwich had already developed into a town before the area became a suburb of London for administrative purposes. Thus the disruptive alterations performed in the Victorian period are less serious here than in other London boroughs.

St.Alfege (Greenwich High Road, SE10): Alfege was Archbishop of Canterbury from 1006 on. He was taken prisoner by Danish troops and finally executed in 1012. A church in his honour was evidently built here shortly thereafter, but suffered severe damage in a storm in 1710. Nicholas Hawksmoor rebuilt it to his own

plans in 1712–28, apart from the tower (1730) which is by John James. The valuable woodwork inside was restored in 1953 after being damaged in the war. Barely a trace survives either of the medieval church or of the village surrounding it.

National Maritime Museum (Romney Road, SE10): The centrepiece of today's building is *Queen's House* (1616), designed by Inigo Jones for Queen Anne, wife of James I. Building stopped after Anne's death and the residence was only completed in *c.* 1635 for Henrietta Maria, wife of Charles I. It originally consisted of two buildings which stood to the left and right of the London-Dover road, and were joined on the first floor by an enclosed bridge. A little later, John Webb, a pupil of Inigo Jones, inserted another two intermediate bridges which gave the

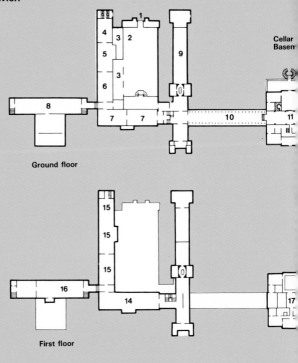

Ground floor

First floor

house its present appearance. Then the road was moved elsewhere and the house was joined together on the ground floor too. Side wings, joined by colonnades, were added in 1809. The entrance hall and Tulip Staircase survive in Inigo Jones's impressive style. The *Royal Naval Asylum*, a school for orphaned children of

sailors, was housed in these buildings until 1934. After this the buildings were comprehensively restored and given over to their present function, namely the exhibiting of instruments, documents and paintings relating to the history of seafaring and naval warfare from the Tudor period to the present.

Old Royal Observatory (Greenwich Park, SE10): The oldest of the observatory buildings was erected for John Flamsteed, the first Astronomer Royal, appointed in 1675. Sir Christopher Wren not only drew up the plans for the house and observatory, but also suggested the site. In this he was opposing plans to build the observatory in Hyde Park or in the

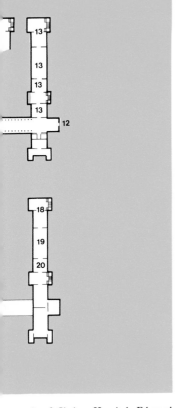

acknowledged as the zero meridian. This 0 line is marked in the paved courtyard of the observatory. Today the buildings are part of the National Maritime Museum.

Royal Naval College (SE10): These buildings stand on the site of the old palace of the Tudors in which Henry VIII, Mary I and Elizabeth I were born. That palace was pulled down in 1694 with the intention of it being replaced by a new one. *King Charles's Building,* which is part of the present complex, dates from that period. The building's foundation stone was laid in 1664, but it was not completed until the late 17C. At that time, it was intended to be a *Naval Hospital* on the model of Chelsea Hospital. *King William's, Queen Anne's* and *Queen Mary's Buildings* were then built in the 1st half of the 18C. Plans for the college were drawn up by Christopher Wren, but the execution displays the influences of his pupil Nicholas Hawksmoor and, in particular, his successor Sir John Vanbrugh. The main façade of the Royal Naval College faces the river and is designed so that Queen's House can be seen in the background. From 1708 James Thornhill carried out the paintings on the walls and ceiling of the famous *Painted Hall* (King William's Building), which is laid out on three levels: the entrance hall with its dome, the Great Hall, and the Upper Hall. The painting on the ceiling of the Great Hall shows William III and Mary II bringing peace and freedom to Europe. The Naval Hospital was dissolved in 1869. Four years later, the Royal Naval College, the training establishment for naval officers, was transferred from Portsmouth to here.

River bank (SE10): The two ships *Cutty Sark* and *Gipsy Moth IV* are to be seen on *Greenwich Pier,* near the *pedestrian tunnel* built under the Thames in 1897–1902 and leading to the Isle of Dogs. Cutty Sark, the famous clipper dating

grounds of Chelsea Hospital. Edmond Halley, after whom Halley's Comet was later named, succeeded Flamsteed in 1720. In 1749, under the aegis of James Bradley, the third Astronomer Royal, the observatory had to be enlarged further in order to house the new instruments. Other annexes were added in 1813 and 1857. The particular functions of the observatory were to improve knowledge of navigation and astronomy, to define the geographic lines of longitude more precisely, and to measure time accurately. In 1880, *Greenwich Mean Time* (GMT) was agreed upon as an international standard of measuring time. Four years later, the geographic line of longitude at Greenwich was internationally

Greenwich, Old Royal Observatory

from 1859, has been in the dry dock here since 1954, and serves as a testimony to England's adventurous seafaring history. Gipsy Moth IV is the ketch in which Sir Francis Chichester became the first person to sail successfully around the world single-handedly (1966/7).

Environs: Charlton (SE7): The area around the church, manor house and green is still rural. The church of *St.Luke* was part of the manor acquired by Adam Newton in 1607. The funds for today's brick church were obtained from his estate. It is one of the few churches to have survived from the reign of Charles I. *Charlton House,* the manor completed for Adam Newton (Prince Henry Stuart's teacher) in 1612, is a choice example of residential architecture from the period of James I (VI). The house later came into the hands of the Maryon Wilson family,

before Greenwich Borough Council acquired it in 1925 and converted it into a community centre. The buildings survive in their original form, except for the N. wing which had to be rebuilt after World War 2.

Eltham (SE9): An old Kentish village on the London-Maidstone road. Certain good buildings in the High Street still call to mind Eltham's past. But the village has changed enormously since the middle of last century, with the construction of several housing estates. There are still some stately mansions in the area of old Eltham. The origins of Eltham Palace date back to the 11C, when the manor was owned by Bishop Odo of Bayeux. In *c.* 1300, Bishop Anthony Bek of Durham presented the palace to the future King Edward II. Geoffrey Chaucer was responsible for the enlarging and conversion work performed in the late

Greenwich, Cutty Sark, old figureheads

14C. The palace was owned by the Crown until the mid 17C, but had been neglected by the Tudors, who preferred Greenwich. The great hall from the time of Edward IV was restored in the 1930s by order of Stephen Courtauld, who had a new house built for his family, and had the park redesigned. The War Office acquired the usufructuary rights to the land towards the end of the war. From the 17C on, *Eltham Lodge* in the park grounds was the real residence. Built by Hugh May for Sir John Shaw in 1664, today it is the headquarters of the Royal Blackheath Golf Club. One very charming historical remnant is *Well Hall* (Well Hall Road). All that survives of the 16C manor house is the former barn which the Woolwich Borough Council converted into an art gallery in the 1930s. In order to enlarge this building, some original parts of the ruins of Eltham Palace were used.

Plumstead (SE18): The districts SE2 and SE28, located in marshes and on the river bank, were entirely amalgamated with other districts when the whole area was industrialized and developed into a suburb. Nevertheless, the originally rural character of the parts around *Plumstead Common* and *Winn's Common,* and also around *Shooters Hill,* has been conspicuously well preserved. The inhabited parts here are loosely spread over a large area. *St.Nicholas* (High Street, SE18) still largely survives in its medieval form. The S. aisle is 12C; the N. aisle was completed in the 15C. Only the tower was rebuilt in 1664. *Greenwich Borough Museum,* with exhibits devoted to the natural and cultural history of the region, is housed in the *Plumstead Library* building in the High Street.

Woolwich (SE18): Early on this medieval fishing village on the Thames saw the start

*Greenwich, Cutty Sark, female
figurehead (Florence Nightingale)*

*Greenwich, Cutty Sark, figurehead
(Amphrite)*

of the region's industrial development. From at least as early as the beginning of the 14C, there was a ferry service on the site of the *Woolwich Free Ferry;* the old municipality also had bridgeheads on the N. bank (Newham) until the area reform of 1965. In 1512 Henry VIII established the *Royal Dockyard* in order to build Great Harry, the flagship of his new navy. The wharves here continued to be of importance right up to the period of steamship building. The *gatehouse* and *clockhouse* (both late 18C) still survive, although most of the land is now occupied by a housing estate. Many 16C freebooters and discoverers put to sea from the Woolwich Docks, including Sir Francis Drake in his Golden Hind. The artillery weapon foundries in the E. of the town were a permanent feature from about the 18C onwards, and some of them were already here in the 16C. Parts of the buildings of the *Royal Arsenal* (Warren Lane), designed by John Vanbrugh in the early 18C, still survive. The military installations in the grounds of the Arsenal were later moved to the slopes of the hill to the S. of Woolwich Common. The late-18C and early-19C barracks buildings (*Royal Military Academy, Royal Artillery Barracks* and *Connaught Barracks*) are still in use. Along with such civilian industries as crockery and glass manufacture, these installations ensured that the area was able to develop as an independent town with a complete infrastructure of its own. This is an exceptional feature for an area so near to London. The *Rotunda Museum of Artillery* (Repository Road) documents the history of land warfare with infantry since the 14C. The building itself was originally built by John Nash in St.James's Park, where it was used for ceremonial receptions to mark the victory over Napoleon. This rotunda was then moved to its present site in 1819. The *Thames Barrier* (SE7), a marvellous achievement of modern engineering, can be seen in the

Greenwich, Cutty Sark

W. of the old dockyard. Spring tides regularly put the low-lying areas of London under water, and the possibility of building a dam as a protection against floods had been under discussion since the mid 19C. The outbreak of war prevented the plans drawn up in the 1930s from being carried out and a project for a dam was later shelved. The present solution to the problem, realised between 1975 and 1982, is exciting both architecturally and technically.

Guildford

Surrey p.190□B 4/5   (GU1, GU2)

This town grew up by a ford across the Wey along the E.-W. ridge of the limestone hills to the S. of London. The town did not expand N. and S. until comparatively late. Guildford is one of the most attractive towns in Surrey; the High Street is especially pleasant, but the town's particular advantage is that it is within easy access of a number of fine stately mansions.

Cathedral (Stag Hill): Henry VIII intended to make Guildford a bishop's seat, but this did not actually happen until 1927. Sir Edward Maufe was commissioned to build a cathedral in 1932. Building began in 1936, in low-key Gothic, but the building was not consecrated until 1961 because of interruptions of the war years. In addition to the architect himself, other contemporary artists contributed to the decorations.

Holy Trinity (High Street): The town's parish church had to be rebuilt in the mid 18C after the tower collapsed. The *Weston Chantry* in the SW survives in its original form; its chapel was consecrated in 1540.

St.Mary (Quarry Street): The exterior was restored in the mid 19C, but the interior is among the best to be found in churches in Surrey. The building's pre-Norman origins are still discernible in the tower, but in other respects the present appearance of the church dates back to the 12C.

Castle (S. of the High Street): A royal castle, it emphasizes the town's importance even in early times. The sentries' lookout hill dates from the 11C; it was given a stone superstructure in the 12C. A watchtower on the E. side of the hill took over the latter's functions in *c.* 1170. The castle reflects the strict functional architecture found under Henry II, a period before the experience of the Crusades stimulated builders into decorating defensive buildings too.

Environs: Clandon Park (3 miles NE): Originally an early-17C stately mansion, similar in style to Holland House in Kensington, it was pulled down to make room for the present Palladian-style building. The new house (1713–29) was built by Giacomo Leoni for Thomas Onslow, although the baroque style is not very marked in the façade, which has led many to doubt whether the Venetian was really responsible for the building as a whole. The baroque style has been fully realized in the interior, however, which is arranged around the enormous two-storeyed entrance hall. The park was designed by Capability Brown in *c.* 1770.

Compton (3 miles SW): The village has an irregular layout with a large number of charming 19C cottages. The church of *St.Nicholas* dates from the Saxon period, but was considerably altered in the 12C, 13C & 15C. One curiosity is the *Cemetery Chapel*, built and decorated in 1896 under the supervision of Mary Watts in memory of her husband, the painter George Frederic Watts.

Godalming (4 miles S.): A very untypical little country town, which had no real centre until the white *Market Hall*, with open arcades on the ground floor, was built in 1814. The church of *St.Peter and*

Clandon Park (Guildford), stately home

St. Paul stands on the same site as the previous Saxon building, and is an unorthodox combination of all the stylistic epochs from Norman period up to the 19C, when the church was restored. Similarly, charming houses of different dates and styles from early Tudor times on can be seen in the town.

Loseley House (2 miles SW): Sir William More, a relative of Sir Thomas More, had Loseley House built in 1661–9, in a conservative Elizabethan style. The present structure consists only of the N. wing of the original design. The W. wing was pulled down in 1835 and it is uncertain whether the E. wing was ever completed. The surviving N. wing, always the main part of the house, is particularly interesting inside where the decoration is largely original. Some say the panelling in the *Great Hall* came from Henry VIII's Nonsuch Palace (see Ewell), and it may

be the work of the same team of artists.

Sutton Place (3 miles N.): In 1521, this manor was lent to Sir Richard Weston, a favourite of Henry VIII. The new building which he then erected followed the same stylistic idea as Layer Marney (see *Colchester*) but, in contrast to that building, Sutton Place was actually completed. However, the towers and gatehouse on the N. side of the courtyard were pulled down in 1786, so that a direct comparison is not possible. In *c.* 1640, another courtyard with offices was attached.

Wisley Gardens (7 miles NE): The garden of the *Royal Horticultural Society* was laid out in the early 20C to the S. of the attractive hamlet of *Wisley*. The aim of these gardens is to collect and document all kinds of garden plants. They also include an experimental garden for new vegetables and ornamental plants. The

Clandon Park (Guildford), grotto

hamlet itself has a Norman church and, standing beside this, *Church Farm* with some 16C timber-framed buildings.

Hackney (Borough of Greater London)

London County p.190☐D 3   (E5, E8, E9, N16)

Today's borough comprises the former districts of *Hackney, Shoreditch* and *Stoke Newington.*

HACKNEY (E8, E9): At the time of the Domesday Book, Hackney was probably a small hamlet in the possession of the manor of Stepney (see *Tower Hamlets*). The town's first parish church seems to date from *c.* 1300. All that survives of this church of *St.Augustine*, which may have been founded by the Knights Templar, is

the tower. Aristocrats and rich citizens began building themselves large houses here from the 15C on. In the 17&18C Hackney was famous for its recreational gardens and amusement facilities. However, 19C industrialization altered the entire area in the S., and the old splendour was largely lost as a result.

St.John (Mare Street, E8): A cruciform church (1798) by James Spiller, with space for 4,000 people, replaced the old parish church of St.Augustine. The new tower and entrance hall were added shortly after. The building was restored in 1955 after suffering fire damage.

Our Lady and St.Joseph (Tottenham Road, Kingsland, N1): In 1856, a former factory shop was converted into a Roman Catholic church, which occupies the first floor of the building.

Sutton House or **St.John's Institute** (near Sutton Place in Homerton High Street, E9): The only manor house in Hackney to survive from the Tudor period, today it is administered by the National Trust. The house was built and decorated in the early 16C. *Thomas Sutton,* who founded Charterhouse School and Almshouses, lived here at the turn of the 17C.

Victoria Park (E9): This was the first park which London's administrators deliberately planned as a recreation area for the working population of the East End of London. James Pennethorne designed it in the tradition of landscape gardens, and it was provided with suitable buildings (such as the pagoda). It opened to the public in 1845, before building work had been completed.

Environs: Shoreditch (EC2, E1, E2, N1): This originated as a settlement in the Roman period and was always important because of its proximity to London. *St.Leonard* (Shoreditch High Street, E1) was founded in the 12C. The present structure was begun by George Dance the elder in 1740 and completed in 1840. *The Theatre* and *The Curtain,* the first permanent theatre buildings, were built here under Elizabeth I, but the only reminder of them today are *Curtain Road* (EC2) and the actors' tombs in St.Leonard. In 1914, the poorhouses (Kingsland Road, E2) founded by Sir Robert Geffrye in 1715 were converted into the *Geffrye Museum,* which documents interior decoration from Elizabeth I until the 1930s. Individual rooms are each decorated in a single style. **Stoke Newington** (N16): Stoke Newington's palaeolithic finds clearly indicate that it was the oldest area of human settlement in today's borough. Initially a refuge for the Nonconformists who had been banned from London; later, poor immigrants from the Caribbean, India and Cyprus flocked here. Sadly, it suffered severely from 19C developments.

The centre of this area today is *Stoke Newington Church Street,* where today's shabby façades do at least give a hint of former importance. The two parish churches are interesting for their difference; late-medieval *Old St.Mary's* is still clearly recognizable as a village church, while the dimensions of the new church (1858) clearly reflect the pride of a growing suburb.

Hammersmith (Borough of Greater London)

London County p.190□C 3
(SW6, W6, W12, W14)

This borough unites the former districts of *Fulham* and *Hammersmith.*

HAMMERSMITH (W6, W12): This name for the district first appears in documents dating from 1294. Hammersmith's location on London's arterial roads W. and NW (which become the M4 and M40 respectively) has not been without its influence on local history. Throughout the Middle Ages, Hammersmith was a part of Fulham Manor, which was itself a possession of the Bishops of London from the 8C onwards. The original value of good communications is documented by some fine 18C houses which have survived, although today Hammersmith almost drowns in traffic. Groups of 18C town houses, are mainly to be found only along the river bank around *Hammersmith Bridge,* to the S. of the major traffic routes.

Linden House and **Sussex House** (Upper Mall, W6): Both houses date from the 1st quarter of the 18C, but Sussex House is the more conspicuous example of the classical style of the time.

Kelmscott House (Upper Mall, W6): Built in the 1780s. *William Morris,* the artist and writer, lived and worked here between 1878 and 1896.

Hammersmith Terrace (W6, between Upper Mall and Chiswick Mall): An impressive group of 17 terraced houses from the mid 18C. The houses face the river, their gardens extending down to the river bank.

St.Peter's Square (W6): Another attractive group of early-19C houses for the upper middle classes. The church of *St.Peter*, part of this group, is the oldest surviving church in Hammersmith.

Environs: Fulham (SW6): Until the late 19C this area, with its scattered villages, was a centre of vegetable growing in London. Until the 19C, *All Saints* (Church Gate) was the parish church for the entire area of today's borough. Only the tower still survives of the medieval structure; the rest of the church was rebuilt in *c.* 1880. Tombs in the church and graveyard are witness to the parish's former significance. *Fulham Palace* (Bishop's Avenue) was probably a summer residence of the Bishops of London from the 11C onwards (until 1973). *Fitzjames Quadrangle,* which is the oldest surviving section, dates from the early 16C, while the most recent enlargements are from the 2nd half of the 19C. The rare species of trees in the park were probably introduced by some bishops in the 17C. *Sandford Manor House* (near King's Road) derives in its present form mainly from the 17C. A workshop was set up in this house in 1762, which was bought up by the Imperial Gas Company in 1824. For a time the Gas Company used the Manor House as homes for their executives.

Shepherd's Bush (W12): A suburban housing area which owes most of its power of attraction to the *BBC Television Centre.* The redevelopment of the *White City* (Wood Lane) led to housing development, which began in the 1920s. The brothers Kiralfi built the White City for the Franco-British Exhibition in 1908. In the same year, the White City Stadium was the venue for the Fourth Summer Olympics. Another exhibition was held here in 1910 to celebrate the Anglo-Japanese Alliance. In the period between the two World Wars, the white stucco buildings, which had become neglected, were almost completely replaced by new residential buildings.

Haringey (Borough of Greater London)

Middlesex p.190☐D 2

(N4, N6, N8, N10, N15, N17, N22)

Since 1965, the former districts of *Hornsey, Tottenham* and *Wood Green* have been united in this borough.

HORNSEY (N8): A village of Saxon origin. Until the 19C, its development, and also that of its municipal districts of *Crouch End, Highgate, Muswell Hill* and *Stroud Green,* was influenced by their location at the edge of the hunting ground belonging to the Bishops of London. When the railway station was opened in 1850, suburban housing estates began to develop; small and medium-sized workshops and industrial enterprises also became established. All that survives of the old parish church of *St.Mary* is the tower (*c.* 1500) in Hornsey High Street. The new church (late 19C) stands a bit further E. Today almost the entire area is part of London's housing development, although the large number of parks ensure the outskirts are open and not too urban.

Alexandra Palace (Alexandra Park, N22): An exhibition building dating from 1862 was rebuilt here in 1873 to compete with the Crystal Palace as a leisure and amusement centre. However, Alexandra Palace was never able to attain the same popularity. German prisoners of war were kept here after World War 1, and these were employed in laying out the park. The BBC opened its first television centre here in 1936, but in 1956 this moved to Shepherd's Bush (see Hammersmith).

Today, parts of the studios are used for Open University programmes. Parts of the building were destroyed in a fire in 1980.

The Broadway (Crouch End, N8): A Victorian shopping street, typical of Hornsey. At the N. end of the street is *Topsfield Parade*, a four-storeyed shopping centre built in the late 19C on the site of *Topsfield Hall*, which had been pulled down shortly before.

Muswell Hill Broadway (N10): This street with its three churches is the centre of the suburban estate called *Muswell Hill*, which was largely planned and designed by W.J. Collins around the turn of the century.

Environs: Tottenham (N15, N17): Clearance of forest land for housing purposes began here in Saxon times and by the late 17C nothing was left of the forest in which Henry VIII had hunted. The area's appearance in the late 17C was characterized by farms and fine homes. In *Church Lane*, the 14C parish church of *All Hallows*, the vicarage and Bruce Castle all stand within a short distance of one another. The façade of the early-17C *vicarage* was redesigned in the early 18C. *Bruce Castle*, an Elizabethan mansion, today houses a museum with collections relating to local history, the history of the postal service, and the Middlesex Regiment. The name of the house is a reminder that this possession belonged to the Scottish royal family until the 14C. In the last quarter of the 19C the entire district became transformed into a workers' suburb. *Tottenham Hotspur*, the famous football club, was founded here in 1880.

Harlow

Essex p.190☐E 1   (CM17)

In 1947, this little old town (along with

the surrounding villages) was chosen as one of the places to be developed into towns to relieve the pressure on London. Frederick Gibberd was the architect and the whole project proved to be so successful that today the majority of the inhabitants find work within the town of Harlow and do not have to commute to London. The old village churches have largely survived.

St.Mary (Great Parndon): This church still preserves its 15C form.

St.Mary the Virgin (Latton): Originally Norman, the present structure is mainly 15&16C. Good monuments from the 15C to 17C.

St.Andrew (Netteswell): 13C nave and choir; the tower was added in the 15C.

St.Mary-the-Virgin (old part of town): The town's medieval parish church was first altered in *c.* 1709; in its present form it is heavily Victorian (rebuilt 1878–80). The *Stafford Almshouses* from 1630 survive near the church, in Churchgate Street.

Environs: Bishop's Stortford (Hertfordshire, 7 miles N.): This is the birthplace of *Cecil Rhodes* (1853–1902) and a *museum* has been set up in the house where he was born. The impressive 15C parish church of *St.Michael* has a 12C marble font.
Hatfield Broad Oak (Essex, 7 miles NE): This village has a homely character, and contains secular buildings from the 15C on (e.g. *Town Farm*). The church of *St.Mary-the-Virgin* is a remnant of the Benedictine abbey founded in 1135. The present church is mainly 15C, but some parts of the previous 12C structure were included in the building. A library was added on the S. side in 1708.
Sawbridgeworth (Hertfordshire, 4 miles NE): *Great St.Mary's* church is witness to this little town's historical importance.

Bishop's Stortford (Harlow)

Most of it is 14C and there are a large number of tombstones and monuments. **Stansted** (Essex, 9 miles NE): The third important and most modern airport in the London region, is gaining in stature, particularly due to the increase in charter flights from the European continent. In *Stansted Mountfitchet* (about 1 mile to the NW of this) stands the church of *St.Mary-the-Virgin* which is mostly late 17C and 19C, although many parts of a previous Norman church were included in its structure.

Harrow (Borough of Greater London)

Middlesex p.190☐C 2/3

(HA1, HA2, HA3, HA5, HA7)

HARROW-ON-THE-HILL (HA1): A

pilgrimage site, which may even have had this function in the pre-Christian era. In 767, King Offa of Mercia presented it to the Abbot of St.Albans. The Domesday Book records that its possession had in the meantime passed to Lanfranc, Archbishop of Canterbury. The surrounding countryside was densely wooded until at least the 16C. The inns in Harrow, for example the *King's Head*, were used as bases for royal hunting parties even as late as the time of Henry VIII. The foundation of *Harrow School* in 1572 had a decisive effect on the area's further development. Harrow and its environs are so well endowed with splendid buildings that preservation orders have been issued in respect of no less than eight districts.

St.Mary (Church Hill): This church is visible far and wide and forms the centre

Bishop's Stortford (Harlow), High Street

not only of Harrow-on-the-Hill but also of the surrounding localities. Founded by Lanfranc in 1087, it was consecrated in 1094 by Anselm, his successor as Archbishop of Canterbury. The slender, steep tower dates from 1450. The church was altered by Sir George Gilbert Scott in 1847. The stained-glass windows high up in the nave show scenes from the history of Harrow from the 9C to the 19C.

Harrow School (between High Street and Church Hill): One of England's great public schools. In 1572, Queen Elizabeth I granted to John Lyon, a free farmer, the privilege of founding this school. It appears that an old school building, which already stood on this site, was initially used for lessons until the new buildings were completed in 1615. The oak-panelled classroom *(Fourth Form Room)* from that

period still survives in its original form. Most of the buildings added later are 19C, but their style is in parts very carefully assimilated to that of the original structures. The lake in the grounds, which comprise sports grounds and a park, was designed by 'Capability' Brown in 1767.

Environs: Pinner (HA5): Like Harrow itself, the community or parish of Pinner was initially owned by the Abbey of St.Albans, and later by the Archbishops of Canterbury; it originally extended far into Hertford, where its oldest branch chapel still stands in *Oxhey* on Pinner Hill. *St.John-the-Baptist* (High Street) dates from 1321. Pinner is unexpectedly rich in old houses from the 16C and later. Many interesting houses are to be found along *Church Lane* and *Moss Lane. Headstone Manor*, the best of the large houses in the environs, stands in the *Headstone Recreation Ground* (HA2). Built in the late 16C and the 17C, it was part of the Archbishops' possessions; the *chapel* may be an adaptation of the hall which was here previously.

Stanmore (HA7): The original Neolithic settlers who lived here were replaced by the Celts in *c.* 100 BC; they later fought here against Julius Caesar (54 BC) in a battle commemorated by an *obelisk* from 1750 which now stands in the grounds of the *Royal National Orthopaedic Hospital.* The region remained rural until the 20C, and some of that character has lasted to the present. An interesting group of houses, now under preservation orders, stand around *St.John-the-Evangelist* in the *Great Stanmore* district of town. The church itself, built in 1632, revealed severe structural damage in the 19C, but has still survived as a roofless ruin (a new church has been built next to it). However, the half-timbered *Church House* and the old tithe barn survive in their original form. *Bentley Priory* is one of the large houses. A monastery was founded here in 1170,

and passed into secular hands in the 16C. Today's buildings were erected in 1777 to plans by Sir John Soane. The house was converted into a hotel in the late 19C, and later into a girls' school. Today it is owned by the *Royal Air Force,* who used it as a headquarters in World War 2. For *Canons* (Canons Park, Little Stanmore), see *Edgware* (Barnet).

Havering (Borough of Greater London)

Essex p.190☐E 2   (RM1, RM2, RM3, RM5, RM7, RM11, RM12, RM13, RM14)

This borough unites the two former districts of *Hornchurch* and *Romford.* The name is derived from the historical royal free zone of Havering.

Romford (RM1): Today Romford is the administrative centre of the borough. The town developed along the course of the old Roman road from London to Colchester. The right to hold a market in the town

Bishop's Stortford (Harlow), St.Michael, font (detail, left), arch (right)

was granted in 1247; the medieval centre was around *Old Church Road* (RM7). The River Rom frequently flooded, and in the 15C the settlement moved a little way to the N. The old church of *St.Edward* on this site was pulled down in the 19C and replaced by the present structure, which is 14C in style. *Church House* dates from the first phase of building in the 15C. Originally used as a priest's house it was converted into an inn when coach traffic became of economic importance to the area; today the *Cock and Bell* is again used for religious purposes. A few other inns *(The Golden Lion, The Lamb)* are almost the only notable witnesses to the town's past. The town became a Victorian suburb and in the past 30 years it has again been subjected to comprehensive redevelopment and modernization.

Environs: Havering-atte-Bower (RM4): The district gets its name from a small village on its N. edge. From the time of Edward the Confessor until the reign of James I (VI), the rising ground was overlooked by a royal *palace* which for a long period was the official residence of the English queens. Parliament sold the possession, and one of the palace chapels became the first parish church in this community. The present church of *St.John* replaced it in 1876–8. The locality still resembles a village in character. *Bower House* (Orange Tree Hill) was the first work of Henry Flitcroft the elder. This house appears to have been be built mainly of materials from the old palace.
Hornchurch (RM12): In 1159, Henry II placed this area at the disposal of the monks of St.Bernard who built a hospice here. This stood on the site of the present church of *St.Andrew*, whose architectural history dates back to the 13C. The church makes an astonishingly urban impression considering how rural its surroundings were at that time. Hornchurch owes its wealth to leather manufacture. When it developed into a dormitory town on the outskirts of London, most of the town's

old picturesque places disappeared, but individual elements of the old village are still visible between the *King's Head* and the church (High Street and Church Hill). *Drury Falls*, the earliest buildings of which were completed in the 16C, stands in the E.
Rainham (RM13): Settlement in this area dates back to the Stone Age. Finds from the prehistoric and early historical periods have been discovered and these are now in the British Museum. Finds from Saxon burial sites suggest quite an important tribe settled here. The church of *St.Helen and St.Giles* in the old village centre, the oldest building in the entire borough, is totally Norman and has remained practically unaltered for 900 years. *Rainham Creek* was a port from the late 12C until the 19C; it was also a profitable distribution centre, particularly in the 18C. John Harle, the owner of Rainham Wharf at that time, built himself the house called *Rainham Hall* beside the church in *c.* 1729. This hall is a very attractive three-storeyed house whose interior decorations still preserve a large number of original features. Today, National Trust tenants

Harrow-on-the-Hill (Harrow), house

live in Rainham Hall. Other interesting buildings include *Bretons* (18C), which stands at the W. edge of town and is now a leisure centre and *Albyns* in the E., a 16&17C timber-framed building, with 18C alterations to the façade.

Upminster (RM14): The area around Upminster and the urban district of *Corbets Tey* in the S. is distinguished by a number of buildings which have been the subject of preservation orders. They range in size from cottage to country house. Part of the church of *St.Laurence* stands on the foundations of a 7C Saxon church. The present structure, begun in *c.* 1100, attained its final shape in the course of the 13C. Between 1689 and 1735, William Denham, scientist and local parish priest, used the tower for experiments in measuring the speeds of light and sound, because he was able to see the Woolwich parade ground from here. He also wrote a theory of clocks. *Upminster Hall* (Hall Lane) dates from the 15&16C; the N. wing may be 17C. At the time when it was built it was a hunting lodge belonging to the Abbots of Waltham Abbey. The mid-15C *Upminster Tithe Barn* (Hall Lane) was restored recently and now this impressive wooden structure houses a museum of local agriculture. *Clock House* (St.Mary's Lane), a two-storeyed brick building from the 1770s with a little clock tower from the same period, was at that time the stable building of *New Place,* the residence of the Esdaile family, which no longer exists. *Upminster Windmill* is a former linen factory, built in 1803 and fitted with a steam engine eight years later. It continued operating until 1934, and the County of Essex and the borough of Havering have preserved it as an industrial monument.

Hemel Hempstead

Hertfordshire p.190□C 1/2   (HP1, HP2, HP3)

This is one of the large towns which stand on the NW outskirts of London and which was built to relieve the pressure on the capital. However, the old town centre has been preserved because the new centre was built a little further to the S. The *High Street*, with its buildings which grew up over the course of time, runs along a slope, and its E. and W. sides are of different heights.

St.Mary (High Street): The town's parish church stands in an open square in the side of the valley. After St.Albans, it is the best example of a Norman church in this region. Built between *c.* 1150 and *c.* 1175, the windows were enlarged in the 14&15C and redesigned in Gothic style.

Environs: Abbots Langley (4 miles SE): *St.Lawrence,* the church of this little town, was originally Norman, although its final shape is 14C. The wall paintings of the patron saint, Lawrence and of St.Thomas of Canterbury also date from this period.

Great Gaddesden (3 miles NW): The charming church of *St.John-the-Baptist* is Norman in origin but was comprehensively redesigned in the 15C.

Redbourne (3 miles NE): This little town also has a church of the type typical of the region; basically Norman (tower and nave) it has 14C Gothic enlargements (choir and S. aisle). A *Lady Chapel* was added to the church of *St.Mary* in the 15C.

Henley-on-Thames

Oxfordshire p.190□A 3   (RG9)

This town developed in the 12C as a port on the Thames, when it was used for shipping timber to London. It was an important town in the 16&17C and today it presents a very 18C appearance, because many houses were given new façades at that time. Today it is primarily home to commuters.

Henley-on-Thames, riverbank road

St.Mary: This church was begun in 1204, but was so altered in the 14&15C that it presents an entirely late-Gothic impression; extensive rebuilding in *c.* 1854, when a second (N.) aisle was added.

Town Hall and **Friar Park:** The Town Hall (1900) by Henry Hare is in the Queen Anne style which was popular in the early 18C. Behind it stands a most fascinating house and garden. *Friar Park,* designed and built in 1896 by its owner Sir Frank Crisp in collaboration with his architect M.Clarke Edwards, has a garden designed as a Swiss landscape, with caves and underground lakes, which in places have quite spooky effects.

Most interesting streets include *Hart Street* (from the bridge over the Thames leading to the Market Place), *Market Place, Bell Street* and *New Street.*

Environs: Hambleden (Buckinghamshire, 3 miles NE): One of the most attractive villages in Buckinghamshire, with fine cottages and church all clustered around the village green. *St.Mary,* of Norman origin, was completed in the 14C; the tower was added in the 18C because the old Norman tower had collapsed. At the N. edge of the village stands the early-17C *Manor House,* and the *Rectory* or *Kendricks* from 1724.

Medmenham (Buckinghamshire, 3 miles E.): *Lodge Farm,* a late-17C mansion, stands on the N. slopes above the church of *St.Peter.* The residential part consists of a charming brick building, while the farm buildings are timber framed. *Medmenham Abbey* stands at the end of Ferry Lane. A mansion (today's E. wing) was built in 1595 on the site of the early-13C Cistercian abbey. The mansion was enlarged in the 18C and again in *c.* 1898.

Henley-on-Thames, St.Mary

Remenham (Henley-on-Thames), country h

Sir Francis Dashwood set up his *Hell Fire Club* (a group of young gentlemen who pursued practices in mockery of religious rituals) here in 1745. The chapel which he designed for these purposes is not open to the public. *Danesfield* to the E. of this was designed by R.Walker at about the turn of the century in the style of a large Tudor house.

Remenham (Berkshire, 1 mile N.): The church of *St.Nicholas* is a Victorian reconstruction of the previous building which dated from the Norman period onwards. The *Temple* (1771) by James Wyatt, standing on Temple Island, has an unrestricted view of Henley-on-Thames; the house was originally part of the *Manor House of Fawley*, which was restored by Wyatt and stands on the other side of the river (in Buckinghamshire). The elegantly proportioned *Culham Court* (about a mile E. of the church) dates from the same period; its architect is unknown. *Park Place* (about a mile S. of the church, opposite Henley-on-Thames) has an interesting garden, which is today shared between several houses. The present house (*c.* 1870) is in French Renaissance style, while the garden was designed more than 100 years earlier by General Conway, the owner at the time. Temples, bridges, etc. in the park are said to have been built out of materials taken from Reading Abbey, and were erected to the General's instructions. *Happy Valley,* which is especially well laid out, is today the garden of the house of the same name.

Hertford

Hertfordshire p.190☐D 1   (SG13, SG14)

The county town of Hertfordshire is today

a delightful little town with only slightly more than 20,000 inhabitants. *Hertford* was a fortified town even in Saxon times; later the medieval castle formed the real starting point for the town's further development. Numerous old buildings have survived and these are still lively in character and well maintained. Only parts of the S. and E. of the town, near the modern bypass, are at all spoilt, although only two of the five medieval churches have survived.

St.Andrew (St.Andrew's Street): The town's main church was rebuilt by J.Johnson jun. in 1869–76; the only original part of the 15C church is the N. entrance. Buildings nearby have fared better, e.g. the *Old Verger's House* (No. 43), a 15C building.

Castle: The castle is the oldest building in the town. Built in *c.* 1100, it was in royal hands until the reign of Elizabeth I. James I sold it to William Cecil, Earl of Salisbury, and it has remained in his family's possession ever since. Parts of the 12C and 15C structures are included in the present buildings.

Lombard House (Bull Plain): In the 17C, the Hertford Clubhouse was inhabited by *Henry Chauncy,* a historian and the judge who presided at the last trials of witches to be held in England. The house's façades were adapted according to 18C taste.

Environs: Broxbourne (4 miles SE): The dimensions of the late-15C church of *St.Augustine* indicate that this little town on the River Lea was quite important in the late Middle Ages. It is possible that the church may have been built by the same architect who designed St.Margaret's Westminster.

Stanstead Abbots (4 miles E.): The 15C village church of *St.James* has 18C interior decorations and is surrounded by a number of early-17C houses, e.g. *Baesche Almshouses, Old Clockhouse* and *Red Lion Inn.* Standing on the Hertford side of the village street there is a house built in red brick which is thought to be one of the earliest domestic examples of imitated Gothic.

Ware (2 miles NE): The *High Street* and *Baldock Street* are rich in 16C, 17C and 18C houses. *Place House* (Bluecoat Yard), a 15C half-timbered structure, and the old manor of Ware, was used as a school from 1674–1761. The *Priory,* which today houses the council offices, includes some of the old buildings of the Franciscan monastery, which had been founded in 1338 by Thomas Wake, who owned the manor. The *Corn Stores* (Star Street), a group of unusual 17C storehouses, are arranged around a courtyard and are interesting because access to their upper storeys could only be gained by ladders on the outside.

Hertford Castle

High Wycombe

Buckinghamshire p.190☐A 2(HP11, HP12, HP13)

High Wycombe, an expanding town at the edge of the London catchment area, is also a successful industrial centre. In appearance it is rather a hotch-potch of buildings of indeterminate architectural style and date, including many erected in the present century during various phases of expansion, but also some dating back to the town's 18C heyday. High Wycombe geographical location is of interest, for it is situated in the narrow valley of the River Wye which cuts deeply into the chains of hills at this point.

All Saints: The town centre is dominated by this spacious neo-Gothic church (*c.* 1755) by Henry Keene. Only the lower part of the tower which replaced the tower of the medieval church sometime before 1520, is still genuinely late Gothic (Perpendicular).

Guildhall: The Guildhall (1757), also by Henry Keene, stands at the W. end of the

High Street, also mainly 18C. The open ground floor is formed of Tuscan arcades. A historical painting by J.H. Mortimer, showing St.Paul converting Druids, is to be found in a room on the upper storey.

Wycombe Abbey School (Marlow Hill): In 1896, this stately home belonging to Lord Shelburne, founder of the Guildhall, and his family, was converted into a school for which W.D. Caroe erected additional buildings in the years following. The main building (1795) is by James Wyatt, who also initially supervised the construction work and the entire complex is of a playful character.

Environs: Bledlow (8 miles NW): The church and *manor house,* with 18C barn and 18C cottage form an attractive group. *Holy Trinity* church is based on an enlargement of the Norman building which dates from *c.* 1200. Further alterations were completed in the 13&14C.
Chinnor (Oxfordshire, 8 miles NW): A little town on the slope of *Wain Hill,* which gives a far-ranging view over the surrounding area. In the SE of the town is *Bledlow Cross.* 65 ft. high and 15 ft. wide, it was hewn direct from the hill's limestone, and is probably 17C.
Hughenden Manor (1 mile N.): An originally rather plain 18C house, which E.B. Lamb redesigned in 1862 for *Benjamin Disraeli,* the owner. Apart from the library, practically the whole building adopted the neo-Gothic taste of the times. The late-19C church of *St.Michael* by Sir Arthur Blomfield is built on the site of a medieval church, and stands by the drive leading to the manor. This church is mainly of interest for its falsified tombstones by which the Wellesbourne family in the 16C attempted to prove it was descended from Simon de Montfort.
Penn (3 miles E.): Some good late-17C buildings around the church. *Holy Trinity* itself is a rather haphazard but very attractive mixture of medieval architectural styles and 18C rebuilding.

The 17C *Parsonage Farmhouse* in half-timbered style is about half a mile S. of the church.
West Wycombe (2 miles NW): This village is completely dominated, if not actually overwhelmed by the landscaping and house, both of which are the work of Sir Francis Dashwood (1708–81). However, parts of West Wycombe are older than this, and the village's rural architecture makes a more unified impression than do these more recent features. *West Wycombe Park* was built in the early 18C when it was surrounded by a formal French garden. Sir Francis began redesigning the possession in *c.* 1750 and the work was completed shortly before his death. The house is irregularly designed and surprises the onlooker mainly by its interior decorations. There are some ornamental open fireplaces, but the most striking features are the frescos, which were modelled on Raphael's frescos in the Villa Farnesina and his loggias in the Vatican Palace, and also on Carracci's ceiling paintings in the galleries of the Palazzo Farnese. Shortly after Dashwood's death, Humphry Repton lightened the impression made by the *landscaped garden,* but the statues and little temples which are still present in abundance suggest the exuberance with which the park was decorated. The park continues on the other side of the London-Oxford road (A40), which was itself completed in 1752 and therefore also ran through the original landscaped garden. At that time, the medieval church of *St.Lawrence* in this W. part of the park was altered into a Georgian building and the tower was given a golden sphere. Seats were installed in this sphere and it is said to have been used as a tavern. (The church belonged to a village which formerly occupied the site and was abandoned at an earlier date.) Beside the church is the Dashwoods' *mausoleum,* an unroofed hexagonal structure designed by John Bastard the younger. Halfway between the church and the village are the *Caves,* where the Hell

Fire Club is thought to have met, in addition to its other meeting place in Medmenham Abbey (see *Henley-on-Thames*). The group gave itself the name of 'Brotherhood of St.Francis' or 'Dashwood's Apostles'. The elaborate system of caves was enlarged between 1750 and 1752 by local workers supervised by Sir Francis Dashwood.

Hillingdon (Borough of Greater London)

Middlesex p.190□C 3   (UB3, UB4, UB7, UB8, UB9, UB10, HA4, HA6, TW6)

This borough was created in 1965 by combining the districts of *Hayes and Harlington*, *Ruislip-Northwood*, and *Uxbridge*, as well as *Yiewsley* and *West Drayton*.

HILLINGDON (UB10): Formerly the centre of a large medieval community which developed as a result of the integration of the manors of Hillingdon and Colham. From the late 13C onwards large parts of the estates were owned by the Bishops of Worcester. When the *Grand Union Canal* was enlarged in the early 19C, industrialization came to the area. The rapid increase in population then caused the area to be divided into six municipalities. *Cedar House*, *Cottage Hotel* and *Red Lion Inn*, all 16C, still give the church's surroundings a rural character.

St.John-the-Baptist   (Uxbridge Road/Royal Lane): Rebuilt and enlarged by Sir George Gilbert Scott about the mid 19C, the aisles, however, are still essentially 15C. The tower was rebuilt in 1629; its oldest parts date back to the 13C.

Environs: Harefield (UB9): The 17C half-timbered *King's Arms* and *Lady Egerton's Almshouses,* which stand in the *High Street* and *Park Lane,* have survived the passing ages. The 16C church of *St.Mary's* may contain parts of the 12C church belonging to the order of St.John of Jerusalem.

Hayes (UB3): From the 11C to the 16C, the manor of Hayes and Harlington was in the possession of the Archbishops of Canterbury, whose ownership of the parish church, which was their own private church, continued until the 19C. The really large mansions from the 16C to the 18C have unfortunately disappeared because of industrial expansion, but some fine town houses survive here and there.

Heathrow (TW6): The largest international airport, it was opened on 31 May 1946 on land hived off from the districts of Hayes and Harlington to form a separate area of its own. The modern terminals 1 to 3 were opened in 1955, and Terminal 4 in 1986. Heathrow is the only one of London's large airports to be linked to the inner city by a direct underground railway connection *(Piccadilly Line)*.

Ruislip (HA4): The building materials used in the old village survive almost entirely intact around the parish church of *St.Martin* at the N. end of the High Street. The church was completed in the mid 13C; the tower dates in its present form from *c.* 1500. There are some more good buildings further N., in *Bury Street*.

Uxbridge (UB8): From the 12C to the 19C, this town was the market centre of W. Middlesex and particularly important for grain. This prosperity left its traces, but the appearance of Uxbridge today is chiefly characterized by its development into a suburb in the 19&20C. *St.Margaret's* was orginally a branch church of Hillingdon, and only in 1827 did it become an independent parish church. The original church was built in *c.* 1200 and radically redesigned in the 15C. The S. aisle was formerly a guild chapel and is accordingly lavishly decorated.

West Drayton and **Yiewsley** (UB7): Today these districts are busy suburbs, whose character has been dictated by the presence of the M4 motorway and Heathrow Airport. Obviously, there are good communications links with central London. *The Green* in West Drayton still preserves a degree of its previously rural appearance. The *De Burgh Arms* and *Yiewsley Grange*, both 17C buildings in Yiewsley, are the only interesting older houses in the area.

Hounslow (Borough of Greater London)

Middlesex p.190☐C 3   (W4, TW3, TW4, TW5,
                          TW7, TW8, TW13, TW14)

This borough was formed by combining the former districts of *Brentford, Chiswick, Feltham, Heston* and *Isleworth.*

Hounslow (TW3, TW4): In 1215, after Magna Carta had been passed, the barons held a tournament in Hounslow and in the *Forest of Staines;* the report of this tournament contains the town's first documentary mention. Lying on the London-Exeter road, Hounslow was largely dependent on travellers and because of this the most important industry, right up until the mid 19C, centred on the stables and inns. The present suburban structure of Hounslow itself, especially the W. part of the borough, resulted from the opening of the railway in *c.* 1840, and from Hounslow's inclusion in the London underground railway system in the 1930s.

Holy Trinity (TW3): This church was originally a chapel attached to the hospice of the Brothers of the Holy Trinity, which was set up here in the early 13C. A new church was built on this site in *c.* 1829. Burned down in 1943, it was replaced by the present church, a work by W.E. Cross, in 1963.

Hounslow Heath (TW4): Part of this survives as a recreational area. From 1919 on, this heathland was the site of London's first civilian airport.

Environs: Brentford (TW8): Brentford was of some importance even in the 8C, because of the ford over the River Brent. However, until the 19C, the residential buildings here were mostly confined to the *High Street.* Industrialization came after this and entirely altered the town. The old church of *Ṣt.Lawrence* near Brentford Bridge has been closed since 1961. It replaced a 12C church in 1764. Its 15C tower survives from the previous church. *The Butts* (a little to the N. of the High Street) is the only place in the town where a fairly unified group of good houses from the 17C and early 18C is still to be found. The most interesting mansion is *Boston Manor House* (Boston Manor Road), built in its present spacious form in 1662. There was a manor on this site from at least as early as the 14C when it was in the possession of the nuns of St.Helen Bishopsgate. It was re-opened in 1963 after war damage had been repaired. Today it contains flats as well as the state rooms.

Chiswick (W4): Until the 19C, this part of London consisted of large mansions with small villages interspersed between them. Chiswick House (Burlington Lane, W4) and the pair of houses called Gunnersbury House and Gunnersbury Park (W3), bear witness to the area's past. *Chiswick House* (1725–9) was built by the third Earl of Burlington modelled on the work of Palladio. It was decorated by William Kent and others. The two houses in *Gunnersbury Park* were built in the early 19C, possibly to plans by Alexander Copland, on the site of a former large stately home. The larger house, which is itself known as Gunnersbury Park, now contains a museum with exhibits related to archaeology, social history and local history. A number of delightful houses from the old core of the village are to be seen in *Church Street* and *Chiswick Mall,* where the parish church of *St.Nicholas* (1252) is also to be found.

Feltham (TW13): This very old town was almost entirely destroyed by a fire in 1634; the rest fell victim to 18&19C

developments. Even the medieval church of *St.Dunstan's* (St.Dunstan's Road) was rebuilt in 1802 and enlarged some 50 years later. The priest's house (today the *Church Centre*) survives from the 17C, apart from its 18C façade. Mid-18C *Feltham House* (Elmwood Avenue), and early-19C *Hanworth Park House,* are two mansions in the area.

Osterley (TW7): This little village at the S. edge of Osterley Park was entirely swallowed up by 20C suburban housing estates. However, *Osterley Park* and *Osterley Park House* are sights worth seeing. Today the park and its lakes are unfortunately cut in two by the M4 motorway. Sir Thomas Gresham built himself the house as a country seat and landscaped the garden in the 16C. From the late 1750s on, when it was owned by the Childs, a family of bankers, the house was redesigned on classical models. Sir William Chambers was mainly responsible for the building's exterior, while from 1761 onwards Robert Adam was in charge of the interior design, including the stucco. It took 19 years to carry out his sophisticated requirements. Osterley Park House was a private residence until 1949; today it is administered by the Victoria and Albert Museum.

Syon House (Syon Park, Isleworth, TW8): A Brigittine monastery stood here in the 15C and fell to the Crown in 1534. In *c.* 1550, Edmond Seymour, Duke of Somerset, began to replace the monastery by a large house which forms the core structure of the present building. Inigo Jones was commissioned to improve the house's appearance in the 1630s. Jones's alterations were largely left in place by Robert Adam when the latter was commissioned to redesign the building in 1762. Adam limited himself to designing the interior, and to carrying out enlargements on the W. side of the house. Charles Fowler designed the *Great Conservatory* in the 19C. This conservatory is said to have given Joseph Paxton, who built the Crystal Palace, the inspiration to draw up the plans for that building. The *Botanical Gardens* in Syon Park were opened to the public in 1837.

Islington (Borough of Greater London)

London County p.190□D 3

(EC1, N1, N5, N7, N19)

Since 1965 this borough has also included *Finsbury*, which is the S. part of the borough. (Parts of Finsbury, particularly The *Clerkenwell* area are described in the central London section of this book.)

ISLINGTON (N1): When this area was still part of the forest of Middlesex, it was divided among six manors and at that time Islington itself was the last overnight stopping-place outside the city walls. Most of the houses standing here in the 16C were owned by aristocrats, and two were even owned by Henry VIII who enjoyed hunting nearby. Some exalted courtiers, such as Sir Thomas Fowler and Sir Walter Raleigh, had houses here in the reign of Elizabeth I. Indeed, the village on the top of the hill was known as 'merry Islington' until the 18C. However, Islington also experienced less joyous events and the region was used as a refuge for evacuees, both during plague epidemics and also after the Great Fire of London. Many nonconformist clergymen and their communities and schools moved here too. In the 18C some of the City Companies (guilds) acquired land and built poorhouses and other social facilities. Industrialization began in the 19C when Regent's Canal and the railway were built and this led to the area's becoming densely built up, much as it is today, although at that time parts of Islington were slums. Since the 1960s the area has become increasingly gentrified and as the area has become more and more middle class so the Victorian and Edwardian appearance of the streets has been preserved in appropriate style. Elegant streets of well-maintained houses make a walk around this part of the borough most interesting.

St.Mary's (Upper Street, N1): Built in the 12C, it was comprehensively restored in the 15C and 18C. Recent reconstruction was completed in 1956.

Angel Islington (Islington High Street, N1): From the early 17C the Angel in Islington was one of the leading coach houses in the N. of London. It was converted into a large hotel in *c.* 1819, and later altered again and enlarged. The company ceased its operations in *c.* 1960. The branch of a bank was opened here in 1982 after careful restoration work.

Canonbury Tower (Canonbury Place, N1): This former mansion, the finest historical building in Islington today, possibly occupies a site which was important even in prehistoric times. Even in its present form the building includes proto-Roman elements; the tower and much of the house were probably designed by William Bolton, last prior of St.Bartholomew's Priory in Smithfield, in the 1st third of the 16C; the house takes its name from the canons of that priory.

Royal Agricultural Hall (Liverpool Road, N1): Since 1981 this has been a centre for trade exhibitions. Completed in 1862 to designs by Frederick Peck from Maidstone, its original purpose was to provide a venue for the annual agricultural and cattle show called the Smithfield Club. It soon became used as a multipurpose hall for other exhibitions, concerts, balls, etc.

Kensington and Chelsea (Borough of Greater London)

London County p.190☐D 3 (SW3, SW5, SW7, SW10, W8, W10, W11)

The *Royal Borough of Kensington and*

Chelsea—its complete and correct title—comprises the two formerly independent districts of *Chelsea* and *Kensington*, and also parts of what was formerly *Paddington*. As regards the fine buildings in the E., such as *Kensington Palace* and *Chelsea Hospital*, the reader is referred to the descriptions in the part of the book devoted to central London.

KENSINGTON (W8): Until the 17C this was merely a small country town to the W. of London. Developing out of an Anglo-Saxon settlement around *Church Street*, it later extended along the *High Street*. The area retained a distinctly rural appearance until the 19C, but the large number of fine houses in the neighbourhood provided the roots of an urban lifestyle from the early 17C onwards. The population increased almost twentyfold with the building of some estates of fine houses in the 19C, indeed, it was in this way that most of *South Kensington* was built along with the preparations for the international exhibition of 1851. The borough was given the title Royal in 1901 to commemorate the fact that Queen Victoria was born and grew up in Kensington at Kensington Palace.

St.Mary Abbots (Church Street, W8): A Saxon church probably occupied the site originally. The abbot of Abingdon built a church in the 12C and this was comprehensively rebuilt in 1370 and again in 1696. At the latter date it was also used as a royal chapel. The present church is a reconstruction of 1872 by Sir George Gilbert Scott. Some 18C houses still stand near the church.

Holland House (Holland Park, W8): After the bomb damage of World War 2, only part of the house could be restored, but its present use as an open-air theatre and restaurant preserves something of exuberant social life which the house formerly experienced. The original mansion owned by Sir Walter Cope (*Cope*

Kingston-upon-Thames, Market Place

Castle) was completed at the beginning of James I's reign. Later it came into the possession of the Earls Holland by marriage, and it was finally acquired by Henry Fox, first Baron Holland, in 1763. Renovation and reconstruction was carried out under the fourth Baron Holland in the 19C.

Leighton House (Holland Park Road, W 14): This red brick house, which has a rather inconspicuous exterior, was built by G.Aitchinson in 1865 for *Lord Leighton*, a famous Victorian painter and sculptor. The surprisingly exotic interior was designed to suit the taste of the master of the house, who was a great lover of Eastern art. The *Arabian hall* extends through two storeys and is spanned by a massive dome; there are exotic mosaic friezes and 13–17C tiles with Islamic decorative motifs. Paintings and sculptures

by Lord Leighton and other contemporaries like Edward Burne-Jones and W.de Morgan can be seen here today.

Environs: Chelsea (SW3): King Offa of Mercia held a synod here in 787. The first permanent church was built in Chelsea, probably in 799, at a time when it was a small village on the limestone shore of the Thames, lying on the edge of the forest of Middlesex. The nobility settled in this area from the 15C onwards. Sir Thomas More built himself a house here in the 16C and Chelsea thereby put itself on the political and intellectual map of London. At one time it was even known as the 'village of palaces'. From the 17C on, the social composition of this district consisted of intellectuals, writers, and later also artists, although today Chelsea is more of a fashionable quarter for rich Londoners. (Recent fame came in the 1960s when

Kingston-upon-Thames, Coronation Stone

Chelsea's boutiques, especially in *King's Road*, became the height of fashion.) The *College of St.Mark and St.John* (King's Road, SW10) surrounds *Stanley Grove*, one of the finest houses in Chelsea. Built for the Stanley family in the late 17C, it remained a private residential house in a charming garden until the mid 19C.. The house became part of St.Mark's College; St.John's College moved here from Battersea (see *Wandsworth*) in 1923 and the campus of the two colleges was further enlarged in the 1950s.

Earl's Court Exhibition Hall (Warwick Road, SW5): The largest reinforced steel hall in Europe, it was opened in 1937 in an area formerly devoted to entertainment where, for example, 'Buffalo Bill's Wild West Show' was performed around the turn of the century. The main hall is 245 ft. wide.

Notting Hill (W 11): This developed into a residential area from the 1830s onwards. Attempts to make the area distinguished with 'good addresses' such as *Kensington Park Gardens* were not entirely successful. Although the slums have disappeared, extremes of living conditions are still apparent. The preponderance of West Indians in parts of the area finds particular expression in the *Notting Hill Carnival* (August Bank Holiday each year), which first took place in 1966, and is to date the largest event of its kind in Europe.

Kingston-upon-Thames (Borough of Greater London)

Surrey p.190☐ C3/4   (KT1, KT2, KT3, KT4, KT5, KT6, KT9)

KINGSTON-UPON-THAMES (KT1; KT2): This town had a strategically important location from earliest times and was the site of the first ford across the Thames. Later it had the only bridge across the lower reaches of the Thames—apart from *London Bridge* (q.v.)—. Kingston has been one of the large Surrey market towns since the privilege was granted by Charles I in 1628, when the holding of other markets within a radius of seven miles was banned. Today the town suffers particularly badly from the great amount of through traffic.

Market Place (KT1): The whole of this area is under a preservation order. A charming Victorian ensemble, especially interesting are the façades of the *Griffin Inn* and the *Druid's Head Inn,* together with certain older buildings. Parts of *Boots* chemist's and pharmacy shop are housed in a 16C half-timbered building. The *Market Hall* (the former town hall) was designed by C.Helman in 1838. *All Saints* in the N. also makes a Victorian impression, although parts of it are 13C.

Environs: Chessington (KT9): Parts of the community developed into a suburban residential area in the period between the 1st and 2nd World Wars, but the region's rural character has still entirely survived in the S. *St.Mary-the-Virgin*, the parish church, has survived with much of its 13C structure; fine wooden columns support the nave. Parts of a medieval house and farm with a defensive ditch are recognizable on *Castle Hill. Chessington Zoo* is the largest privately owned zoo in England. *Burnt Stub*, a Gothic mansion in the grounds, was built in the 19C.
Malden (KT3, KT4): *New Malden* (KT3) is a suburb. Although it began to grow larger in the 19C, its architectural style is largely 20C. The centre of *Old Malden* (KT4) still has a fine village structure and the area around *Church Road* is under a preservation order. The *Manor House* was built in the 17C. The *Plough Inn* is actually 16C, but because its exterior

has been rebuilt this is no longer directly discernible. *St.John-the-Baptist*, the parish church has a 19C extension preserving the original 14C choir as its side chapel. This extension also contains the nave from 1610, when the massive tower was built. That nave now forms an aisle adjoining the Victorian nave.
Surbiton (KT5, KT6): Kingston refused to have a railway line built through the town in the mid 19C and the line to Southampton was therefore extended along the rise in the SE. A new suburb, initially known as *Kingston-on-Railway* was built here. Surbiton became a popular suburb which was soon regarded as queen of the London suburbs. Part of the Victorian group of buildings is under a preservation order. The churches of *St.Andrew* (Maple Road, KT6), *St.Mark* (St.Mark's Hill, KT6) and *St.Matthew* (St.Matthew's Avenue, KT6) in Victorian Gothic all underline this impression. *Southborough House* (Ashcombe Avenue, KT6), designed by John Nash, is an example of the houses which stood here before the railway arrived.

Lambeth (Borough of Greater London)

London County p.190□D 3 (SE 11, SW2, SW4,
SW8, SW9, SW 16)

This borough today includes the districts of *Clapham* and *Streatham*. A description of the large public buildings along the bank of the Thames is to be found under the central London entry.

LAMBETH (SE1, SE 11, SW8, SW9): Nearly the entire area of the borough was a deserted marshland until the 18C, and as such was popular as a hunting ground for ducks. Almost all of today's buildings are 19C, except for *Lambeth Palace*, the

Clapham (Lambeth), St.Mary, portal detail [

Brixton (Lambeth), Brixton Windmill

seat of the Archbishops of Canterbury since 1197. In mid-18C maps, only the river bank is shown as built up. Some of today's districts are discernible as tiny hamlets. However, in the 19C, industrial enterprises and the slums which surrounded them changed all that. The present, distinctive appearance of the whole area dates from the Victorian era onwards.

Churches: Apart from *St.Mary's*, which is the medieval parish church outside the walls of Lambeth Palace, the best of the numerous churches are the four late-Georgian buildings: *St.Luke's* (Knight's Hill, West Norwood, SE 27) from the 1820s with a colonnaded portico which is put to great effect because of the church's hilly location; *St.Mark's Kennington* (SE 11); *St.Mary-the-Less* (Black Prince Road, SE 11), by the same architect as St.Luke's,

but designed in Gothic style and completed in 1828; and the *Congregational Church* in St.Matthew's Road, SW2 from 1828.

Secular buildings: As mentioned, these buildings mainly date from the last 150 years. Around *Herne Hill* (SE 24) and *Denmark Hill* (SE5) on the border with Southwark stand once-fine villas, while groups of Georgian and Victorian terraced houses have resisted the changing times in *Kennington* (SE 11, SW8, SW9).

Lambeth Walk (SE 11): The street market here dates from the early 19C, and today forms one of the few London markets open seven days a week.

Oval Cricket Ground (Kennington Oval, SE 11): The headquarters of the *Surrey County Cricket Club* have been here since 1845. Like most of Kennington, the land is owned by the Duchy of Cornwall, i.e. by the Prince of Wales. Today's pavilion was built in 1898. Apart from the county club matches, the final matches in the Test Match series are traditionally held here.

Environs: Brixton (SW2, SW9): Although the name of this town was first mentioned in 1067, the area developed extensively in the 19C. The parish church of *St.Matthew* (SW2) was consecrated in 1824, at which time the first phase of house building began. Only after 1860, when the railway connection was opened, did the area begin to be densely populated by the less well-off who characterize much of the district today.

Clapham (SW4): This area, today divided between the boroughs of Lambeth and Wandsworth, became a popular residential area after the plague epidemics and the Great Fire of London in the 17C. The first permanent coach connection with the centre of London began in 1690. The affluence of the citizens resident here today is clearly documented in the old houses still surviving around *Clapham Comon* and in *Old Town* and *High Street*. A large number of important historical personalities resided here. *Holy Trinity* (Clapham Common North), with its fine location in the middle of this large area of green, was completed in 1776 and for part of its life acted as almost the private chapel of the *Clapham Sect*, an Evangelical group who lived in the big houses nearby.

Streatham (SW 16): The old village, here since Saxon times, was located around *St.Leonard*, which dated from the 12&14C and was replaced in 1830 by a new edifice which is chiefly of interest for the monuments which came from the old church. Developments since the 17C are comparable with those in Clapham, although those who took up residence here at the time were somewhat better off. However, nearly all memory of this past has disappeared as a result of rebuilding between the wars.

Lewisham (Borough of Greater London)

London County p.190□D 3 (SE4, SE6, SE8, SE 12, SE 13, SE 14, SE 23, SE 24)

Today's borough was enlarged by the addition of *Deptford* and it now extends as far as the Thames.

LEWISHAM (SE 13): In the Middle Ages this community was in the possession of the abbey of St.Peter in Ghent. At that time it was a rural settlement around the parish church of *St.Mary* (Lewisham High Street), which George Gibson rebuilt in the 1770s. The area became a fashionable suburb from the late 16C on, and over the two following centuries mansions alternated with farmhouses in determining the area's character. Here too, the scattered nature of the residential settlements was replaced from the mid 19C onwards by affluent layers of plainer housing estates built around the newly opened railway stations. The fine houses along the *High Street* gradually gave way to the shops and today these have given way to a modern shopping centre. Of the really old buildings, only the former *vicarage* (Ladywell Road/High Street) from the 1690s still survives.

Environs: Blackheath (SE3): The real high heath, from which the area takes its name, is today in the borough of Greenwich, but the part with the longest history of human settlement is *Blackheath Village*, lying on the W. side of the former heath in Lewisham. Here too, expansion only began in the late 18C, when a few individual large houses were built on the edge of Greenwich Park. A construction boom then began in the mid 19C as the railway opened up the area. At the same time, a suburban settlement for well-off citizens developed, soon devouring large parts of the heath. Larger free areas now remained between Blackheath Village and *Shooters Hill Road*, and today these give pleasant emphasis to the Victorian housing with its free-standing houses and smaller groups of terraced houses. *Morden College* (St.German's Place, SE3), in the E. of the area around Shooters Hill Road, was founded by Sir John Morden in 1695. He acquired the land in 1669 and commissioned Sir Christopher Wren to design this 'poorhouse' with its generous dimensions. The foundation was intended to provide board and lodging for merchants who, like Sir John, pursued trade with the Turks, but became impoverished through no fault of their own, such as by losing ships. Today, the house is maintained as an old people's home, and the requirements for qualification are still similar.

Catford (SE6): This hamlet was redesigned over the last hundred years and became a busy modern suburb, where even the 19C buildings had to gave way to modernization. Today Catford is the borough's administrative centre.

Deptford (SE8, SE 14): The borough's industry is still concentrated here, but the shipyards and docks, formerly so important have almost entirely disappeared. Henry VIII began to enlarge the English fleet here and a number of splendid ships were built in the Deptford shipyards in the 16&17C. Peter the Great came here in 1698 to study shipbuilding. Today the area is covered with more recent housing estates and firms. The only two structures which still clearly document this great past are *St.Nicholas* (Deptford Green, SE8) from the late 17C (the substructure of its tower dates from the turn of the 16C), which was repaired and made smaller after World War 2, and *St.Paul* (High Street, SE8), built by Thomas Archer between 1712 and 1730 and carefully restored in 1976. In *New Cross* (SE 14) in the SW, some fine houses from the Georgian period survive along

the road to Dover. To the S. of this, around *Pepys Road*, the Haberdashers' Company, who were the landowners, made sure that the residential building work carried out since the last few decades of the 19C was good quality and pleasing to look at.

Lee (SE 12, SE 13): Until far into the 19C, this was an idyllic town in the middle of an agricultural area to the S. of Blackheath. Lee developed along the winding *Old Road* (SE13) before the area was altered by suburban town planning, which prescribed a regular grid of streets. Two fine old houses are *Manor House* from 1771, and *Pentland House*. The design of the latter dates from *c.* 1680 but the building was later altered.

Sydenham (SE 26): Until the 17C this was a rather rough area with cottages and gardens along today's *Sydenham Road* supplying the London markets. The discovery of mineral springs (*Wells Park*) made the area attractive from the mid 17C until the 19C, but large-scale development did not begin until the 19C. The fine buildings of the rich stood in *Upper Sydenham*, but from the late 19C onwards they were increasingly replaced by large residential blocks reminiscent of the Wilhelminian style in central Europe. *Crystal Palace Park*, has been a particular attraction since 1854, when the building was transferred here from the international exhibition in Hyde Park (1851). Sadly Crystal Palace itself burned down in 1936 and only parts of the foundations can still be seen.

Luton

Bedfordshire p.190□C 1   (LU1, LU2)

Luton is by far the largest town in Bedfordshire and the car industry employs about one sixth of the inhabitants. The indiscriminate spreading of low-density housing estates has taken its toll on Luton's townscape and the few surviving historical buildings scarcely stand out among the sea of modern buildings. A large charter airport for the London region stands on the town's E. edge.

St.Mary: The parish church and the central religious building of a large and rich town, it is unhappily dwarfed by the cooling towers of the power station and the *College of Technology* and the church seems smaller than it actually is. The exterior in Perpendicular style is mostly 14C, although the building was extensively renovated after the 2nd half of the 19C. Inside, some decorative elements survive from the 12C, but the overall character is early 14C in style.

Moat House (Moat Lane, Biscot): Luton's only medieval architectural monument (late 14C), it was given a new up-to-date roof in *c.* 1500. Restoration work on the building began in the mid 1970s.

Wardown: A town house (1875) of rich but not very imaginative design. Used today as an art gallery and museum.

Luton Hoo (Luton), stately home

Water Tower (West Hill Road): The lively design of this building (1901) well exemplifies the design of the Arts and Craft Movement around the turn of the 20C.

Someries Castle (Copt Hall): The ruins of the castle belonging to the Someries and Wenlock families are here, half a mile E. of the Vauxhall works. The castle dates from the 2nd half of 15C and was the first brick building in this area. Apart from the *gatehouse* and the *chapel*, only a few remains of walls survive.

Environs: Flamstead (Hertfordshire, 4 miles S.): The 12C church of *St.Leonard* has interesting wall paintings from the 12–15C (now carefully restored), showing Christ's Passion and Glory. Norman church tower.
Luton Hoo (2 miles S.): A magnificent mansion in a park laid out by 'Capability' Brown. The country seat was originally built by Robert Adam in the 1760s for the Earl of Bute who was Prime Minister at the time. It was later (*c.* 1627) altered by Sir Robert Smirke. Its present design dates

from 1903, when it was remodelled by the architect Mewès of Mewès & Davis. The work of Adam and Smirke can still be discerned in many details.

Whipsnade (5.5 miles W.): This little town owes its attractions to its *Zoological Garden*, for which Berthold Lubetkin & Tecton built some timelessly modern structures, like the elephant house. The church of *St.Mary Magdalene* was built of brick throughout, and combines an 18C nave with a 16C tower.

Maidenhead

Berkshire p.190□A/B3 (SL6)

Maidenhead (Berkshire, SL6): The town developed as a railway station for travellers from London to Bath. The *railway bridge* to the S. of the road bridge over the Thames was completed by Brunel in 1838. When it was built, its arches extended across the greatest area spanned by a brick structure. The bridge appears in Turner's painting *'Rain, Steam and Speed'*. *Smyth's Almshouses* (Bridge Street), a row of houses from 1659, are probably the best group of historical buildings in Maidenhead. The *Henry Reitlinger Donation*, a collection of ceramics from China, Persia, Peru and Europe, along with African and European objets d'art, is housed in a distinguished town house (1890s).

Environs: Bisham (Berkshire, 9 miles NW): *All Saints* church which stands on the river bank has a late–12C tower. The church itself was practically rebuilt in 1849, but preserves good 16C monuments to Sir Philip and Sir Thomas Hoby. A little further up river is *Bisham Abbey*, originally a house of the Knights Templar; it was also a priory of the Augustine hermits for two centuries, and a Benedictine abbey from 1537–40. After this the Hobys had the building converted into a private residence. All phases of its varied history are recorded in the surviving

structures. About a mile further W. are the remains of *Hurley Priory*, a Benedictine monastery founded shortly after the Norman Conquest. The nave of the monastery church became today's parish church of *St.Mary*. The monastery refectory to the N. of it is today part of a house.

Cliveden (Buckinghamshire, 3 miles NE): This was last the private country seat of Lord Astor in the 1930s. Sir Charles Barry designed the house (originally 17C) in its present form in 1850. The landscaped garden is by 'Capability' Brown and the garden pavilions by Giacomo Leoni.

Maidstone

Kent p.190□F 4 (ME 14, ME 15, ME 16)

The Romans built an enlarged military post here. This little town was much dependent on the court of the Archbishops of Canterbury in the Middle Ages, but it grew constantly from the 16C onwards until it assumed its present function as the administrative centre of Kent.

All Saints (on the river bank of the Medway by the archbishops' palace): Archbishop Courtenay of Canterbury completely rebuilt the church in 1395 on the site of a previous church. Today it is the largest and most splendid church in Kent from this period.

Archbishop's Palace (N. of the church): The core of the palace is also from Courtenay's period, but the façade and interior decorations were rebuilt in Elizabethan style when the house became a private residence of the Astleys in the 16C. The N. façade and windows were rebuilt in 1909. The complex also includes a 13C house, known as the *Gatehouse*, and the *tithe barn* to the E. of the church.

Old College (S. of the church): The

buildings founded by Archbishop Courtenay for a master and 24 curates were completed in 1396–8. The *Master's House* at the S. end of the complex is today a centre of the *Kent Music School* and seems to have been built before that period. But the free-standing *Master's Tower* was built under Courtenay. It was probably the main gate by which the college could be entered from the riverside.

Museum (St.Faith Street): This consists mainly of *Chillington Manor*, built in 1561 but altered by renovation work in 1875. The collection contains objets d'art and material relating to natural history and archaeology.

Town Hill (High Street): An impressive building (completed 1763), with wall paintings and rococo stuccoes in the council chamber.

Environs: Aylesford (3 miles): The village, overlooked by its church which stands on a gentle slope, still has some older houses and one of the first medieval bridges over the Medway. The most important building is *The Friars* at the W. edge of the village, which was the first monastery of the Carmelite order in S. England. Founded *c.* 1240, the 14C cloister still survives. The Carmelites acquired it again in 1949, rebuilt it, and gave it a new church (since 1958).
Boughten Monchelsea Place (3.5 miles S.): A manor house was built here around a square courtyard in *c.* 1570. The entrance is the E. wing of today's house, whose S. wing was rebuilt in *c.* 1819. Surrounded by a park with red deer.
Leeds Castle (5 miles E.): This fortress is considered to be the finest castle in the world, its rural setting lending support to such a claim. The castle stands on two islands in a quiet lake amidst wooded landscape. There seems to have been a fortification here since the 9C. It was used as a royal fortress from 1272–1547, but

Henry VIII was responsible for converting the previously Norman structure into today's carefully restored palace. The interior decorations have largely survived. Additional attractions include a unique collection of dog collars dating from the Middle Ages, and a collection of Impressionist paintings.
Otham (2.5 miles SE): This town is famed for its well-preserved half-timbered buildings. Parts of *Wardes* are 14C, and it was restored in 1912. *Synyards* was built in the early 16C and repaired in 1905. Best of all is the small late–15C manor house of *Stoneacre*. Restored by Aymer Vallance in 1920, it was enlarged using sections from other houses from the same period to form an interesting edifice resembling a museum.

Maldon
Essex p.190□C 4 (CM9)

Maldon (Essex, CM9): A town snugly and charmingly embedded in the countryside near mouth of the Blackwater river. *All Saints*, the town's parish church, has a surprising triangular tower (13C). Apart from this it is a mixture of constructions and renovations from the 14C–19C. *St.Mary-the-Virgin*, Norman in origin, has some 14C additions. The best secular structure is doubtless *Moot Hall* (High Street), a plain brick tower (*c.* 1435), overlooked to the rear by a staircase tower. The colonnaded portico and today's windows are 19C.

Environs: Beeleigh Abbey (1 mile NW): A Premonstratensian monastery dating from *c.* 1180. The surviving structure dates from the 1st half of the 13C, and includes the chapterhouse and the vaults below the dormitory.
Bradwell-on-Sea (9.5 miles E.): One of the oldest churches in England survives here. St.Cedd, the bishop of the East Saxons, built *St.Peter-on-the-Wall* in 654

above that wall of the Roman fortification which faces the sea.

Only a few remains of the *fort* are to be seen. The chapel choir is in ruins, but the nave survives in its entirety. *St. Thomas*, the parish church (14C) lies some 2 miles inland. *Bradwell Lodge*, the former priest's house from the Tudor period, stands on the opposite side of the village green, and has some late–18C additions. Robert Adam and Angelica Kauffmann are said to have carried out some of the interior decorations.

Tolleshunt D'Arcy (6 miles NE): The church of *St. Nicholas* is a perfect example of Perpendicular style. The *Hall* (*c.* 1500), with later enlargements, is a country house surrounded by a castle moat reached only by a bridge over the river built in 1585.

Merton
(Borough of Greater London)
Surrey p.190☐D3/4 (SW 19, SW 20, SM4, CR4)

MERTON (SW 19; SW 20): The name has been documented since the 10C. The area was probably in royal hands under King Harold; William the Conqueror certainly held it. *Merton Priory* was set up for the Augustinian monks here in 1114, to the S. of today's *Station Road* (SW 19). The remains of the chapterhouse are known today as *Merton Abbey*, and derive from that priory. Hugenot immigrants began to set up calico bleaching and textile printing along the Wandle in the 16C. *Merton High Street* was the centre of the village at that time; the original village lay a little further to the W.

St. Mary (Church Lane, SW 19): Towards the end of the 11C, the Domesday Book records there was a church here, but this was evidently replaced quite soon after by the present structure (Norman aisle from 1115, early-13C Gothic choir). The original roof beams have survived.

Merton Park (SW 19, SW 20, to the SW of the church): This area used largely for agricultural purposes was acquired by John Innes a businessman and enlarged between 1871 and 1904 into today's village, which is subdivided into many sections of differing appearance. It may also have given Victorian and Edwardian architects the idea for their purposive planning and design of garden cities in the larger area around London.

Environs: Mitcham (CR4): An area settled since Anglo-Saxon times, this locality, with its large *common*, preserves some rural character; fine 18C mansions add to the interest of the region. The parish church of *St. Peter and St. Paul* was founded in the 13C. Today's church is a combination of the medieval tower and a structure from 1822.

Morden (SM4): A large number of modern housing estates have been built here since the 2nd quarter of this century, although the originally rural character of the locality surrounding *St. Lawrence* (London Road) has survived to some extent. The church was built in 1636 on the site of the medieval village church (late 12C). A Georgian villa (completed 1770) stands in *Morden Park*. The *Old School House* (1731), founded for twelve poor children of the parish, survives at the beginning of *Central Road*. At the E. end of Central Road the visitor comes upon *Morden Hall*, a 17C house last converted in *c.* 1840. Its enclosure with red deer is another attraction in this region. *St. Helier* to the SE, towards Mitcham, is an enormous council house estate on the garden-city model, built by London County Council in the early 1930s.

Wimbledon (SW 19): The administrative centre of the borough, the district's character is largely that of a modern town, mainly because the medieval core around the *High Street* and *Church Road* was comprehensively cleaned away in the 19C and the medieval buildings were not preserved. The old centre of Wimbledon enjoyed its heyday in the 16&17C. The *Old Rectory* (*c.* 1500) stands beside the church, which is an almost entirely new building as a result of renovation work in 1788 and 1843. *Eagle House* (1613) and the late–17C *Rose and Crown* inn, two buildings which have survived, stand not far from the beginning of the High Street. However, Wimbledon's real fame comes from the tennis courts of the *All England Lawn Tennis and Croquet Club*, which organizes the Wimbledon Championships each year—without doubt the most important tennis competition in the world. The battle for the title has been held here since 1877, and since 1922 it has been held on the new premises in Church Road. A *tennis museum* with a library adjoining was opened here in 1977 on the centenary of the championships.

Newham
(Borough of Greater London)
Essex p.190☐D/E3 (E6, E7, E12, E13, E15, E16)

This borough was created in 1965 by uniting the districts of *East Ham* and *West Ham*, and also parts of *Woolwich* on the N. bank of the Thames.

EAST HAM (E6, E7, E 12): Today this town is the borough's administrative centre. Its origins may lie in a Roman settlement, but the community remained a thinly populated agricutural area until well into the 19C, being given a more varied appearance by some stately mansions, particularly those belonging to Henry VIII's courtiers. The practice of calling modern streets after the names of Henry's wives originated here. From the 1880s onwards, East Ham developed into one of the large London dormitory towns. Industry was confined to the area surrounding the docks in the S.

St.Mary Magdalene (High Street South, E6): This Norman parish church (*c.* 1130) has preserved its original form, apart from some minor changes and the 16C addition of the tower.

Environs: Canning Town (E16): One of the workers' housing estates conjured

Wimbledon (Merton), tennis museum

up from nowhere in the 19C to add to the docks and industrial esates on the N. shore of the Thames. Its poor architecture and hygiene were criticized from the outset. Matters were not improved until private humanitarian initiatives tackled the problem.

Plaistow (E 13): This medieval village became a centre of industrialization in what is now the borough. Factories in the 16&17C wove silk and treated leather. Today the town's appearance has completely changed, because of the expansion of the docks in the S. from the mid 19C onwards.

Silvertown (E 16): Another workers' and industrial estate built about the mid 19C. The ruins of the church by S.S. Teulon (1860's), which burned down in 1981, are a fine sight amidst the docks.

Stratford (E 15): From 1135–1538, the Cistercian *Stratford Langthorne Abbey* owned more land here than anyone else, extending over much of what is now Newham. The town itself was an economic centre from earliest times on. *St.John* (1834) in The Broadway is an example of the Gothic Revival. A monument in the graveyard commemorates thirteen Protestant martyrs who were collectively burned at the stake under Queen Mary in 1556.

West Ham (E 15): For a while, the whole W. section of the borough bore the name of this locality to the S. of Stratford. Its history corresponds to that of Stratford, and the Cistercian abbey was actually in the West Ham urban district. *All Saints* (Church Street) is a mixture of widely differing stylistic periods and phases of reconstruction, but clearly dates back to the 12C. Some fine buildings in the SW of this urban district are *Abbey Mills Pumping Station* and the Three Mills. The pumping station in Abbey Road is used for the London drainage system. Outside, it looks like a palace, flanked by towers resembling minarets; its ornate interior is reminiscent of a Byzantine church. Sir Joseph Bazalgette completed it in 1868 as

Polesden Lacey (Reigate), stately home

part of the drainage system, and it reflects the high esteem in which engineering was held at the time. *Three Mills* (Three Mills Lane) are the largest surviving tidal mills in England. Two buildings still stand: *Clock Mill*, with the clock tower from 1753 and the section rebuilt in 1817 (today offices), while *House Mill* (1776) is to be made operational again for use as a museum devoted to the technology of those times. The *Botanical Garden* in *West Ham Park* (E 15, E7) was founded by Dr.John Fothergill from 1762–80.

Redbridge
(Borough of Greater London)

Essex p.190☐D/E 2   (E 11, E 18, IG1, IG2, IG3, IG4, IG5, IG6, RM6

This borough takes its name from a former

bridge which crossed the river Roding and linked up the districts of *Ilford*, *Wanstead* and *Woodford*, all of which now are known as Redbridge.

Ilford (IG1): Inhabited ever since prehistoric times, this area came into the possession of Barking Abbey. Abbess Adeliza set up a hospital for lepers here in *c.* 1140. Abbess Mary Becket, sister of Archbishop Thomas Becket, enlarged this foundation in *c.* 1180 in memory of her murdered brother. *Ilford Hospital* (High Road) on the slope of Ilford Hill includes buildings from that foundation, namely the 14C chapel and the 18C poorhouses, now rebuilt. *Valentines* (*c.* 1700) in Valentines Park is the only surviving mansion in the area. Today it is a local council building. Suburban estates typify the whole area as far as the postal districts IG2 and IG3. *Barkingside* (IG6), another

suburb like Ilford, was built from the 1830s on.

Environs: Wanstead (E 11): This locality is surrounded by woodland and greenery surviving from Epping Forest. These give Wanstead a character of its own, although it is totally surburban in character now. The mansion in *Wanstead Park* was unfortunately pulled down in 1824 and its building materials sold, but parts that are left in the park and the elegant church of *St.Mary* (Overton Drive) give an idea of its former splendour. The early–18C *Manor House* (High Street) survives in good condition.

Woodford (E 18): This medieval village in the possession of Waltham Abbey was divided up into rural estates after dissolution. The parks of those estates were covered over with suburban housing developments from the 2nd half of the

Polesden Lacey (Reigate), lion in park (left), painting (right)

19C on, but a number of the Georgian buildings survive around *St.Mary* (High Road; E 18).

Redhill

Surrey p.190□D 4/5   (RH1)

This little town did not arise until the last century, after the opening of the road (1807) and railway line (1841) to Brighton. Given these circumstances, Redhill contains a surprisingly large number of town houses in the classical style of the 1st half of the 19C. An impressive example of these is *The Firs* (Brighton Road), some 900 yards S. of the town centre. Completed in *c.* 1830, it was somewhat clumsily extended in 1936.

Environs: Bletchingley (2.5 miles E.):

This little country town, which owes its prosperity to its old status as a market, grew up ribbon-like into a very fine village along a main road. The church of *St.Mary-the-Virgin* on the valley side of the town was built in *c.* 1090 on the site of a previous Saxon building. 13C and 15C enlargements produced the Perpendicular Style seen today. There are a number of good monuments inside. On the hillside above the town stand the remains of a *castle*, destroyed in 1264 in the disputes between Henry III and Simon de Montfort. The first buildings in the NW of the town are the *Brewer Street Farmhouses* (15C), surrounded by cottages. The three houses standing independently in the countryside are: *Pendell Manor House* (*c.* 1730), the smallest of the group; *Pendell Court* (1624), in a very conservative Tudor style; and *Pendell House* was built twelve years later. According to tradition, the

Richmond-upon-Thames

latter it said to be by Inigo Jones; the layout and articulation of its interior are perfectly symmetrical.

Reigate

Surrey p.190□D 5   (RH2)

Hardly any genuinely old domestic architecture survives in this town. The town's parish church of *St.Mary* has arcades from *c.* 1200, and was rebuilt by George Gilbert Scott junior; a monument of 1730 commemorating Richard Ladbroke is the work of the relatively unknown artist, Joseph Rose the elder. All that survives of *Reigate Castle* to the N. of the High Street is the lookout hill with its watchtower. Today this is a public rose garden. Opposite is *Reigate Priory* (High Street), which was founded for the

Augustinian canons in 1235 and converted into a Tudor house in 1541. Today's buildings are 18C, but in the *hall* there are some surprising features (such as the *Holbein Fireplace*) which may be original decorations from the mid 16C. The *Old Town Hall* (1728) in the High Street stands out prominently among its mediocre surroundings.

Environs: Dorking (5.5 miles W.): The church of *St.Martin* (1868−77) by Henry Woodyer dominates the town which, with its winding *High Street*, has a pleasant appearance without having any particularly good individual buildings. **Juniper Hall** (5.5 miles NW): This house, built in *c.* 1770, was redesigned externally to no very good advantage some hundred years later, but the room decorations and some of the old structural elements have survived. The very ornate

Sculptured Drawing Room in Robert Adam style is attributed to Lady Templeton. Madame de Staël and Talleyrand lived in this house as emigrants during the Napoleonic Wars.

Norbury Park (7 miles NW): This house stands in a vantage point W. of Mickleham and was built by Thomas Sandby from 1774 on. The position of the house, and the design of the *Painted Room* (1783), are an eloquent testimony to a love of the countryside. The bay window in the latter room is framed by paintings on the ceiling and walls showing landscapes on a scale corresponding to the landscape visible through the window, all of which gives the illusion of open space.

Polesden Lacey (7.5 miles W.): A fine house stood here in the Middle Ages and that was replaced in 1631 by a new building which *Richard B. Sheridan*, author of the plays 'The School for Scandal' and 'The Rivals', later acquired as his residence. His wife began to lay out the gardens of the house. The house itself was rebuilt again in 1824, this time to plans by Thomas Cubitt; its present appearance derives from alterations to the design by

Ambrose Macdonald Poynter in 1906. The villa has a fine collection of furniture, wall hangings and paintings.

Richmond-upon-Thames
(Borough of Greater London)

Surrey, Middlesex p.190□C 3   (SW 13, SW 14,
    TW1, TW2, TW9, TW 10, TW 11, TW 12)

Since 1965 this borough has included the districts of *Barnes, Hampton, Richmond, Teddington* and *Twickenham*. It is the only London borough to have territory on both sides of the Thames.

RICHMOND-UPON-THAMES
(Surrey, TW9, TW 10): Until 1499 the town, like the manor, was called *Shene*, and was probably only a small fishing village on the Thames. At that time Henry VII began to rebuild a mansion which had burned down, and named the town after his county in Yorkshire. This new building took on the dimensions and significance of a palace, and thus contributed to the town's development

Hampton Court (Richmond), window frames by Gibbons

over the following centuries. The palace itself fell into disrepair in the 18C. The only structures surviving are the gate leading on to the green, and an annexe in *Old Palace Yard*. Today, Richmond is an important business centre and has fine early–18C town houses, such as the rows of houses in *Richmond Hill* and *Maids of Honour Row*. Richmond is surrounded by a number of splendid spacious parks, including *Richmond Park, the Old Deer Park* and *Kew Gardens*.

Environs: Barnes (Surrey, SW 13): This locality has been the subject of wide-scale replanning since the 19C, but the town centre (High Street/Church Road) has preserved some of its rural openness, especially around the duck pond and where it passes into *Barnes Common* in the S. *Barnes Terrace* still has some 18C and early–19C houses, some of which have fine terraces with ornamental iron balustrades facing on to the river. A group of houses with charming gardens facing the Thames stands a little further to the W. around *Leyden House* (Thames Bank, SW 14), which is a 15C half-timbered

building with an 18C rough cast façade.
Ham (Surrey, TW 10): Some delightful 18C town houses survive around *Ham Common* and along *Ham Street*, leading down to the river. The late–17C *Manor House* (Ham Street) was extensively enlarged in the 18C. The house and its well laid-out garden are still privately owned. *Ham House*, the former home of John Maitland, Duke of Lauderdale, stands a little nearer the Thames. The house (1610) by Sir Thomas Vavasour was enlarged by the Lauderdales from 1672 on. After this, contemporaries took the view that the only villas possibly surpassing it in elegance were some few Italian structures. It has survived largely unaltered. The park still has its formal 17C design, and has not been transformed into a landscaped garden.
Hampton (TW 12), **Hampton Court** (KT8), **Hampton Hill** (TW 12) and **Hampton Wick** (KT 11): Today these are the sections into which *Hampton Manor* in Middlesex is divided. The manor was in the possession of the order of St.John of Jerusalem from 1236 on. Thomas Wolsey took on the lease of this

Hampton Court, entrance (left), fountain courtyard (right)

Hampton Court Palace, lower storey 1 Entrance to Public Gardens **2** Fountain Court **3** Cloister **4** Chapel **5** Chapel Court **6** Tudor Kitchen **7** King's Kitchen **8** Great Hall **9** Anne Boleyn's Gatehouse **10** Clock Court **11** Henry VIII Wine Cellar **12** Round Kitchen Court **13** King's Staircase **14** Orangery. **Upper storey 15** Queen's Suite **16** Queen's Gallery **17** King's Suite **18** Guard Room **19** King's Gallery **20** Fountain Court **21** Royal Rooms **22** Communication Gallery **23** Guard Chamber **24** Presence Chamber **25** Public Dining Room **26** Prince of Wales Suite **27** Chapel. **Upper storey 28** Royal Seats **29** Haunted Gallery **30** Queen's Staircase **31** Wolsey's Closet **32** Round Kitchen Court **33** Great Hall **34** Henry VIII Watching Chamber **35** Horn Room **36** King's Kitchen, upper storey.

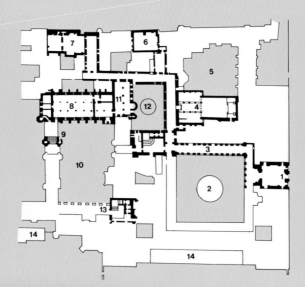

possession in 1514, and started to replace the manor house by a palace. The parish and the urban district both had their administrative offices in Hampton. The Hampton Wick district of town, located some way away, was able to develop fairly independently. The 'new town' of Hampton dates from the early 19C. A number of interesting town and country houses survive in this area, such as *Bushy Park House* (late 18C) and *Hampton Court House* (*c.* 1757). *Bushy Park* and *Hampton Court Park* formed an enclosed royal hunting ground under Henry VIII, but were opened to the public in 1547. Bushy Park is laid out as a landscaped garden, but Hampton Court Park has a formal design oriented on the Palace. The centre of the whole area is of course *Hampton Court Palace*. Wolsey originally planned that there should be 280 rooms for guests here, and lodgings for some 500 servants and administrators. When the King took over the Palace in 1529, he immediately began converting and enlarging it. New façade ornaments and the Astronomical Clock by Nicholas Oursian were added to Wolsey's gatehouse, which was re-named *Anne Boleyn's Gatehouse*. Henry VIII also had an influence both on the layout of the gardens and on the care and protection of the game in the two parks. The works carried out by Sir Christopher Wren for King William III and Queen Anne are the best of the additions and alterations made to the palace under later rulers. Under Queen Victoria, the palace was opened to the public, and the Crown transferred the responsibility for its upkeep to the government.

Hampton Court (Richmond), Edward VI

Ham (Richmond), Ham House, garden

Kew (Surrey, TW9): A group of elegant houses began to develop around *Kew Green* from the 16C on because the area was popular with courtiers owing to its proximity to Richmond Palace. 18C houses still determine the character of the green, and the parish church of *St.Anne* (consecrated 1714) stands in the middle. George III had the church enlarged in 1770 after acquiring Kew Palace. The entrance hall, tower and mausoleum were added in the 19C. The monarch's influence is seen in the church's liberal decorations. *Kew Palace* (Kew Gardens) was built as *Dutch House* in 1631, and Queen Caroline acquired it for her daughters in 1730. From then until 1818 the house was one of the royal residences; the decorations and furniture which can be admired here today date from this last phase. The *Royal Botanic Gardens* (sometimes known as Kew Gardens) were officially established in 1841, but had been laid out in the 18C in land belonging to the Prince of Wales. They may even date back to a late–17C private orangery.

Petersham (Surrey, TW 10): Like many other towns in the country around London, this was discovered in the 17C by well-to-do citizens who had escaped the plague epidemics in the centre of London. Thanks to its rural environs and the river Thames in the W., this town still displays a uniform character and has a large number of very good houses. Some fine examples are *Douglas House* (1680) in Lower Petersham Road, *Petersham House* (*c.* 1674) at 143 Petersham Road, and

Petersham Lodge (1740) in River Lane. The last-mentioned house was later enlarged in several phases. The parish church of *St.Peter* should be noted as a charming example of an 18C country church.

Richmond Park (Surrey, TW 10, SW 15): This is the largest park in Greater London. In 1637, Charles I had it fenced in for use as the park of Richmond Palace. The park has been open to the public since the mid 18C. Herds of red and fallow deer are allowed to run free here. Windsor Castle and the dome of St.Paul's Cathedral can be seen from *Henry VIII's Mound* near Pembroke Lodge. During World War 2, the *Thatched House Lodge*, built for the park keepers in *c.* 1673, was assigned to General Eisenhower as his lodging. Since 1963 Princess Alexandra has lived here.

Teddington (Middlesex, TW 11): In the 19C, this farmers' village on the edge of Bushy Park was overrun by the suburban estates along the railway line. The contrast can be seen today in the parish churches of *St.Mary* and *St.Albans* (Ferry Road), which stand side by side. St.Mary dates in its present form from the 18C, and is

Ham (Richmond), Ham House, Drawing Room

a homely village chapel; St.Albans (1887) shows some of the signs of an ostentatious town church, but its W. end is unfinished.
Twickenham (Middlesex, TW1, TW2): Although this is now mainly a residential suburb from the late 19C and the 20C, the rural serenity which made this a popular area for building country houses in the early 18C can still be felt along the bank of the Thames. Except for the medieval tower *St.Mary-the-Virgin* (Church Street, TW1) was rebuilt in 1714/15 at the suggestion of Sir Godfrey Kneller, the court painter, in order to make it fit in better with the increasingly elegant surroundings. *Marble Hill House* (Richmond Road, TW1), one of the large residences, was carefully restored by the London County Council after 1901, and was given a valuable collection of early Georgian paintings, furniture and prints. These were installed to complement the house, which was built in 1724–9 for Henrietta Howard, mistress of George II and a spirited lady with good taste. Today an art gallery showing non-permanent exhibitions is housed in what remains of *Orleans House* (Riverside, TW1), built in

1710. Both houses stand in well-designed parks and have a free view of the Thames. *Strawberry Hill* (Waldegrave Road, TW1), the most imposing house in Twickenham, is now *St.Mary's College*, a Roman Catholic teacher training college, but its fame came from the activities of Horace Walpole who, from 1748 on, enlarged a small villa into a Gothic castle.

Rochester

Kent p.190☐F 4   (ME1, ME2)

There was a settlement here on the ford over the Medway even before the Romans came and built a bridge and the fortified town of *Durobrivae*. St.Augustine established the bishopric in 604 and thus increased the town's importance. Interesting historical houses survive in the town in spite of extensive industrialization.

Rochester, **Cathedral 1** W. façade with portal **2** Font **3** Lady Chapel **4** S. transept **5** Monument to Sir Richard Watts and memorial stone to Charles Dickens **6** Sacristy **7** Choir **8** Entrance to crypt **9** Chapterhouse **10** Sanctuary **11** St.John's Chapel **12** Gundulf's Tower **13** Jesus Chapel **14** N. transept

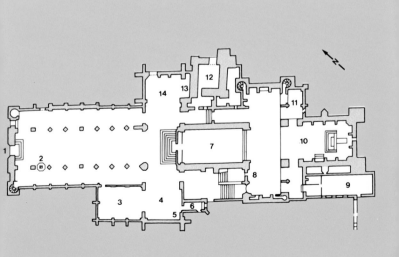

Cathedral: Built by King Ethelbert of Kent in 604. Bishop Gundolf arranged for the first phase of reconstruction, carried out between 1077 and 1108, and he also founded a Benedictine priory. This early, Norman part of the structure can still be clearly seen in the crypt. Extensive building continued until the 14C.

Castle: This fortress on the limestone rock high above the Medway has stood here since 1086 at the latest. In 1610 it was pulled down, except for the fortified tower (completed by Archbishop de Corbeuil in 1126) and the outer limiting wall. Its height of 120 ft. makes it the highest fortified tower in England.

St.Nicholas: Built as a parish church in the grounds of the cathedral graveyard, and consecrated in 1423, it was restored in 1624 after a fire.

Environs: Chatham (1 mile SE): The town became important because a dockyard was set up here under Henry VIII. Until recently the town depended almost totally on the docks. Admiral Nelson's *'Victory'* was launched here in 1795. Some early–18C buildings survive in the dockyard, such as *Admiral's House* (1703). The *Museum of the Corps of Royal Engineers* documents the history of the corps.
Cliffe (6 miles N.): The 13C church of *St.Helen*, at the centre of a large medieval parish, is unexpectedly ornate. It was redesigned in the 14C and altered in the 19C. *Manor Farm* in West Street is an Elizabethan house with charming and original architectural features.
Gillingham (2 miles E.): The church of *St.Mary-the-Virgin* is all that survives of the medieval village. The oldest sections date from *c.* 1200, but the church was largely redesigned when it was restored in the 19C. About half a mile to the E. of it are the ruins of *Grench Manor* (Grange Road) from the 1380s; the house stands by the road, and behind and to one side are the remains of the chapel.

Rochester Cathedral

Sittingbourne (10.5 miles E.): The *Court Hall Museum*, a collection of regional archaeological finds, occupies a small mid–15C house, formerly used as the manor's court. The *Sittingbourne and Kemsley Light Railway* is a narrow-gauge railway of interest to railway enthusiasts.

Royal Tunbridge Wells

Kent p.190□E/F 5   (TN1)

A picturesque spa which gradually developed after springs containing iron carbonate were discovered here in 1606. The church of *King Charles-the-Martyr*, an affront to the Puritans of those times, was built in 1676 and enlarged twice before 1690. Its articulation is unorthodox. *The Pantiles*, which are the covered walks beside the fountain, were built before the

Civil War. The present arrangement of the area dates from 1687. The rest of the town was enlarged in a rather haphazard manner, apart from *Calverley Park* and *Holy Trinity*, a group of buildings designed by Decimus Burton in the 1830s and stimulated by John Nash's project in Regent's Park.

Environs: Chiddingstone (6 miles NW): This impressive village consists almost exclusively of original 16&17C houses. The 14C church was most recently rebuilt in *c.* 1629 after a fire. The present appearance of the *castle* is early 19C, but it stands on the site of a fortified medieval manor. It contains collections devoted to the history of the Tudor and Stuart rulers, and also objets d'art from ancient Egypt, Japan and India.
Hever Castle (7.5 miles NW): This late−13C castle was acquired by the Boleyns in 1452. William Waldorf Astor, its American owner, restored it in exemplary fashion after 1903 without depriving it of its medieval character. Anne Boleyn, second wife of Henry VIII and mother of Queen Elizabeth I, spent her childhood and youth here. The formally designed garden is decorated with sculptures which Astor brought with him from Italy.
Lamberhurst (6 miles SE): The village itself makes a very picturesque impression and it is also the starting point for at least two interesting excursions. *The Owl House* (half a mile W.) is a 16C cottage formerly used by wool smugglers as a hideout. The extensive garden, well known for its rose-growing, is open to the public. *Scotney Castle* (half a mile SE) is a ruined group of buildings fortified in the late 14C. The castle moat surrounds two islands, on one of which one of the round fortified towers

St.Albans Abbey, nave

survives to its original height. Parts of a 16C attempt to redesign the complex, and the completed section of the impressive country house planned in the 17C, may also be seen in the grounds.

Penshurst (4.5 miles NW): This village is dominated by *Penshurst Place*, the manor house in which Sir Philip Sidney was born. All the main periods of domestic architecture employed in large country houses can be found in its design. The central section consists of *Great Hall, Queen Elizabeth Room* and *Tapestry Room* (1st half of 15C). The *Long Gallery* was completed *c.* 1600. Restoration and enlargement have continued until modern times, but without eliminating the old features. Penshurst Place is still privately owned by the Sidney family.

Tonbridge (4 miles N.): The N. section of the *High Street*, leading uphill from the bridge over the Medway, consists of an impressive group including the remains of the castle built here from the Norman period onwards in order to guard the bridge. The imposing *gatehouse*, completed *c.* 1300, replaced the old defensive tower on the lookout hill.

Saffron Walden

Essex p.190☐E 1   (CB 10)

This small country town was originally known as Walden. The addition to its name results from the saffron plantations which occupied the surrounding area from the 14C until the 18C. The streets are rich in old houses. The church of *St.Mary-the-Virgin*, almost 200 ft. long, was restored in the 15&16C. It is perhaps the finest church in the whole of Essex. *Ring Hill* in the W. of the town is an Iron Age hill

St.Albans Abbey, tower (left), detail of shrine (right)

fort, an indication of the length of time this area has been settled. Ruins of a Norman fortified tower survive from the *castle*.

Environs: Audley End House (1 mile W.): The Benedictine abbey of Walden stood here, and in 1538 Henry VIII transferred it to Lord Audley. In the early 17C, his uncle Thomas Howard, Earl of Suffolk, began to build an enormous stately home, the largest existing in those times. Only a fragment of that building survives. The house's picture collection is an additional attraction.
The garden was originally laid out by 'Capability' Brown (*c.* 1760).
Clavering (6 miles SW): An attractive village with some good houses. In the street leading to the 15C *church* there is a 17C half-timbered house which has a brick façade and a shop front with a storeroom behind it. This house is

decorated with wall paintings. The remains of *Clavering Castle* stand to the N. of the church.
Thaxted (6 miles SE): Knife-cutlers made this a rich town in the 14&15C. The large and proud church of *St.John-the-Baptist* bears witness to that past, and so do the *Guildhall* and the *Recorder's House* (house of an town hall official) from the 15C.
Tilty (8.5 miles SE, near Broxted): The fine village church of *St.Mary-the-Virgin* was a chapel outside the gates of the former Cistercian abbey (founded 1153) which stood to the N.

St.Albans
Hertfordshire p.190□C 2　　　　(AL1)

The area was settled by a Belgian tribe before the Romans built *Verulamium*,

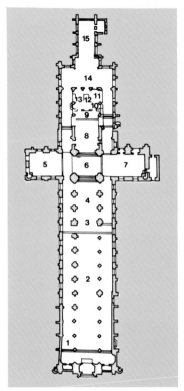

St.Alban's Cathedral 1 Font **2** Nave **3** Choir screen **4** Choir **5** N. transept **6** Crossing **7** S. transept **8** Sanctuary **9** Altar rail **10** St.Alban's Chapel **11** Tomb monument to Humphrey Duke of Gloucester **12** Marble shrine of St.Alban **13** Watching loft **14** Retrochoir **15** Lady Chapel

which has been well documented by excavations carried out from the 1920s onwards. The monastery was the determinant factor in the development of the town throughout the Middle Ages, from about the 8C on. The town itself, however, remained fairly small and had only about 6,000 inhabitants in *c.*1800. The core of the old part of town around the early–15C *Clock Tower* is rich in interesting buildings from different periods, probably the oldest are to be found in *French Row.*

Abbey: All that survives of this today is the 11C church, the length of which was increased in the 13C. After the monastery was dissolved, its church was used as a parish church and the *Lady Chapel* was converted into a Grammar School. Since 1877 the church has been the cathedral of the newly established diocese.

St.Michael: The church's nave and choir are Saxon in origin (10C). In the 12C they were enlarged by the addition of aisles. The church has a *monument to Sir Francis Bacon.*

Environs: Gorhambury (2.5 miles W.): *Gorhambury House* was built in 1784 to the designs of Sir Robert Taylor as a residence for the Earls of Verulam, relations of Sir Francis Bacon. The ruins of the 16C *manor house* where Sir Francis lived can be seen in the grounds of *Gorhambury Park.*
London Colney (2 miles SE): The church of *St.Peter* (1825), designed by George Smith, is a very early example of neo-Romanesque. The church's glass windows are by the widowed Marchioness of Waterford, a friend of John Ruskin.

Sevenoaks

Kent p.190☐E 4   (TN13)

Sevenoaks has now become a dormitory town for London. This is reflected in the fact that the more recent residential areas are all N. of the old part of town. The S. part of *High Street* forms the old town centre and the buildings grouped around the church are almost exclusively 18C.

St.Nicholas The town church was built in its present imposing size in the 13C, but was partly altered in two 19C renovations.

Sevenoaks School: Founded by Sir William Sennocke in 1432 in order to educate poor children free of charge. The present group of buidings dating from 1724–32 were built to the designs of Lord Burlington; parts of the school include former almshouses.

High Street: *The Chantry, Old House* and *The Red House* stood here in *c.* 1700. The best 18C buildings are *Manor House, Oak End* and the *Old Vicarage.* Manor House, the most recent of this group, is set back from the High Street and is also architecturally distinct from the other houses. 19C *White House* and *Temple House* fit in well with these surroundings.

Environs: Ightham (4.5 miles E.): The 14&15C village church of *St.Peter* has some good monuments. At the N. edge of the village is *Ightham Court*, a mansion from *c.* 1575 which was comprehensively altered over the following centuries, especially in its interior design. *Ightham Mote*, a small medieval manor house, is some 2 miles S., near Plaxtol. Impressively embedded in the countryside, and surrounded by a *moat*, it has repeatedly been adapted to its inhabitants' changing needs, but has not lost its original character. The showpiece of this complex is the *Great Hall* (mid 14C). To the E. of *Plaxtol*, a village built around the 17C church, stands *Old Soar Manor*, which is remarkable for including in its structure the residential section of a late–13C knight's castle. The *hall* was replaced by a brick structure in the 18C.

Knole Park (SE of Sevenoaks High Street): This was a palace of the Archbishops of Canterbury from *c.* 1460 on, and was later privately owned by the Sackvilles; after its enlargement (completed 1608) it was one of the largest private houses in England.

Sundridge (2.5 miles W.): The *church, manor house* and *Old Rectory* form a charming group standing in a park. *Old Hall*, a half-timbered building from the 2nd half of the 15C, stands on the NE edge of the town. It was carefully restored in accordance with old documents in 1923. *Combe Bank* (early 18C) by Roger Morris stands to the NW of Sunbridge. This splendid house has now been converted into a girls' school.

Westerham (5.5 miles W.): This small

St.Albans Abbey, ceiling

St.Albans, Verulamium

town is the birthplace of *General James Wolfe*. At the battle of Quebec in 1759, Wolfe successfully enforced England's claims to Canada in the face of French opposition. Wolfe himself suffered the fate which was later to befall Admiral Nelson and though his troops won, he himself failed to survive the battle. His memory is kept alive by his *statue* on the green and by a commemmorative exhibition in *Squerryes Court*. This house (1681) also has a collection of Dutch paintings. It is only the name of *Quebec House* on the E. edge of the town that relates this early–17C building to the town's history. Early–18C *Grosvenor House* stands on the opposite side of the street. *Squerries Lodge* (Market Square) is an charming 18C house which includes some sections from a 13C stone house. The *statue of Sir Winston Churchill* on the green is a reminder of *Chartwell*, Sir Winston's country house,

which stands 2 miles to the S. and is now preserved in his memory.

Sheerness

Kent p.190□F 3   (ME 12)

Sheerness is the main town of the *Isle of Sheppey*. The sheep from which the island takes its name still graze in the lush meadows, but today the area is an industrial zone. Its development began in the late 17C, when the first large docks were built up in Sheerness. Today's *dockyards* were built by Sir John Rennie in 1824, although they were enlarged in the course of the 19C and adapted to new requirements and circumstances. The main building by Rennie is the *quadrangle*. It still survives in its simple and impressive proportions.

Environs: Minster-in-Sheppey (2.5 miles SE): One of the earliest nuns' convents in England was founded here in c. 674. The abbey church of *St.Mary and St.Sexburgha* has Saxon stonework work in the N. wall. The church's subdivision into one section for the nuns and another for the congregation can still be seen today. Interestingly, at one time the convent's rule was that of St.Augustine, but at a later stage it adopted the rule of St.Benedict. Augustinian canonesses were living here when the order was dissolved under Henry VIII.

Southend-on-Sea

Essex p.190□F 2   (SS1, SS2)

Today Southend is one of the large English seaside resorts in the Thames Estuary, Southend's past has been, however, rather undistinguished. Little development occurred until the middle of last century, its importance as a seaside resort being largely due to the good railway connections with London. Travelling time of less than an hour meant that the town attracted less well-off visitors from the E. end of London.

Prittlewell Priory Museum (Priory Park): The surviving sections of the 12C Benedictine priory contain a regional museum devoted to natural and cultural history. The building is surrounded by charming gardens.

Southchurch Hall (Southchurch Hall Close): This mid–14C mansion stands in a small and rather formal garden. The half-timbered building with medieval decorations also contains a library.

The 13C church of *St.Mary-the-Virgin* (North), and the church of *St.Andrew* (South), which is mostly Norman, are interesting buildings in the **Shoebury** district of the town.

Environs: Canvey Island (6 miles W.): This island was regained from the sea in the early 17C by drainage and the building of defensive walls. The building which houses the *Dutch Cottage Museum* survives from this period (c. 1620), when Dutch workers were employed in making the newly gained land secure.

Foulness Island (7.5 miles NE): Like the surrounding islands, this is known for its rich variety of wildfowl. *St.Mary-the-Virgin* (1850) by William Hambley is Early English.

Leigh-on-Sea (3 miles W.): By now this has become part of Southend-on-Sea, but the church and High Street have a character of their own. 15C *St.Clement*, which was rebuilt and enlarged in the 19C, stands high above the sea; steps lead down to the *High Street*, which still has the character of the pre-Victorian fishing village. A little further to the W. are the ruins of the late–14C *Hadleigh Castle*, where Catherine Parr, Henry VIII's last wife, was incarcerated for a time. The small Norman church of *St.James-the-Less* stands in the town of Hadleigh.

Paglesham (6 miles NE): A small village with the Norman church of *St.Peter*, and an 18C *church hall*. *Lunts*, a spacious country house from 1804, stands to the E., a little way outside the village.

Southwark
(Borough of Greater London)

London County p.190□D 3   (SE1, SE5, SE 15,
                                                SE 16, SE 17, SE 21, SE 22)

Today's borough comprises the former districts of *Bermondsey, Camberwell* and *Southwark*.

SOUTHWARK (SE1): This area developed from the Roman fortifications on the S. bridgehead of *London Bridge* and as such it was a stopping point for travellers. Southwark was also a market town in Saxon times, although trade pursued here never seriously rivalled that of the city of London, which acquired the district of Southwark from the Crown in 1550. From about that time on the area became known for diverse forms of entertainment e.g. *Globe Theatre* of Shakespeare's time. Until the mid 18C, however, the only real area to be settled was along the bankside road known as *Borough High Street* as far as the parish church, *St.George-the-Martyr*, (1736) built by John Price on the site of a previous structure. The days of horse-drawn coaches is remembered in the *George Inn* (Borough High Street), the S. wing of the coach house built here in 1676. *Holy Trinity* (Trinity Church Square) is surrounded by houses from the 1820s. For the *Imperial War Museum* and *Southwark Cathedral*, see the descriptions under central London.

Environs: Bermondsey (SE1) and **Rotherhithe** (SE 16): From the Norman Conquest on, this area was largely in the possession of the Benedictine abbey, founded in Bermondsey. The monks also built the first harbour here. A relatively small-scale economic development, with harbour facilities, docks and warehouses, continued until the 19C. From that time, the absence of a broader infrastructure led to the area's decline. At present, efforts are under way to redevelop and revive the area. The parish church of *St.Mary Magdalen* (1680) is in Bermondsey Street, SE1; the parish church of *St.Mary* (St.Marychurch Street, SE 16) was rebuilt in 1715.

Camberwell (SE5): Here, in the administrative centre of the new borough, post 1930s suburban development has completely overrun the rural past. Even the medieval church of *St.Giles* (Camberwell Church Street) had to be rebuilt in 1844 after a fire; rebuilding was according to plans by the two Victorian architects W.B. Moffatt and G.G. Scott. *Camberwell Grove* is worth visiting for its fine Georgian houses.

Dulwich (SE 21): The medieval village developed under the name of *Dulwich Village*, while the manor was in the possession of Bermondsey Abbey. The actor Edward Alleyn acquired the property in 1605, and in the following years he founded the *College of God's Gift*, today's *Dulwich College*. This institution inherited the entire estate of the childless Alleyn, and his foundation had a decisive influence on the area's subsequent development. Most of the existing buildings were designed in the 1860s by Charles Barry the elder.

Dulwich Picture Gallery (College Road, SE 21): The first public art gallery in England was opened in 1814 based on Edward Alleyn's private collection, which had been assembled at a much earlier date, and other collections. The gallery is housed in a building designed by the neoclassical architect Sir John Soane, which was extensively restored after World War 2. Some 300 paintings are on display in the twelve rooms of this gallery. The 17C and 18C are well represented, with works by Rembrandt, Rubens, van Dyck, Murillo, and Watteau, Canaletto, Tiepolo, Gainsborough and Hogarth.

Newington (SE1): The 'new town' here is documented from the 13C on. The most interesting building historically is the *Metropolitan Tabernacle* (Newington Butts), completed by W.W. Pocock in 1851 for Charles Haddon Spurgeon, a popular Baptist priest. Only the portico survives in the original. The building behind it was restored in 1959 after bomb damage. The name Tabernacle derives from the model of the Mosaic tabernacle, because Spurgeon, the Baptist priest (1834–92), held that mankind was on a journey through the desert.

Peckham (SE 15): From the 17C on, this was a refuge for prominent nonconformists. It was converted into a suburb in the Victorian period, but redevelopment and housing construction over the last thirty years have wiped out the traces of those times too. However, *Peckham Rye*

Southwark Cathedral, N. aisle

Common and *Park* are still largely surrounded by good 19C buildings.

Staines

Surrey p.190☐B/C 3   (TW 18)

The population has increased tenfold since 1900, but the central area of town still provides a fine historical backdrop. The *Blue Anchor* (High Street) dates from *c.* 1700, and *Clarence Street* has a fairly intact row of late-Georgian town houses.

Environs: Great Fosters (2 miles SW): A country house built in brick, with two square staircase towers. The plain design is fairly typical of such late-16C houses in the area around London. Buildings in the grounds were built by local craftsmen after 1930.

Royal Holloway College (3 miles W.) and **Holloway Sanatorium** (3 miles SW): The college was one of the first academic educational institutions for women. Both institutions, which were financed by Thomas Holloway, occupy buildings which must be some of the most surprising Victorian buildings in the counties around London. The architect was W.H. Crossland who, acting on Holloway's instructions, used a guildhall in Ypres as a model for the sanatorium, while the château of Chambord on the Loire was his model for the college. The sanatorium was opened in 1884, and the college was built in 1879–87.

Runnymede (2.5 miles W.): The English understanding of legal matters was founded on this meadow on the bank of the Thames on 15 June 1215, when King John, coming from Windsor, and the barons arriving from their assembly in

Staines, met here and agreed on the contents of *Magna Charta*. The King placed his seal on the draft of the text. The *Coopers Hill Memorial* by Sir Edward Maufe on the rising ground behind this is in memory of the 20,000 members of the Allied airmen's units who died from 1939–45. The names of all the fallen are recorded here on this memorial, which includes an observation tower rising above the treetops.

Sutton
(Borough of Greater London)
Surrey p.190□D 4(SM1, SM2, SM3, SM5, SM6)

SUTTON (SM1, SM2): A rural settlement from about the 6C on, Sutton received an impetus for growth when the London-Brighton road was opened in 1755. Widescale housing development began in the 2nd half of the 19C, and both villas and terraced houses were built. In the 20C some of these were replaced by more modern structures, including high-rise buildings. The parish church of *St.Nicholas* (probably 7C) in St.Nicholas Way, was replaced in 1862 by a neo-Romanesque structure by Edwin Nash. Some of the shops in the *High Street* have good façades.

Environs: Beddington (SM6): From the 14C on this possession was in the hands of the Carew family. *Carew Manor* is the result of their long period of affluence; its *Great Hall* is still largely as it was in the 15C. The whole group of buildings to the S. of *Beddington Park* was last added to in about the mid 19C; today the house contains a school.
Next to this is *St.Mary's*, mainly 13&14C, with later renovations.
Carshalton (SM5): Parts of *All Saints* church (Church Hill) are 12&13C, although it was comprehensively rebuilt and redesigned around the turn of the present century. The early–18C

Carshalton House (Pound Street) has a beautiful and extensive garden, and is now a monastery school.
Cheam (SM3): In the 1930s, Tudor-style houses were added to some genuine 17C buildings in the centre of Cheam. *White-hall* (Malden Road) is a half-timbered house (*c.* 1530) open to the public.
Wallington (SM6) and **Woodcote Village** (SM6, CR3): Since the late 19C these two hamlets have developed into urban housing estates.

Tilbury
Essex p.190□F 3   (RM 18)

Here there is a variety of functional buildings from different historical periods. *Tilbury Docks* were built from 1880–6 and added to in the late 1920s. *Tilbury Fort* in the W. and E. (1670–83) was built to guard the Thames against the immediate danger of attacks by the French and Dutch. These fine buildings exhibit London's elegance and good taste despite their functions, and probably also its financial strength.

Environs: Grays Thurrock or **Grays** (RM 17, 2.5 miles NW): The *Thurrock Local History Museum* has a good collection of regional archaeological finds, including objects from the Palaeolithic period, the early and late Bronze Ages, Roman times, and the pre-Christian Saxon period. The collection is supplemented by an exhibition on the more recent social history of the region, including documentation concerning the railway and fire brigade.

Tower Hamlets
(Borough of Greater London)
London County p.190□D 3   (E1, E2, E3, E 14)

Since 1965 the borough has comprised the

former districts of *Bethnal Green, Poplar* and *Stepney*.

BETHNAL GREEN (E2): Today this is a heavily built-up area. Until the 17C, wealthy Londoners had country houses in this region. When textile factories, and later entire industrial complexes, moved here construction began on an intensive scale. The entire surrounding area then suffered a decline in the 19C. *Nettleswell House* and other 18C buildings (Victoria Park Square) are to be found behind the *Bethnal Green Museum of Childhood* (Cambridge Heath Road). The *Trinity Almshouses* (1695) are in Mile End Road, E1, opposite a group of 18C houses. For *Spitalfields* and *Whitechapel*, see the description in central London.

Environs: Bow (E3): This developed in parallel with Stratford, but on the other bank of the Lea. *St.Mary* (*c.* 1311) was originally a filial church of Stepney. The original structure largely survives in spite of later renovation. Here, in the late 19C, the organization of female factory workers into trade unions began.

Poplar and **Isle-of Dogs** (E 14): In the early 19C, the 'landscape' created by the *West India* and *Millwall Docks* came to replace an enormous marshy area used for agricultural purposes. Christopher Wren's buildings in Greenwich are optically oriented towards the S. tip of the Isle-of-Dogs. *All Saints* (East India Dock Road), built in 1823, and *Montague Place* behind it, form a fine architectural group. *St.Anne's Limehouse* (Commercial Road) is by Nicholas Hawksmoor.

Stepney (E1): In the early 16C, several churches dating from Anglo-Saxon times were replaced by *St.Dunstan* (Stepney Green).

Waltham Abbey
Essex p.190□D 2   (EN9)

This little country town forms a pleasant background to the remains of this rich abbey. King Harold refounded it in 1060, and after his death in the Battle of Hastings he was buried in the buildings he founded.

Waltham Cross (Waltham Abbey), detail

Waltham Abbey, nave

The *Abbey Church of the Holy Cross and St.Lawrence* is a Norman church with a nave and two aisles. The monastery was dissolved in 1538 and converted into the town's parish church; the W. tower was added at that time. The only other structures still surviving are the abbey *gatehouse* and the 14C bridge leading to it.

Environs: Theobald's Park (Hertfordshire, EN8, 2 miles W.): The country seat of William Cecil, Lord Burleigh, stood here. In 1607, at the request of James I, the family were obliged to exchange it for Hatfield Palace. No trace of the house survives. In 1763 George Prescott built *Theobald's Park*, a new house in the park. Henry Meux and his family, the new owners, had this building enlarged and converted in the 19&20C. It was also Henry Meux who ordered *Temple Bar*, the W. gate of the City of London, to be renovated and set up in the entrance to his park in 1888. Temple Bar was originally built in Fleet Street in 1672 to the plans of Christopher Wren. The park also contains *Temple House* and *Old Park Farm*, themselves 18C, but not so altered as Theobald's Park.

Waltham Cross (Hertfordshire, EN8, 1.5 miles W.): The town takes its name from the still-surviving cross which was set up here in 1291 to commemorate Queen Eleanor's funeral procession. The idea of these richly decorated memorial crosses was taken up by King Edward I, although they were designed and built by Alexander of Abingdon. Since the last restoration in the 1950s, the original statues have been in the *Cheshunt Public Library*.

**Waltham Forest
(Borough of Greater London)**
Essex p.190☐D 2/3   (E4, E 10, E 11, E 17)

The modern borough comprises the former districts of *Chingford*, *Leyton* and *Walthamstow*.

WALTHAMSTOW (E 17): Evidence indicates there were settlements here in the Bronze and Iron Ages. These were set

Waltham Abbey, Abbey Church, rose window

in the wooded region later called *Epping Forest*. In the 19C the region became a densely populated and fully developed industrial town. Fortunately, some remains of the elegant buildings begun in the 15C still survive. 18C examples include *The Chestnuts* and *Cleveland House* (Hoe Street), and *Water House* (Forest Road) where William Morris formerly lived. It now houses the *William Morris Gallery*. *Forest School* (1834) has a chapel with lead-glazed windows designed by William Morris. To the S. of *Walthamstow Common*, near the school, some attractive Georgian houses have survived. The area around *St.Mary* (Church End) is of interest; the church itself was practically rebuilt in the 1530s and enlarged in the 19C.

Epping Forest Museum (Rangers Road, E4): This attractively situated Tudor house from the early 16C was formerly used as a hunting lodge in the nearby forest. It was a favourite resort of Elizabeth I.

Environs: Chingford (E4): *All Saints* (late 13C) may have been built on the foundations of a 12C church. The new building was restored in the 15C and rebuilt in 1930 as a filial church for the new parish church of *St.Peter and St.Paul*. The town centre has moved from *Old Church Road* to *Chingford Green* in the NE. *Queen Elizabeth's Hunting Lodge* (Ranger's Road) survives from *Fairmead Park*, planned by Henry VIII.

Leyton (E 10) and **Leytonstone** (E 11): The parish church of *St.Mary-the-Virgin* (Church Road, E 10) was founded in the 12C. However, today's church was completed in several phases, beginning in the early 17C. Some older town houses were included in *Leytonstone House* and *Whipp's Cross Hospitals*, two hospital complexes (E 11).

Wandsworth
(Borough of Greater London)
London County p.190☐D 3　　(SW8, SW 11, SW 12, SW 15, SW 17, SW 18)

Today's borough comprises the former districts of *Battersea* and *Wandsworth*.

Waltham Abbey, Abbey Church, Lady Chapel, fresco

Wandsworth (SW 18): In addition to the agricultural community, some form of industry seems to have developed here along the river Wandle since the 13C. This tendency has certainly intensified since the 18C, when Flemish and French Protestant immigrants came here. Ever since then, large commercial enterprises and country houses have existed side by side in this area. The mixture of residential and industrial buildings has survived, but the impressive buildings have been largely crowded out. *All Saints* parish church (High Street) stood here since 1234, and its history partly reflects the general situation: the tower dates from 1630; the other extensions were added in 1724, 1780 and finally 1841. Individual well-preserved groups of houses can be seen beside the *church* (Wandsworth Plain), and also further E. around *Wandsworth Common*.

Environs: Battersea (SW 11): The village and manor originated in Saxon times around today's church. *St.Mary* in Battersea Church Road was completed in its present form in 1777. Henry Yevele,

Watford, pub sign

the architect of Westminster Abbey, took part in building the 14C church. The few really good buildings in the district are nearby: the late–17C *Old Battersea House* was recently carefully restored; the *Raven Pub* dates from the same period. The *Vicarage* and *Devonshire House* (18C) supplement this group. *Battersea Park* was laid out to plans by Sir James Pennethorne and opened in 1853. Today this park offers a multitude of facilities for recreation and amusement. Further to the E., the *New Covent Garden Market* (Nine Elms, SW8) was opened in 1973.

Putney (SW 15): From the 16C on, impressive country houses belonging to courtiers and rich Londoners were built here along the bank of the Thames. The improvement in communications (*Putney Bridge*, 1729; railway, 1846) led to an increase in population. However, the town continued to be purely a residential area, mainly for artists, writers and City employees. Little has changed since the period between the two World Wars, and today Putney is a homely area thickly concentrated with Victorian and Edwardian terraced and semi-detached houses. Formerly, the more wealthy members of the community preferred the S. suburb of *Roehampton* (SW 15), where fine mansions were built from the mid 17C on. An impression of the splendour of the time can be glimpsed at in *Roehampton Lane*, where *Queen Mary's Hospital* is housed in *Roehampton House*, built for Thomas Cary the merchant in 1710–12 to plans by Thomas Archer. It was last enlarged by Sir Edwin Lutyens, before it was converted to its present function during World War 1. *Manresa House*, the Roman Catholic priests' seminary, was built for Lord Bessborough in 1750. *Garnett College*, the former *Downshire House*, dates from *c.* 1770. *Grove House* (*c.* 1777), the former *Roehampton Great House*, was probably built by James Wyatt (enlarged *c.* 1850), replacing Sir Richard Weston's house dating from 1630. **Tooting** (SW 17): In the 18C this became a popular area for Londoners' country houses, but its appearance changed greatly around the turn of the present century. Buildings which survived around the old village centre *(Church Lane, Tooting Graveney)* include the Schoolhouse (1828), the parish church of *St.Nicholas* (1833), and the late–18C *Hill House* (today part of *St.Benedict's Hospital*).

Watford
Hertfordshire p.190☐C 2   (WD1)

Although this is a large and economically independent town, it still comes under the influence of London. The underground railway connection is by no means the only evidence of this. *St.Mary* (High Street) is mainly 15C, with parts of the previous early–13C church. The *Morison* chapel was added in 1597 as a family memorial chapel. The *High Street* and *The Parade* are now an architecturally attractive pedestrian zone. *Cassiobury Park* was laid out by Humphry Repton in 1802. Some buildings still survive from the country house that once stood in the park and these include the late–17C *Dower House (Little Cassiobury)* and the stables which have been converted into a housing block *(Cassiobury Court)*.

Environs: Elstree (4.5 miles E., WD6): Something of the former village structure is preserved in the *High Street*. To the N. of the church stand *Schopwick Place*, a Georgian house, *Hollybush Inn*, where some of the rooms still retain their medieval appearance, and individual cottages. Towards the S., come *St.Nicholas School* and a group of late–19C *poorhouses*; *Hill House* (completed 1779) stands at the end of the High Street. The *Manor House* near the railway station was given a new façade in 1880 and is now a community centre; the building itself is 17C with 18C additions. *Borehamwood* to the E. has developed into a town since the 1950s.
Moor Park (2.5 miles SW): One of the finest manor houses in Hertfordshire. Built for the third Earl of Bedford in 1620, it was altered in 1720 by Giacomo Leoni who converted the original brick building

Moor Park (Watford), stately home

Moor Park (Watford), hall in stately home

into the present structure. The house has a fine art collection.

Welwyn Garden City

Hertfordshire p.190□D 1   (AL7, AL8)

This town built to a drawing-board design is of interest for two reasons. First, in contrast to other garden cities in Great Britain, it was designed from the outset not as a suburb in the countryside, but as a community which was to function entirely independently, both socially and economically. Secondly, two phases of contemporary architectural thought are exemplified here. It was first designed in the 1920s for a maximum of 20,000 inhabitants and later, in the 1950s and 1960s, it was enlarged in the N. into a town to relieve the pressure on London,

with a housing capacity for up to 50,000 inhabitants in all. The architect Louis de Soissons was in charge of both the phases of work in which the last-mentioned district of town was built.

Environs: Ayot St.Lawrence (3.5 miles NW): Apart from the charming village church, *Shaw's Corner* is this town's real point of attraction. *George Bernard Shaw*, the writer and dramatist, lived from 1906–50 in this late–19C house, which is now preserved unaltered as a memorial to him.
Brocket Park (1 mile W.): This landed possession was acquired by the lawyer Sir Matthew Lamb in 1746. James Paine designed *Brocket Hall* for him. Building works on the house proceeded from *c.*1760–*c.*1780. Splendid interior decorations.
Hatfield (nearly 2.5 miles S.): *Hatfield*

Hatfield (Welwyn Garden City)

New Town developed along with the second phase of building Welwyn Garden City. One consequence was that *Old Hatfield* has largely retained its historical character. *Fore Street, Park Street* and *Church Street* are charming historical buildings. *St.Etheldreda* was rebuilt in 1872 by David Brandon, who preserved the choir and transept of the old church; the Cecils' chapel (1618) also survived. Access to *Hatfield Palace* and *Hatfield House* is gained to the E. of and behind the church. The palace was completed in 1497 for Bishop Morton of Ely, and fell to the Crown in 1538; Mary and Elizabeth spent large parts of their childhood here under house arrest. In 1607 James I exchanged the palace for Theobald's Park (see Waltham Abbey), belonging to Robert Cecil. Cecil evidently felt that the building made too defiant an impression, because he ordered large sections of it to be pulled down and used as building materials for Hatfield House. However, he preserved the palace's splendid *banqueting hall*.

Splendid Hatfield House (completed 1611) is still the private residence of the Cecil family. It also has a rich collection of memorabilia devoted to Queen Elizabeth I.

Knebworth House (5 miles N.): This is the stately home in *Old Knebworth*, the *Great Hall* of which dates from Henry VII's time. Other parts of the original building were torn down in 1812 and replaced by new and different structures. When Sir Edward Bulwer-Lytton, the well-known politician and author ('The Last Days of Pompeii'), inherited this stately home in 1843, he ordered the building to be converted to its present Gothic design. The house's decorations and furniture are largely original items from the 17&18C.

City of Westminster, Regent's Park, Park Crescent (left); Windsor Castle, Norman Gate (right)

Welwyn (2.5 miles N.): Like Old Hatfield, this old town benefited from the fact that a new town was built close by, so that the necessary shopping centres and industrial enterprises were therefore also set up there. Consequently today Welwyn is a pleasing little town with a great deal of historical flair and attractive living conditions.

City of Westminster (Borough of Greater London)

London County p.190☐D 3   (WC2, SW1, W1, W2, W9, NW1, NW8)

Today's borough includes the formerly independent district of *St.Marylebone*, and also parts of *Paddington*. The areas to the S. of Regent's park and to the E. of Hyde Park have already been described under the central region of London, so that only a few additions are required here.

ST.MARYLEBONE (W1, NW1): The section of St.Marylebone described here is that to the N. of *Marylebone Road*. That section's history is closely related to John Nash's conception and design for Regent's Park. The district's name is a slurring of the name of the old parish. This was *St.Mary-by-the-Bourne* (that is, 'on the river Tyburn'). *Regent's Park* (NW1) was originally planned as an enormous landscaped garden which was to form the surroundings for a district of impressive villas. Only three such villas, *The Holme, Nuffield Lodge* and *St.John's Lodge*, were actually built and still survive. The park was completed shortly before 1830. A zoological garden, today's *London Zoo*, was

Windsor Castle

built to the NE by Decimus Burton, who was commissioned by the *Zoological Society of London*, which had been founded shortly before. The zoo was opened in 1828. The Royal Botanical Society laid out a garden in the Inner Circle. In the 1930s this garden was converted into *Queen Mary's Rose Garden*. The performances of the *Open Air Theatre* are held here in the summer months. Elegant residential blocks were built around the park in the 1830s. One of these, *Park Crescent* (NW1), was recently very carefully restored. These buildings are fine examples of classical style from the Regency period.

Environs: St.John's Wood (NW8), **Maida Vale** (W9) and **Kilburn** (NW6): These NW suburbs were also enlarged in the 1830s. *Hamilton Terrace* (NW8) still gives a good impression of this initial phase. But this construction work was only

completed once the Victorian estates had been built. These rows of plainer houses can be seen to good effect in *Maida Avenue* (W9) and *Queen's Park Estate* (S. of Kilburn Lane; NW6). It was in this area that J.L. Pearson built one of the finest examples of the Victorian Gothic: this is *St.Augustine* (Kilburn Park Road, NW6), built between 1870 and 1880 on the model of Albi cathedral in S. France. Within the Paddington district proper, *St.Mary Magdalene* (Woodchester Square, W2) by G.E. Street was consecrated in 1878. The crypt underneath the side aisle is an unusual feature for London churches.

Windsor
Berkshire p.190☐B 3   (SL4)

The development of this picturesque town

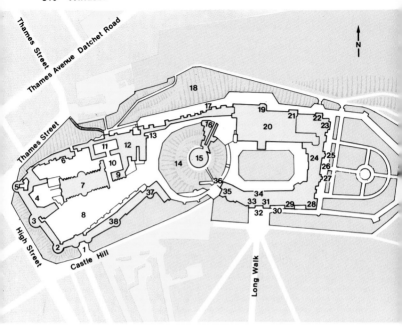

Windsor Castle 1 Henry VIII's Gateway **2** Salisbury Tower **3** Garter Tower **4** Horseshoe Cloisters **5** Curfew Tower **6** Canon Residences **7** St.George's Chapel **8** Lower Ward **9** Albert Memorial Chapel **10** Dean's Cloister **11** Canon's Cloister **12** Deanery **13** Winchester Tower **14** Middle Ward **15** Round Tower **16** Norman Gateway **17** North Terrace **18** Home Park **19** George IV's Tower **20** State Apartments with splendid carvings by Gibbons. The rooms include: The Inner Entrance Hall with etchings by great artists. The China Museum with sumptuous china works. The Grand Staircase (1866) with a statue of George IV by Chantrey, weapons, and armour belonging to Henry VIII. The King's Dining Room with ceiling fresco by Verrio. The King' Drawing Room with paintings by Rubens. The King's State Bed Chamber. The King's Dressing Room with ceiling by Wyattville and sumptuous paintings. The King's Closet. The Queen's Drawing Room with a van Dyck painting (1637) of Charles I's five eldest children. The Queen's Ball Room. The Queen's Audience Chamber with ceiling fresco by Verrio, French tapestries, and late-18C wall tapestries. The Queen's Presence Chamber, similar to the Audience Chamber. The Queen's Guard Chamber with: weapons; a 16C suit of mail; busts of the Duke of Marlborough, Wellington and Churchill; the bullet that killed Nelson; and the sword with which the Japanese Supreme Commander surrendered to Lord Mountbatten in 1945. The Garter Throne Room, where members of the Order of the Garter hold private events. St.George's Hall. The Great Reception Room, probably the most beautiful and most sumptuously decorated room. Waterloo Chamber. The Grand Vestibule with weapons, Coronation and State vestments of George IV, and a statue of Queen Victoria **21** Cornwall Tower **22** Brunswick Tower **23** Prince of Wales Tower **24** Private Apartments **25** Chester Tower **26** East Terrace **27** Clarence Tower **28** Victoria Tower **29** Augusta Tower **30** South Terrace **31** York Tower **32** George IV's Gateway **33** Lancaster Tower **34** Visitors' Apartments **35** Edward III's Tower **36** St.George's Gateway **37** Henry III's Tower **38** Military Knights' Residences

was evidently dependent on the royal palace, but secular buildings such as the *Guildhall of Holy Trinity* (today *Three Tuns*) from 1518, and the *Town Hall* (High Street) designed by Sir Thomas Fitch and completed by Sir Christopher Wren in 1690, are witness to a well-established social structure. William the Conqueror probably began building *Windsor Castle* at the same time as the *Tower* (q.v.) of London. The original

Eton (Windsor), College, courtyard

building probably consisted of a lookout hill and two watchtowers, surrounded by palisades. The 12C stone fortifications were completed on their present scale in *c.* 1272. Unlike today, Windsor was formerly not the chief residence of the reigning monarch, but it has always been very popular as a royal castle. Thus, most monarchs contributed to the decoration and beautification of the castle. Edward III had a kind of guild chapel built for the Knights of the Garter in 1348, and Edward IV replaced this between 1475 and 1480 by today's *St. George's Chapel*, one of the best late-Gothic religious structures in all England. The interior design of the residential sections was improved at the wish of Charles II. Today's decorations in the State rooms date mainly from the 19C. The medieval *Windsor Park* was an enormous wooded area which stretched from Guildford to

Buckinghamshire and was reserved for royal hunting parties. Today's park, laid out in the 17&18C, is divided into *Home Park* (closed to the public) and *Great Park*. Great Park is about two-and-a-half times the size of Richmond Park, which is the largest park in Greater London. Garden buildings and castle annexes stand here and there in both Home Park and Great Park.

Environs: Ascot (Berkshire, 5.5 miles SW): This little town is internationally known for the *Royal Ascot horse races*, which are the event of the season. When Queen Anne instituted the races here in 1711, their character was rather that of a private court entertainment. The Duke of Cumberland, who had a stud farm housed in Cumberland Lodge in Windsor Great Park, developed the races into a serious sporting contest. From the late 18C on,

King, Queen and heir to the throne were all regular spectators. Not until the 19C was the public also gradually admitted. Nothing survives of the old *Royal Enclosure*. There is room for some 10,000 invited guests on the new stands (1961—4).

Eton (Buckinghamshire, half a mile N.): The town of Eton appears to be only a projection of Eton College, the famous public school on the bank of the Thames opposite Windsor Castle. In this the town resembles Windsor and its relationship with Windsor Castle. However, the traveller walking along Eton *High Street* will sense or perceive that this little town has preserved a historical character of its own. Henry VI founded *Eton College* in 1440 as a collegiate church to which a grammar school and poorhouses were attached. In parallel with this, Henry also founded *King's College* in Cambridge, where the Eton pupils were to pursue further studies. Of the original buildings at Eton, only the *hall* and the kitchen complex still survive. The *chapel* (begun 1449) was completed in the 1480s, and has remained essentially unaltered ever since. Many of the old college buildings were completed in the late 15C. The *Cloister Court* was completed in the early 16C when its W. façade facing School Yard and including *Lupton's Tower* was completed. The 19&20C enlargements now make it possible for some 1,200 pupils to be accommodated and educated here.

◁ *Windsor, The Royal Albert House, detail*

Index of artists

art theoretician 179,
181
Reynolds-Stevens,
William (19C), architect
207
Ricci, Sebastiano
(1659–1734), Italian
painter 86
Riley, W.E. (19/20C),
architect 212
Rodin, Auguste
(1840–1917), French
sculptor 125
Romney, George (1734–
1802), painter 181
Rose the elder, Joseph
(18C), sculptor 283
Roubiliac, Louis François
(1702/05–62), French
sculptor 73 f., 80, 174
Roumieu, R.L. (19C),
architect 230
Rovezzano, B. de (16C),
Italian sculptor 63
Rowntree, Fred (19/20C),
architect 239
Rubens, Peter Paul
(1577–1640), Flemish
painter 83, 165, 181 f.,
298
Rysbrack, John (18C),
sculptor 73, 75, 133,
174

Saint-Gaudens, Augustus
(1848–1907), American
sculptor 129
Salvati, mosaic artist 75,
123
Sandby, Thomas (18C),
architect 284
Sanderson, John (18C),
architect 234
Savage, John (19C),
architect 48
Scheemakers (18C),
sculptor 91
Scott, Sir George Gilbert
(1811–78), architect
54, 75, 103, 123, 134,

219, 226, 255, 264,
267, 298
— jun., George Gilbert,
architect 283
— Sir Giles Gilbert
(20C), architect 91,
100
— J.J. (19C), architect
210
— J.Oldrid (19C),
architect 210
— Lady (19/20C), sculp-
tress 132
Sedding, J.D. (19C),
architect 38
Seddon, J.P., sculptor
132
Semper, G. (19C), ore
founder 63
Shaw, John (19C),
architect 43
— Norman (20C),
architect 232
Simonds, George, sculp-
tor 124
Simpson, Sir John (20C),
architect 204
Sloane, Charles (18C),
joiner and architect
239
Smirke, Sir Robert
(1781–1802), architect
88, 158, 275
— Sydney (19C),
architect 158
Smith, George (19C),
architect 294
— Robert (19C), sculptor
130
— Sidney (19C), architect
178
Snow, W. (17/18C),
painter 50
Soane, Sir John
(1753–1837), architect
82, 86, 176, 232, 256,
298
Soissons, Louis de (20C),
architect 306
Spiller, James (18C),

architect 250
St.Aubyn, J.P. (19C),
architect 202
St.Lot, sculptor 78
Stevens, Samuel (18C),
architect 118
Stone, Nicholas (1586–
1647), sculptor 39, 66
Story, W.W. (19C),
sculptor 130
Strange, Clifford (20C),
architect 204
Street, George Edmund
(19C), architect 46,
231, 309
Sueur, Hubert le (17C),
sculptor 125

Tarver, E.J. (19C),
architect 206
Taylor, Sir Robert (18C),
architect 294
Tecton (20C), architect
276
Templeton, Lady,
architect 284
Teulon, S.S. (19C),
architect 232, 280
Theed, William, sculptor
97
Thornhill, Sir James
(1675–1734), court
painter 61, 243
Thornycroft, Sir Hamo
(19C), sculptor 127,
129
— Thomas (19C), sculp-
tor 125
Tiepolo, Giambattista
(1696–1770), Italian
painter 298
Tijou, J., French metal-
worker 39, 60, 62
Tintoretto, real name
Jacopo Robusti
(1518–94), Italian
painter 165
Tite, Sir William (19C),
architect 107, 238
Titian, real name Tiziano

Alphabetical list of the sights of London

List of boroughs and other areas described in Greater London